Lecture Notes in Computer Science 15195

Founding Editors

Gerhard Goos
Juris Hartmanis

Editorial Board Members

Elisa Bertino, *Purdue University, West Lafayette, IN, USA*
Wen Gao, *Peking University, Beijing, China*
Bernhard Steffen , *TU Dortmund University, Dortmund, Germany*
Moti Yung , *Columbia University, New York, NY, USA*

The series Lecture Notes in Computer Science (LNCS), including its subseries Lecture Notes in Artificial Intelligence (LNAI) and Lecture Notes in Bioinformatics (LNBI), has established itself as a medium for the publication of new developments in computer science and information technology research, teaching, and education.

LNCS enjoys close cooperation with the computer science R & D community, the series counts many renowned academics among its volume editors and paper authors, and collaborates with prestigious societies. Its mission is to serve this international community by providing an invaluable service, mainly focused on the publication of conference and workshop proceedings and postproceedings. LNCS commenced publication in 1973.

Alexis Espinosa · Michael Klemm ·
Bronis R. de Supinski · Maciej Cytowski ·
Jannis Klinkenberg
Editors

Advancing OpenMP for Future Accelerators

20th International Workshop on OpenMP, IWOMP 2024
Perth, WA, Australia, September 23–25, 2024
Proceedings

Editors
Alexis Espinosa
Pawsey Supercomputing Centre
Kensington, WA, Australia

Michael Klemm
AMD and OpenMP ARB
Beaverton, OR, USA

Bronis R. de Supinski
Lawrence Livermore National Laboratory
Livermore, CA, USA

Maciej Cytowski
Pawsey Supercomputing Centre
Kensington, WA, Australia

Jannis Klinkenberg
RWTH Aachen University
Aachen, Germany

ISSN 0302-9743 ISSN 1611-3349 (electronic)
Lecture Notes in Computer Science
ISBN 978-3-031-72566-1 ISBN 978-3-031-72567-8 (eBook)
https://doi.org/10.1007/978-3-031-72567-8

© The Editor(s) (if applicable) and The Author(s), under exclusive license to Springer Nature Switzerland AG 2024
Chapter "Event-Based OpenMP Tasks for Time-Sensitive GPU-Accelerated Systems" is licensed under the terms of the Creative Commons Attribution 4.0 International License (http://creativecommons.org/licenses/by/4.0/). For further details see license information in the chapter.

This work is subject to copyright. All rights are solely and exclusively licensed by the Publisher, whether the whole or part of the material is concerned, specifically the rights of translation, reprinting, reuse of illustrations, recitation, broadcasting, reproduction on microfilms or in any other physical way, and transmission or information storage and retrieval, electronic adaptation, computer software, or by similar or dissimilar methodology now known or hereafter developed.
The use of general descriptive names, registered names, trademarks, service marks, etc. in this publication does not imply, even in the absence of a specific statement, that such names are exempt from the relevant protective laws and regulations and therefore free for general use.
The publisher, the authors and the editors are safe to assume that the advice and information in this book are believed to be true and accurate at the date of publication. Neither the publisher nor the authors or the editors give a warranty, expressed or implied, with respect to the material contained herein or for any errors or omissions that may have been made. The publisher remains neutral with regard to jurisdictional claims in published maps and institutional affiliations.

This Springer imprint is published by the registered company Springer Nature Switzerland AG
The registered company address is: Gewerbestrasse 11, 6330 Cham, Switzerland

If disposing of this product, please recycle the paper.

Preface

The OpenMP API is a widely used application programming interface (API) for high-level parallel programming in Fortran, C, and C++. The OpenMP API has been supported in most high-performance compilers and by hardware vendors since it was introduced in 1997. Under the guidance of the OpenMP Architecture Review Board (ARB) and the diligent work of the OpenMP Language Committee, the OpenMP specification has evolved to version 5.2, which was released in November 2021, and version 6.0 is imminent with an expected release in November of this year. OpenMP supports parallelism at several levels: offloading in heterogeneous systems; task-based processing across processors; and vectorization in SIMD units. It also goes beyond parallel computing, with support for sequential loop transformations and processor affinity and through policies and mechanisms for using memory and for matching directives and functions to computing environments.

Many of these advances were realized through major new features in version 5.0: context selectors and the declare variant construct and metadirectives that use them; the requires directive; memory allocators and support for deep copy of pointer-based data structures; acquire and release semantics; task (memory) affinity; the descriptive loop construct; reverse offloading; affinity display; and first- and third-party tools interfaces. OpenMP version 5.0 also significantly enhanced many existing features, such as implicit declare target semantics, support for task reductions, discontiguous array shaping in target updates, and imperfectly nested loop collapsing. Versions 5.1 and 5.2 refined these capabilities and augmented them for increased expressiveness and improved ease of use.

With version 6.0 of the OpenMP API specification, the language will include greatly enhanced support for task-based parallelism. Since that support underlies support for the use of non-host devices, these changes are expected to prove to be pervasive in future OpenMP programs. These changes include new concepts such as free-agent threads and transparent tasks, as well as major new constructs including taskgraph. The definition of the OpenMP API specification version 6.0 has been documented in Technical Report 11 (published in November 2022), Technical Report 12 (published in November 2023), and Technical Report 13 (published in August 2024). The reports contain previews of new loop transformations (fuse, interchange, reverse and split directives, and the apply clause); memory scopes for atomic and flush operations; extensions to memory allocators; device selection via traits; improved device support, including the workdistribute construct in Fortran; and further refinements of the OpenMP language.

The OpenMP API remains important both as a stand-alone parallel programming model and as part of a hybrid programming model for massively parallel, distributed memory systems with homogeneous manycore nodes and heterogeneous node architectures, as found in leading supercomputers. As much of the increased parallelism in exascale systems is within a node, the OpenMP API will become even more widely used in top-end systems. Importantly, the features in OpenMP versions 5.0 through 5.2

support applications on such systems in addition to facilitating portable exploitation of specific system attributes.

Each IWOMP, the International Workshop on OpenMP, draws participants from research and development groups and industry throughout the world. After the first meeting in 2005, in Eugene, Oregon, USA, meetings have been held each year, in Reims, France; Beijing, China; West Lafayette, USA; Dresden, Germany; Tsukuba, Japan; Chicago, USA; Rome, Italy; Canberra, Australia; Salvador, Brazil; Aachen, Germany; Nara, Japan; Stony Brook, USA; Barcelona, Spain; and Auckland, New Zealand. In 2020 and 2021, IWOMP continued the series with technical papers and tutorials presented in a virtual conference setting, due to the SARS-CoV-2 pandemic. After a hybrid event in Chattanooga, TN, USA in 2022, we resumed an in-person IWOMP at University of Bristol, UK in 2023. We were delighted to continue the in-person series at Pawsey Supercomputing Research Centre, Perth, Australia. We are grateful for the generous support of sponsors that helped to make this meeting successful; they are cited on the conference pages (present and archived) at the IWOMP website.

The evolution of the specification would be impossible without active research on OpenMP compilers, runtime systems, tools, and environments. The many additions in OpenMP API version 6.0 reflect the contribution by a vibrant and dedicated user, research, and implementation community that is committed to supporting the OpenMP API. As we move beyond the present needs, and adapt and evolve OpenMP to the expanding parallelism in new architectures, the OpenMP research community will continue to play a vital role. The papers in this volume demonstrate the use and evaluation of new features found in the OpenMP API. These papers also demonstrate the forward thinking of the research community, and highlight potential OpenMP directions and further improvements for systems on the horizon.

The IWOMP website (www.iwomp.org) has the latest workshop information, as well as links to archived events. This publication contains the proceedings of the 20th International Workshop on OpenMP, IWOMP 2024. The workshop program included fourteen technical papers, three implementer presentations, and two keynote talks. All technical papers were peer reviewed by at least four members of the Program Committee. The work evidenced by these authors and the committee demonstrates that the OpenMP API will remain a key technology well into the future.

September 2024

Maciej Cytowski
Bronis R. de Supinski
Alexis Espinosa
Michael Klemm
Jannis Klinkenberg

Organization

General Chairs

Alexis Espinosa — Pawsey Supercomputing Research Centre, Australia
Michael Klemm — AMD & OpenMP ARB, Germany

Program Committee Chairs

Maciej Cytowski — Pawsey Supercomputing Research Centre, Australia
Bronis R. de Supinski — Lawrence Livermore National Laboratory, USA

Publication Chairs

Jannis Klinkenberg — RWTH Aachen University, Germany
Sam Yates — Pawsey Supercomputing Research Centre, Australia

Steering Committee

Michael Klemm (Chair) — AMD & OpenMP ARB, Germany
Eduard Ayguadé — BSC, Universitat Politècnica de Catalunya, Spain
Mark Bull — EPCC, University of Edinburgh, UK
Barbara Chapman — Hewlett Packard Enterprise & Stony Brook University, USA
Bronis R. de Supinski — Lawrence Livermore National Laboratory, USA
Rudolf Eigenmann — University of Delaware, USA
William Gropp — University of Illinois, USA
Kalyan Kumaran — Argonne National Laboratory, USA
Simon McIntosh-Smith — University of Bristol, UK
Kent Milfeld — TACC, USA
Matthias S. Müller — RWTH Aachen University, Germany
Stephen L. Olivier — Sandia National Laboratories, USA
Ruud van der Pas — Oracle, USA

Alistair Rendell   Flinders University, Australia
Mitsuhisa Sato   RIKEN Center for Computational Science, Japan
Sanjiv Shah   Intel, USA
Oliver Sinnen   University of Auckland, New Zealand
Josemar Rodrigues de Souza   SENAI Unidade CIMATEC, Brazil
Christian Terboven   RWTH Aachen University, Germany
Matthijs van Waveren   OpenMP ARB, France

Program Committee

Ilkhom Abdurakhmanov   Pawsey Supercomputing Research Centre, Australia
Mark Bull   EPCC, UK
Mark Cheeseman   DUG, Australia
Florina M. Ciorba   University of Basel, Switzerland
Johannes Doerfert   Lawrence Livermore National Laboratory, USA
Alejandro Duran   Intel, Iberia
Deepak Eachempati   Hewlett Packard Enterprise, USA
Jini George   AMD, USA
Joachim Jenke   RWTH Aachen University, Germany
Emily Kahl   Pawsey Supercomputing Research Centre, Australia
Jannis Klinkenberg   RWTH Aachen University, Germany
Melissa Kozul   University of Melbourne, Australia
Michael Kruse   AMD, Germany
Kelvin Li   IBM, USA
Chunhua Liao   Lawrence Livermore National Laboratory, USA
Stephen Olivier   Sandia National Laboratories, USA
Swaroop Pophale   Oak Ridge National Laboratory, USA
Tom Scogland   Lawrence Livermore National Laboratory, USA
Xavier Teruel   Barcelona Supercomputing Center, Spain

Contents

Current and Future OpenMP Optimization

Towards Locality-Aware Host-to-Device Offloading in OpenMP 3
  *Jannis Klinkenberg, Jan Kraus, Christian Terboven,
  and Matthias S. Müller*

Performance Porting the ExaStar Multi-Physics App Thornado On
Heterogeneous Systems - A Fortran-OpenMP Code-Base Evaluation 16
  *Mathialakan Thavappiragasam, J. Austin Harris, Eirik Endeve,
  and Brice Videau*

Event-Based OpenMP Tasks for Time-Sensitive GPU-Accelerated Systems 31
  *Cyril Cetre, Chenle Yu, Sara Royuela, Rémi Barrere,
  Eduardo Quiñones, and Damien Gratadour*

Targeting More Devices

Integrating Multi-FPGA Acceleration to OpenMP Distributed Computing 49
  *Pedro Henrique Rosso, Lucian Petrica, Nusrat Jahan Lisa,
  Marcio Pereira, Sandro Rigo, Hervé Yviquel, Vanderlei Bonato,
  Emilio Francesquini, and Guido Araujo*

Towards a Scalable and Efficient PGAS-Based Distributed OpenMP 64
  Baodi Shan, Mauricio Araya-Polo, and Barbara Chapman

Multilayer Multipurpose Caches for OpenMP Target Regions on FPGAs 79
  Julian Brandner, Florian Mayer, and Michael Philippsen

Best Practices

Survey of OpenMP Practice in General Open Source Software 97
  Tim Jammer, Christian Iwainsky, and Christian Bischof

CI/CD Efforts for Validation, Verification and Benchmarking OpenMP
Implementations 111
  *Aaron Jarmusch, Felipe Cabarcas, Swaroop Pophale, Andrew Kallai,
  Johannes Doerfert, Luke Peyralans, Seyong Lee, Joel Denny,
  and Sunita Chandrasekaran*

Evaluation of Directive-Based Programming Models for Stencil
Computation on Current GPGPU Architectures 126
   Baodi Shan, Mauricio Araya-Polo, and Barbara Chapman

Tools

Finding Equivalent OpenMP Fortran and C/C++ Code Snippets Using
Large Language Models 143
   Naveed Sekender, Pei-Hung Lin, and Chunhua Liao

Visualizing Correctness Issues in OpenMP Programs 161
   Feiyang Jin, Alan Tao, Lechen Yu, and Vivek Sarkar

Developing an Interactive OpenMP Programming Book with Large
Language Models 176
   Xinyao Yi, Anjia Wang, Yonghong Yan, and Chunhua Liao

Simplifying Parallelization

Automatic Parallelization and OpenMP Offloading of Fortran Array
Notation 197
   Ivan R. Ivanov, Jens Domke, Toshio Endo, and Johannes Doerfert

Detrimental Task Execution Patterns in Mainstream OpenMP® Runtimes 210
   Adam S. Tuft, Tobias Weinzierl, and Michael Klemm

Author Index 225

Current and Future OpenMP Optimization

Towards Locality-Aware Host-to-Device Offloading in OpenMP

Jannis Klinkenberg[✉], Jan Kraus, Christian Terboven, and Matthias S. Müller

Chair for High Performance Computing, IT Center, RWTH Aachen University, Aachen, Germany
{j.klinkenberg,terboven,mueller}@itc.rwth-aachen.de,
jan.kraus@rwth-aachen.de

Abstract. The computational demand from scientific and industrial applications has grown significantly, driven by advances in scientific simulations across various fields such as climate forecasting, molecular dynamics, and medicine. This has led to a shift from purely CPU-based systems to heterogeneous architectures that include CPUs and accelerators like General Purpose Graphic Processing Units (GPGPUs), enabling faster computations by offloading demanding tasks to these accelerators. Modern High Performance Computing (HPC) systems nowadays feature Non-Uniform Memory Access (NUMA) designs and are additionally equipped with multiple GPUs that are attached to different parts or sockets of the system. Considering the underlying architecture and proximity between CPU cores on the host and of GPUs during offloading is crucial to achieve good performance. Current programming models like OpenMP lack locality-aware device selection capabilities, necessitating manual code optimization for specific architectures. Our research addresses these issues by exploring CPU-to-GPU offloading performance, suggesting locality-aware host-to-device API extensions for OpenMP, and incorporating these extensions into the LLVM OpenMP runtime. Evaluations on a system with four GPUs demonstrate significant performance improvements through locality-aware device selection.

Keywords: Locality-Aware · Accelerators · GPUs · Device Offloading · Affinity

1 Introduction

In the last decades, the computational demand from scientific and industrial applications continued to grow. Over the past few decades, there has been a significant expansion in the range of research areas employing scientific simulations. These include, but are not limited to, climate and weather forecasting, molecular dynamics, physics, mechanical engineering, medicine and genetics. This persistent effort to advance the breadth and accuracy of simulations has created an ever-increasing requirement for computational resources and processing power.

Nowadays, we can observe a shift from purely CPU-based systems to heterogeneous architectures. Those architectures comprise CPUs as well as one or multiple accelerators such as *General Purpose Graphic Processing Units (GPGPUs)* with the idea to offload demanding computational kernels to accelerators and reduce the time to solution. Reviewing the latest Top500 list [2] of the fastest supercomputers in the world from June 2024, out of the first 30 installations 25 are heterogeneous systems with GPUs.

Further, systems tend to become more complex. While previous cluster generations comprised 1 or 2 GPUs per compute node, recent installations already offer 4 or more, with the trend to increase. Although advances in architectural design or the manufacturing processes and the addition of more compute devices within a node provide more computational power, these designs can also lead to performance variations and inconsistent application behavior. As an example, most modern *High Performance Computing (HPC)* systems today have a *Non-Uniform Memory Access (NUMA)* [6] design, comprising multiple sockets or NUMA domains, each equipped with multiple CPU cores as well a separate memory controller and local physical memory such as DRAM. Sockets within compute nodes are typically connected via an internal fabric such as Intel's *QuickPath Interconnect (QPI)* [12] or AMD's *HyperTransport* technology [4] or more precise *Infinity Fabric*. Local memory can be accessed faster, i.e., with lower latency and higher bandwidth, than the memory attached to a remote NUMA domain or socket. Hence, ensuring data locality becomes a crucial factor to exploit the full potential of such systems [9].

Similarly, with the increasing number of GPUs per node, devices might be attached to different sockets or NUMA domains of the base systems. As a result, accessing different devices and transferring data to or from those devices might also exhibit varying performance or performance variations. Although current programming models such as OpenMP are capable of utilizing multiple devices, they often lack the ability for a locality-aware device selection, and developers have to explicitly tailor source codes to a specific architecture to ensure the best performance. Consequently, in this work, we make the following contributions:

– We investigate the offloading performance between CPU cores and GPUs and analyze kernel launch time and bandwidth on recent systems with AMD and NVIDIA GPUs.
– We propose locality-aware host-to-device API extensions to the OpenMP specification that allow to retrieve device IDs of available GPUs, ordered by distance to the current thread or CPU core. These IDs can then be utilized to offload to close or distant devices.
– We present a prototype implementation in the LLVM OpenMP runtime and discuss implementation details.
– We evaluate our prototype implementation on a recent system with 4 GPUs and demonstrate the impact of a locality-aware device selection for offloading and overall performance.

The remainder of the paper is structured as follows. Section 2 discusses related work. Section 3 demonstrates different heterogeneous architectural designs and analyzes the offloading performance with respect to kernel launch time and bandwidth. In Sect. 4, we introduce our proposed extensions and provide implementation details for our prototype. Section 5 evaluates our approach before we conclude the work in Sect. 6.

2 Related Work

There are some related research activities close to the topic of locality-aware host-to-device offloading. Farooqui et al. [7] present an affinity-aware work stealing scheduler for heterogeneous GPU-based systems that feature *Shared Virtual Memory (SVM)* that is accessible from both the CPU and GPU side. Although they focus more on how work-stealing can be utilized to efficiently balance the load on such heterogeneous hardware, they also consider the hierarchical design and proximity to devices.

Maity et al. [11] propose a data locality-aware computation offloading to *Near Memory Processing (NMP)* 3D hardware in a data-centric computing paradigm that aims at reducing memory transfers between main memory and CPU side. However, they focus on data locality for computational work that is accessing the memory.

While this work tries to maximize offloading performance between host and devices, there are other works that strive to employ locality-aware or load-aware techniques to improve data access and computational performance solely within GPUs. As an example, Hbeika et al. [8] describe a locality-aware, task-queue abstraction that expands task-parallel work on the CPU, organizes tasks by computation type and locality, and executes them in a data-parallel fashion on the GPU. Their aim is to enhance SIMT efficiency and reduce cache pressure on the GPU itself.

3 Analyzing Offloading Performance on Recent Architectures

As discussed in Sect. 1, the number of additional accelerator devices per compute node is increasing. In the past, a common architecture design for HPC system that included 2 GPUs was to attach both of them only to one of the sockets to save costs for material and interconnects as depicted in Fig. 1a. Typically, there are interconnects between CPUs and GPUs such as PCIe and vendor-specific high-performance interconnects between single GPUs such as Nvidia's NVLink [3] or AMD's XGMI, in case they need to exchange data. Accessing GPUs from socket 1 through the internal socket interconnect however might inflict additional latency and experience lower bandwidth.

With increasing number of accelerators, decisions to attach all of them to a single socket changed due to limited scalability and space. Modern systems tend to spread GPUs across the system and attach them to different sockets or NUMA domains, which we will see in the following section. Consequently, selection of the *right* accelerator for offload computations becomes important to reach the best performance. In the following, we will describe two of those systems and present benchmark results for the offloading performance on both.

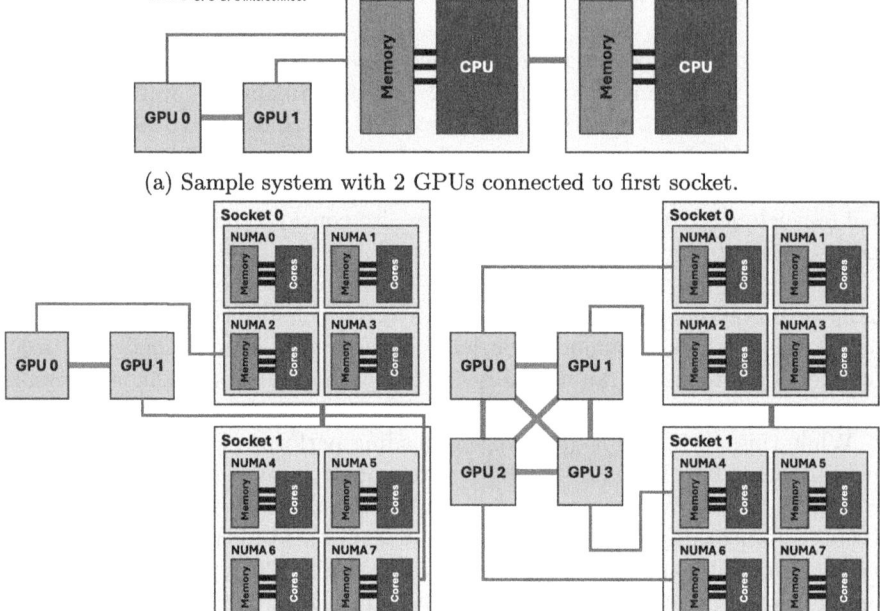

(a) Sample system with 2 GPUs connected to first socket.

(b) Topology of the AMD platform with 2 GPUs, which are connected to NUMA domains 2 and 7.

(c) Topology of the Intel+Nvidia platform with 4 GPUs, which are connected to NUMA domains 0, 2, 4 and 6. GPUs are connected with each other via a faster interconnect.

Fig. 1. System and architecture topologies with different number of GPUs attached.

3.1 Investigated Platforms

In this work, we investigated two different platforms. The first is a 2-socket system, depicted in Fig. 1b, each equipped with AMD EPYC 7F52 processors, with a total of 32 cores running at a base frequency of 3.5 GHz. Further, this system features 8 NUMA domains (4 per socket) with 64 GB DRAM each and 2 AMD INSTINCT MI210, of which one is connected to NUMA domain 2 (socket 0) and NUMA domain 7 (socket 1). It runs under Rocky Linux release 8.9 and Linux kernel version 4.18.0-513.24.1.

```
size_t size = 1000000000;
#pragma omp parallel num_threads(ncores)
{
  int tn = omp_get_thread_num();
  for (int c = 0; c < ncores; c++) {
    if (tn == c) {
      for (int d = 0; d < ndev; d++) {
        char *buffer = per_thread_buffs[tn];
        double ts = omp_get_wtime();
        for (int r = 0; r < REPS; r++) {
          #pragma omp target device(d)
              map(tofrom:buffer[0:size])
          {
            // only touch single element once
            // to avoid optimizing out code
            buffer[0] = 1;
          }
        }
        double elapsed = omp_get_wtime() - ts;
        double avg_time = elapsed / ((double) REPS);
      }
    }
    #pragma omp barrier
  }
}
```

Listing 1.1. Kernel of the fundamental benchmark to measure offloading bandwidth between Host and Device.

The second platform under investigation is a 2-socket system comprising Intel Xeon Platinum 8468 CPUs with a total of 96 cores running at a base frequency of 2.1 GHz, shown in Fig. 1c. Similar to the AMD system, this one is also divided into 8 NUMA domains with 64 GB DRAM each. Additionally, it provides access to 4 Nvidia H100 Hopper GPUs that are attached to NUMA domain 0, 2, 4, and 6. Operating system here is a Rocky Linux release 8.10 with Linux kernel version 4.18.0-553.5.1.

3.2 Assessing Offloading Performance

In order to assess the offloading performance between different cores and GPUs, we constructed fundamental latency (or kernel launch time) and bandwidth benchmarks[1] that apply device offloading but do not execute actual computation in the offloaded region. While for *latency* we only invoke kernel calls on the GPUs, the bandwidth kernel will copy the required data to the device

---

[1] Code available at https://github.com/RWTH-HPC/openmp-device-offloading-benchmark.

before the kernel invocation (HostToDevice) and from the device after the kernel has finished (DeviceToHost). For both benchmarks, we provide three distinct versions: 1. A general OpenMP version that utilizes `omp target` constructs to offload device regions; 2. A CUDA version for Nvidia GPUs; 3. A HIP version for AMD GPUs.

In this work, we conducted tests with the OpenMP version of the benchmarks. The basic kernel of those fundamental tests is illustrated in Listing 1.1. Benchmark runs will execute with `ncores` OpenMP threads, that are bound to physical CPU cores using `OMP_PLACES=cores` and `OMP_PROC_BIND=close`. The kernel iterates over all threads, one by one at a time, and performs offloads to all available devices to determine corresponding latencies or bandwidths from that thread. For bandwidth measurements there are possibilities to test with several buffer sizes, but for this experiment, we selected a fixed buffer size of 1 GB. Additionally, for reproducibility and a fair comparison, each thread is allocating its corresponding chunk of memory close to its location, and we disabled automatic NUMA balancing in the Linux kernel to avoid non-transparent dynamic memory movements by the OS.

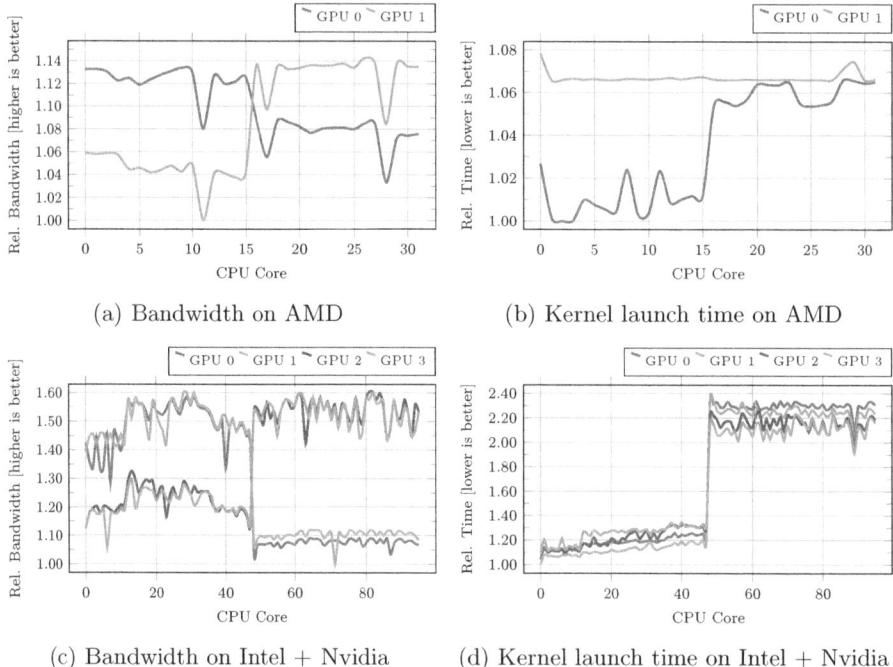

Fig. 2. Bandwidth and kernel launch time performance comparison for offloading operations between CPUs and GPUs. Results are normalized with respect to the lowest value in the corresponding plot.

Results for both platforms are shown in Fig. 2, whereas numbers on the Y-axis have been normalized with respect to the lowest value of the results, which has the value 1. It is clearly observable that on both platforms transferring data between CPU cores and GPUs on the same socket yields higher bandwidth compared to accessing a remote GPU on the opposite socket. On AMD, the average difference is about $1.07 \times$ while effects on the Intel+Nvidia system seem to be more pronounced with $1.32 \times$.

Interestingly, we can detect a different pattern for the kernel launch time behavior. On AMD, the GPU connected to the first socket experiences lower times when accessed from CPU cores on the first socket, while accessing the second GPU results in a high time, independent of the core accessing it. On the Nvidia system, cores on the second socket on average have a $1.85 \times$ higher launch time to all GPUs compared to cores on the first socket, which might be caused by the interaction between OpenMP threads and the hidden helper thread that is spawned by the LLVM runtime system to communicate with GPUs. Although this needs further investigation, first tests with constraining the cpuset to the single NUMA domains could not reproduce this huge difference. Nevertheless, differences in bandwidth are expected to have a higher impact on overall performance as programs typically do not offload very many very small computational kernels to GPUs.

4 Support for Host-to-Device Affinity

The analysis from Sect. 3 demonstrated that the different device selections in OpenMP can have a significant impact on transfer bandwidth and latency. As of now, OpenMP does not provide any means to detect which accelerators are close to an offloading thread. To achieve good performance and avoid performance pitfalls, developers currently need to tailor their source code to a specific architecture design, which might change every 3 to 5 years. In the following, we propose an extension for the OpenMP specification to express host-to-device affinity transparently and further provide implementation details for our prototype extension in the LLVM OpenMP runtime.

4.1 Proposed API Extension

As depicted in Listing 1.2, our proposal consists of adding new type definitions and a new API routine omp_get_devices_in_order, that is intended to find devices that are close to the current requesting OpenMP thread. However, instead of adding a very specific routine for that special case, we aimed at designing the routine in such a way that it can also be used for other purposes and that it can be extended in the future.

The idea of the function is to retrieve devices in a certain deterministic sort order. The first three parameters define the number of desired devices (n_dev) that should be retrieved, an array that will be filled with the corresponding device IDs, and an array filled with the values used to sort the list of devices.

```
// Type definitions
typedef enum {
    omp_dt_lowest_distance = 0
} omp_dev_trait_key_t;

typedef struct {
    omp_dev_trait_key_t key;
    union omp_dev_trait_value_t {
        int i;
        double dbl;
        long l;
    } value;
} omp_dev_trait_t;

// API function
int omp_get_devices_in_order(int n_dev, int *dev_ids, double
    *vals_order, int n_traits, omp_dev_trait_t *traits);
```

Listing 1.2. OpenMP API routine to retrieve list of ordered devices

Additionally, the function accepts a list of traits, that can be used for filtering purposes (i.e. with key-value pairs) or to define sort criteria, in this case *lowest distance*. It is then the responsibility of the OpenMP runtime system to explore the underlying architecture and filter and order the resulting device IDs according to the specified traits. After sorting, array `vals_order` further reveils the values that have been used as basis for ordering device IDs. Currently, the routine only considers a 1-dimensional array for order values. If it is desired to apply multiple sorting criteria, this part needs to be slightly adapted. The routine returns an integer `n_dev_found`, representing the number of devices that are available and match the specified criteria, which can be lower than or equal to `n_dev`. Consequently, only the first `n_dev_found` values in the arrays contain valid entries.

In this work, we focus on returning devices sorted by how close they are to the current requesting thread. However, what *close* exactly means and how different runtimes sort devices might be implementation defined and could exploit very simple metrics such as NUMA distances or more complex mechanisms such as pre-generated bandwidth lookup tables.

Listing 1.3 illustrates an example how this new API routine can be used. Here, a single trait is used to specify the sort order. As traits are designed as key-value pairs and sort order does not need a value, we set it to -1 in this example. After the call, array `dev_ids` contains the desired devices sorted by increasing distance. A program can now utilize that information to either offload to a close device, e.g. `dev_ids[0]`, or a remote device such as `dev_ids[n_dev_found-1]`. Note that, although we reserve space for 20 device entries, it might be that only fewer devices are available or match the search criteria, like on the AMD platform that only has 2 GPUs.

```
int n=20;                // desired number of devices
int n_dev_found;         // actual number found for request
int dev_ids[n];          // buffer with ids returned
double vals_order[n];    // buffer with values used for ordering

// point of view from current OpenMP thread (or core)
n_dev_found = omp_get_devices_in_order(n, dev_ids,
    vals_order, 1, {omp_dt_lowest_distance, -1});

// use closest device
#pragma omp target device(dev_ids[0])
// use remote device (max distance, e.g. on remote NUMA node)
#pragma omp target device(dev_ids[n_dev_found-1])
```

Listing 1.3. Example usage for proposed API extension

4.2 Prototype Implementation Details

For a proof-of-concept of our proposed extensions, we developed a prototype implementation in the LLVM OpenMP runtime system based on LLVM version 18.x[2] which currently only supports the *libomptarget* plugin for Nvidia GPU devices. Behind the scenes, the following steps have been implemented:

1. At initialization, the runtime once iterates over all NUMA domains, sockets and Nvidia devices and identifies where the corresponding devices are connected to. For that we use a combination of hwloc [5] API calls and `hwloc_cudart_get_device_cpuset`.
2. To order devices based on distance, we exploit NUMA distance values that can be retrieved from `libnuma` [1]. With that and information where devices are connected, we are able to create distance lookup tables that can be exploited and reused later. That procedure avoids overhead caused by executing the architecture exploration every time, which is a costly operation.
3. When an OpenMP thread invokes `omp_get_devices_in_order`, the runtime will determine the current CPU core where the thread is executing and with that its assigned NUMA domain via `numa_node_of_cpu(sched_getcpu())`. Then, the runtime can utilize the pre-calculated lookup tables to determine a list of sorted device IDs.

As an example on the Intel+Nvidia platform introduced in Sect. 3.1, calling `omp_get_devices_in_order` from a thread running at NUMA domain 0 would result in the following list: GPU0,GPU1,GPU2,GPU3. Contrary, for a thread running at NUMA domain 6 the list would return: GPU3,GPU2,GPU0,GPU1.

---
[2] Our LLVM prototype implementation is publicly available at https://github.com/RWTH-HPC/llvm-project/tree/thread-to-device-affinity-18.x.

5 Evaluation

To evaluate our experimental LLVM prototype implementation we use a multi-threaded benchmark[3] that conducts a configurable number of independent DGEMM operations, whereas all DGEMM tasks work on square matrices with the same configurable size. Each thread in an application run will allocate memory for data items of its assigned DGEMM operations close to the thread based on the first-touch policy [10] and then trigger the offloading process for the DGEMM tasks. For stability and reproducibility purposes, we again bind OpenMP threads to physical CPU cores this time with `OMP_PLACES=cores` and `OMP_PROC_BIND=spread` and disable NUMA balancing in the underlying OS.

Contrary to the fundamental benchmark described in Sect. 3, all threads can operate simultaneously. Choosing the wrong GPUs to offload to might lead to additional contention. That emphasizes that a locality-aware device selection is imperative to avoid performance declines and yield good performance. Additionally, we added an option to enable or disable the computation in the `omp target` kernel to fully focus on the data mappings and kernel invocations. That also allows us to compare the overall impact on performance with and without computation.

Several tests have been conducted on the Intel+Nvidia platform described in Sect. 3.1 with 12 threads, 60 independent tasks, and matrix sizes ranging from 1024×1024 to 12288×12288. For each test setup, we compare versions where OpenMP threads either decide to offload to one of the closest GPUs (referred to as *best case*) or one of the remote GPUs (referred to as *worst case*), while maintaining a proper load balance within these sets of devices.

Results are depicted in Fig. 3 and report mean values based on 5 individual runs. Figure 3a illustrates performance differences for runs that solely focus on the data transfer and kernel invocation part of the offloading process and not execute any computation in the kernel. Of course, with increasing problem size also rises execution time. However, as expected, we can observe a clear performance improvement when exploiting host-to-device affinity information and select close devices. As an example, with matrix sizes of 10240×10240 and on average, the best case version achieves a $1.38 \times$ speedup over the version that utilizes distant GPUs.

However, there might be cases where the time spent with data mappings and kernel invocation is only relatively small compared to the overall execution time as most time is spent during computations happening on the devices, which does not differ between best and worst case. Consequently, the degree of performance improvement is limited in such cases. As a comparison, we also conducted tests with a version that performs the naïve DGEMM computation in the `target` region. Results in Fig. 3b illustrate that the overall execution time

---

[3] Available at https://github.com/RWTH-HPC/openmp-host-to-device-affinity-demonstrator.

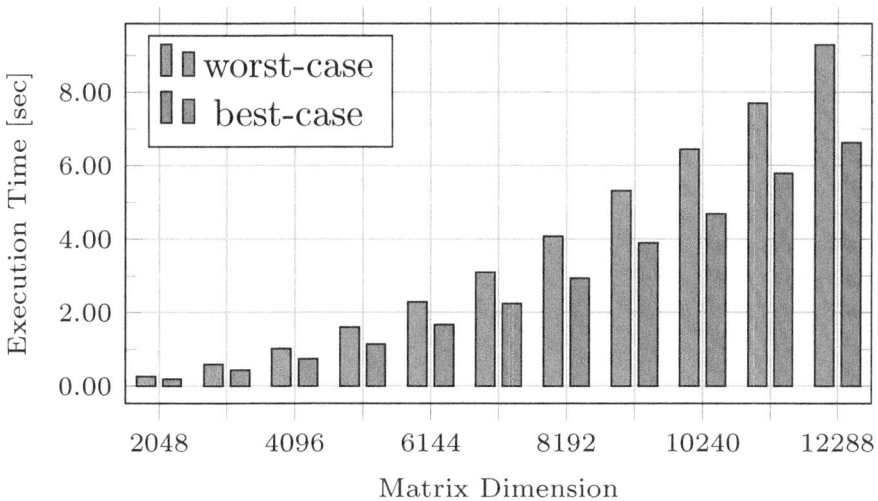

(a) Results without computation in target kernel

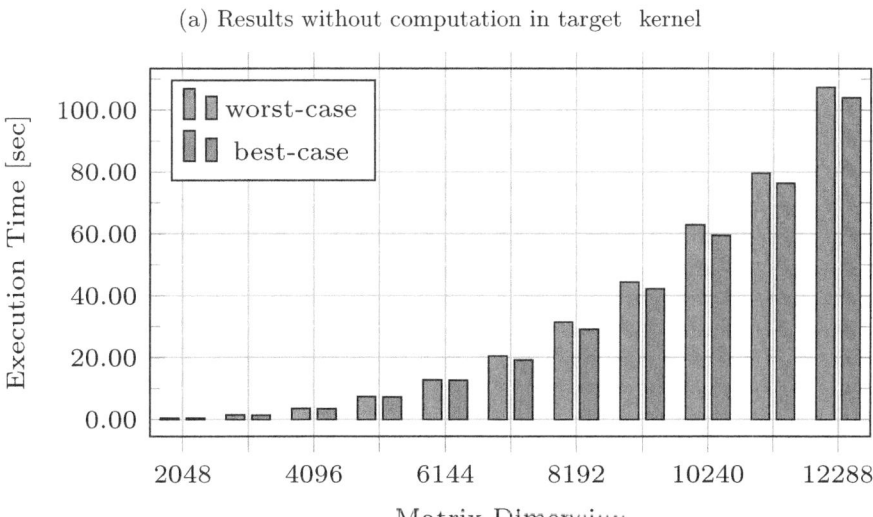

(b) Results with computation in target kernel

Fig. 3. Performance impact of locality-aware host-to-device offloading on the platform that features 4 Nvidia H100 GPUs. Figures show variants where the DGEMM computation was either activated or deactivated within `omp target` kernels.

greatly increases and is dominated by the computational work in the single kernels. Nevertheless, we can also observe slight performance improvements caused by the more efficient device usage and data mappings. For larger matrix sizes such as 10240 × 10240, we can report speedups of up to 6 %.

6 Conclusion and Future Work

In this work, we discuss the challenge of applications that heavily utilize GPU offloading on state-of-the art HPC system, where compute nodes are equipped with multiple GPUs. Proper device selection from offloading OpenMP threads might significantly impact the overall performance of such workloads. We analyzed two recent architectures from AMD as well as Intel + Nvidia and investigated offloading performance with respect to bandwidth and latency (or kernel launch time) between CPU cores and GPUs in the system in an all-to-all manner, reporting differences of up to $1.32\times$ for bandwidth and $1.85\times$. Further, we introduced an API extension for the OpenMP specification to better support locality-aware host-to-device affinity and suitable device selection, followed by detailing our prototype implementation in the LLVM OpenMP runtime system. In our evaluation with a multi-threaded application that performs multiple offloads, we demonstrate the effectiveness of our approach, yielding speedups of up to $1.4\times$, when focusing on data mappings and kernel invocation.

There are several directions for future work. We plan to generalize our Nvidia-based LLVM runtime implementation to add support for AMD and other accelerators. Following on that, we want to conduct more experiments with various HPC system architectures from different vendors and other applications that utilize device offloading. Further, we plan to expand our locality-aware concept to support data-to-device affinity to select devices that are close to the physical location of data buffers on the host or select devices, where large parts of required data is already present due to previous mappings to minimize data transfer costs as much as possible.

Acknowledgments. Special thanks go to Michael Klemm for his insights on recent architecture design and his guidance during the implementation of the latency and bandwidth benchmarks. We would also like to thank Vivek Kale for his feedback on application use cases.

Simulations were performed with computing resources granted by RWTH Aachen University under project rwth0900.

References

1. NUMA - Linux Programmer's Manual. https://man7.org/linux/man-pages/man3/numa.3.html. Accessed 05 May 2023
2. Top500 List - June 2024. https://top500.org/lists/top500/list/2024/06/. Accessed 19 June 2024
3. Whitepaper Nvidia ® NVLink Tm High-speed Interconnect: application performance. https://api.semanticscholar.org/CorpusID:18764353
4. Anderson, D.: HyperTransport Architecture. Addison-Wesley Longman Publishing Co., Inc, USA (2003)
5. Broquedis, F., et al.: hwloc: a generic framework for managing hardware affinities in HPC applications. In: 2010 18th Euromicro Conference on Parallel, Distributed and Network-based Processing, pp. 180–186 (2010). https://doi.org/10.1109/PDP.2010.67

6. Cox, A., Fowler, R.: The implementation of a coherent memory abstraction on a NUMA multiprocessor: experiences with PLATINUM. SIGOPS Oper. Syst. Rev. **23**(5), 32–44 (1989). https://doi.org/10.1145/74851.74855
7. Farooqui, N., Barik, R., Lewis, B.T., Shpeisman, T., Schwan, K.: Affinity-aware work-stealing for integrated CPU-GPU processors. In: Proceedings of the 21st ACM SIGPLAN Symposium on Principles and Practice of Parallel Programming. PPoPP 2016, Association for Computing Machinery, New York, NY, USA (2016). https://doi.org/10.1145/2851141.2851194
8. Hbeika, J., Kulkarni, M.: Locality-aware task-parallel execution on GPUs. In: Ding, C., Criswell, J., Wu, P. (eds.) LCPC 2016. LNCS, vol. 10136, pp. 250–264. Springer, Cham (2017). https://doi.org/10.1007/978-3-319-52709-3_19
9. Klinkenberg, J., et al.: Assessing task-to-data affinity in the LLVM OpenMP runtime. In: de Supinski, B.R., Valero-Lara, P., Martorell, X., Mateo Bellido, S., Labarta, J. (eds.) IWOMP 2018. LNCS, vol. 11128, pp. 236–251. Springer, Cham (2018). https://doi.org/10.1007/978-3-319-98521-3_16
10. Lameter, C.: NUMA (Non-Uniform Memory Access): an overview: NUMA becomes more common because memory controllers get close to execution units on microprocessors. Queue **11**(7), 40–51 (2013). https://doi.org/10.1145/2508834.2513149
11. Maity, S., Goel, M., Ghose, M.: Data locality aware computation offloading in near memory processing architecture for big data applications. In: 2023 IEEE 30th International Conference on High Performance Computing, Data, and Analytics (HiPC), pp. 288–297 (2023). https://doi.org/10.1109/HiPC58850.2023.00019
12. Ziakas, D., Baum, A., Maddox, R.A., Safranek, R.J.: Intel® QuickPath interconnect architectural features supporting scalable system architectures. In: 2010 18th IEEE Symposium on High Performance Interconnects, pp. 1–6 (2010). https://doi.org/10.1109/HOTI.2010.24

Performance Porting the ExaStar Multi-Physics App Thornado On Heterogeneous Systems - A Fortran-OpenMP Code-Base Evaluation

Mathialakan Thavappiragasam[1]($\boxtimes$)[iD], J. Austin Harris[2][iD], Eirik Endeve[2][iD], and Brice Videau[1][iD]

[1] Argonne National Laboratory, Lemont, IL, USA
{mthavappiragasam,bvideau}@anl.gov
[2] Oak Ridge National Laboratory, Oak Ridge, TN, USA
{harrisja,endevee}@ornl.gov

Abstract. The heterogeneity of HPC systems requires efficient host-to-device porting of compute kernels and high-bandwidth data communication. This capability varies from one system to another depending on system architectures and environments. New vendors such as AMD and Intel are entering the GPU field, creating a software portability challenge. Major scientific simulation code bases rely on Fortran and require portable programming models for performance porting to HPC systems with high software productivity. Even though OpenMP target offloading features support portability, most Fortran-OpenMP code bases face significant challenges. Hence, in this work, we motivated an evaluation of a) the computing capability of heterogeneous systems for Fortran-OpenMP-based multi-physics code bases, and b) the performance portability of the astrophysical supernova simulation code Flash-X on heterogeneous systems. For this study, three HPC systems were chosen: Sunspot, a test-bed system of the Intel-PVC GPU featured supercomputer Aurora and Polaris, an NVIDIA system accelerated by A100 GPU, both located at the Argonne Leadership Computing Facility (ALCF), and the AMD-MI250-based Frontier at the Oak Ridge Leadership Computing Facility (OLCF). We discuss challenges and solutions for performance porting the compute-intensive module Thornado, which can be incorporated as an external library in Flash-X to model neutrino transport. We show that the performance of test apps improved by approximately 24× using the relevant optimization strategies + compiler-and-system updates. Further, this study helped improve the intel OneAPI-OpenMP compiler by providing bug reports and reproducers internally.

Keywords: Fortran-OpenMP code base · Multi-physics toolkit · Porting to heterogeneous systems · OpenMP target offloading · OpenACC · Intel's PVC GPU · Concurrent multi-tasking

1 Introduction

Emerging and next-generation supercomputers enhance their computing throughput and communication bandwidths by introducing novel/evolving technologies. Because of existing/upcoming diverse architectures and supporting software suites, we need to port/migrate application tools over those systems using appropriate programming models, such as vendor-specific APIs e.g. CUDA for NVIDIA systems [27], directive-based APIs e.g. a portable model OpenMP [28], OpenACC [42], etc. Novel architectures, supportive novel system software, and compiler suites must be evaluated for their performance, capability, and robustness. Even though various micro-benchmarking tool sets [29] exist for the evaluation, a broad range of real applications can indict bugs and the ability to provide useful insights for system software developers as well as for architecture designers [39]. In this work, we evaluate HPC systems, specifically Intel+HPE-built Aurora [2], and the accompanied software suite, OneAPI while porting the Fortran code-base Thornado using OpenMP target offloading.

Within the ExaScale Computing Project (ECP), ExaStar aims to develop computational tools for exascale systems to model astrophysical sites for heavy element production, such as core-collapse supernovae and binary neutron star mergers. Computational models of these multi-physics phenomena use operator splitting approaches to evolve a coupled system of partial differential equations (PDEs) for hydrodynamics, gravity, nuclear reaction kinetics, and neutrino transport [18]. One of the main application codes developed for astrophysical simulations by ExaStar is the multi-physics simulation software instrument Flash-X [15]. Thornado, also developed by ExaStar, provides modules enabling Flash-X to solve PDEs that model the transport of neutrinos and their interaction with matter. Thornado approximates the neutrino radiation field by solving for angular moments of the kinetic distribution function in a multi-species spectral two-moment approach [8,37]. Thornado uses the discontinuous Galerkin (DG) method [13] to discretize the moment equations in phase-space (see [11,24,25] for details). After discretization with the DG method, the moment equations reduce to a system of ordinary differential equations (ODEs) of the form

$$\dot{\boldsymbol{u}} = T(\boldsymbol{u}) + C(\boldsymbol{u}), \tag{1}$$

where $\boldsymbol{u}$ represents the global solution vector of neutrino moments. In Eq. (1), the transport operator T models the free-streaming of neutrinos in phase-space, while the collision operator C models interactions between neutrinos and matter. Implicit-Explicit (IMEX) [6,34] methods are used to integrate the ODE in Eq. (1) forward in time. One of the simplest IMEX schemes, consisting of a combination of forward and backward Euler steps, evolving the moments from $u^n = u(t^n)$ to $\boldsymbol{u}^{n+1} = \boldsymbol{u}(t^n + \Delta t)$ with time step Δt can be written as

$$\boldsymbol{u}^* = \boldsymbol{u}^n + \Delta t \, T(\boldsymbol{u}^n), \tag{2a}$$
$$\boldsymbol{u}^{n+1} = \boldsymbol{u}^* + \Delta t \, C(\boldsymbol{u}^{n+1}). \tag{2b}$$

Here, the transport operator is integrated with an explicit method, while the collision operator is integrated with an implicit method. Equations (2a) and (2b) constitute the main computational kernels in Thornado. The nonlinear implicit part in Eq. (2b) contributes the majority of the computational cost. In this paper, we consider the performance of the algorithms implemented in Thornado with two representative tests: Streaming Sine Wave (SSW; [25]) and Relaxation [24]. The SSW test solves Eq. (1) with $C(\boldsymbol{u}) = 0$, using a two-stage Runge–Kutta time integration method, which consists of two updates of the type listed in Eq. (2a). Limiters are applied after each stage to recover physical realizability of the numerical solution by modifying the element-local polynomial representation (see Sect. 5.2 in [25]). For this test, the main computational kernel is the recovery of primitive from conserved moments, which is done using a fixed-point iteration method [25]. The Relaxation test solves Eq. (1) with $T(\boldsymbol{u}) = 0$, using the backward Euler method, which is equivalent to Eq. (2b) when $\boldsymbol{u}^* = \boldsymbol{u}^n$. For this test, the main computational kernels are opacity interpolations and collision rate evaluations (matrix-vector multiplications). The nonlinear collision solve is done with a nested fixed-point algorithm [24]. Together, the SSW and Relaxation tests provide valuable insights into the performance of the IMEX scheme used to incorporate Thornado in Flash-X. We mention that the neutrino moments depend to spacetime coordinates $(\boldsymbol{x}, t)$ and momentum space coordinate ε (neutrino energy). The energy dimension is discretized with 32 points. Then, with four moments and six neutrino species, the moment model evolves $32 \times 4 \times 6 = 768$ degrees of freedom per spatial point. Moreover, the collision solve in Eq. (2), while being local in space, couples neutrinos across energies, species and moments. The large number of unknowns and their coupling makes the neutrino transport solve computationally demanding, and efficient use of HPC systems is essential.

In this work, we were motivated to find answers to the questions: 1) do heterogeneous systems have features to build complicated Fortran-based codes?, 2) can a Fortran-based code be accelerated by OpenMP target offload for performance portability over different heterogeneous systems?, and 3) would newly introduced HPC architectures be competitive with the existing applications?. And, our contribution for this paper includes: 1) performance enhancing Thornado via multi-level optimization strategies/methodologies. 2) helping to improve Fortran OpenMP compilers by providing missing features and prioritizing expected future specifications, and 3) performance porting Thornado to the heterogeneous systems Aurora, Frontier, and Polaris using OpenMP target offloading features.

1.1 Design and Structure of Thornado

Thornado is a Fortran code, accelerated by OpenACC and OpenMP directives to utilize GPUs or multi-core CPUs. The code leverages vendor-optimized linear algebra libraries (e.g., LAPACK, OneMKL, cuBLAS, rocBLAS). Thornado is primarily a single MPI rank code that can be executed on a GPU. However, it is able to be used in a modular way to independently evolve regions of a physical domain, such as those provided by the domain-decomposition in an adaptive mesh refinement framework of a multi-physics application (e.g., Flash-X). Thornado includes three major tasks: *Apply limiters* to recover physical realizability of the numerical solution, *Explicit updates* for neutrino advection (related to the SSW app), and *Implicit updates* for neutrino collisions (related to the Relaxation app). Since Thornado uses a two-stage IMEX time integration scheme, both advection and collision updates are executed twice with intermediate calls to *apply-limiters* to maintain realizability and conservation. The SSW app uses explicit second-order strong stability preserving Runge–Kutta (SSPRK-2) time stepping. Figure 1 shows major tasks involving on the computation of neutrino advection for the SSW app. The process begins on a host with the initialization of driver and fields data. On device, the scheme for SSW is evolved for `nsteps` time-steps. This evolution consists of four major tasks: a *precomputing* which includes mesh generation and geometry computation, *update-advection*, *apply-limiters*, and *increment-parameters*. Finally, errors are computed and results are recorded during the post-computation process on host. The Relaxation app relies on an implicit, single-stage, backward Euler scheme for time stepping, and follows the same tasks as SSW. However, it uses implicit-update for neutron-matter collisions instead of the explicit-update advection method.

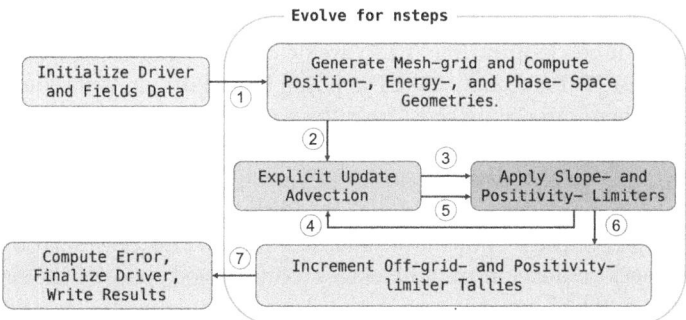

Fig. 1. Top-level workflow diagram for SSW

1.2 Related Work

Thornado is closely related to that used by others to study core-collapse supernovae [7,22,23,38], but these codes have yet to publish demonstration of GPU usage. Within the larger astrophysics community we refer to [1,26,36,40], which use GPUs to solve the equations of reactive hydrodynamics, magnetohydrodynamics (MHD), and radiation-MHD. We also mention the work in [41], which solves an energy-integrated (grey) two-moment model coupled with hydrodynamics and adaptive mesh refinement using GPUs.

2 Performance Porting and Optimization

In this section, we discuss the performance porting effort on heterogeneous systems (specifically focusing on Aurora using OpenMP-target-offloading), including code-, compiler-, and system-level optimizations, major milestones achieved and challenges faced during this performance optimization and enhancement work, and suggest possible solutions. The code base is already ported to the NVIDIA-V100 based system Summit and optimized for OpenACC.

Kernel Level Optimizations. Dominant compute-bound and memory-bound kernels were identified using their single and/or double precision FLOPs and arithmetic intensities from the roofline plots and profiling data obtained by using profiling tools: iprof and Intel-Advisor on Intel systems, Nsight-Sys and Nsight-Compute on NVIDIA systems, and rocprof and omnitrace on AMD systems.

A. Hierarchical Parallelism and Kernel Fission: In several places, the implementation of nested loops are identified as working points for the improvements of prallelization. We mainly used three methods to reorganize the code for the performance enhancement: i) organize task dependencies, ii) make collapsible loops, and iii) decompose loops. In Listing 1.1, `!$OMP TARGET TEAMS DISTRIBUTE` is used for the outer loop in line 1 and `!$OMP PARALLEL DO SIMD` is used for the inner loop in line 4 hierarchically. Instead, using `!$OMP TARGET TEAMS DISTRIBUTE PARALLEL DO SIMD` [9,35] for a flat loop will reduce the time significantly. Therefore, we moved *Computing 1* to inside the inner loop as shown in Listing 1.2 and collapsed the loops. We notice that by rearranging the code as described, the task *Computing 1* is being iterated for nm times instead of n times. Even though this redundant computation may consume more time, the larger loop-collapse avoids additional overheads. This optimization helps to improve the performance on running across a linear-ized space of the size nm [12]. For example, a 2D bi-linear interpolation kernel, implemented in the WeakLib library, reflects the same pattern as described in Listing [17] (-shown as *kernel_1* in Fig. 2 in the performance-evaluation section). The Relaxation app invokes this kernel with outer-loop size n=4096 which is much larger than the inner-loop size m=3. Hence, the loop-flattening results in significant performance improvement. We identified the same issues on the code structure shown in Listing 1.3. In addition to flattening the loops by reorganizing the tasks, we decompose the loops into two code segments (Listing 1.4). Since *Computing 2* neither depends on *Computing 1* or *Computing 3*, it can be separated among them and easily linearized and supports an even work-load distribution among the threads. In our code-base, *Computing 1-3* can be mapped to a set of tasks of the interpolation module in the WeakLib library: *1)* Pre-computing table indexes and interpolation weights for density, *2)* Computing rectangular loop indexes from collapsed triangular loop, and *3)* Computing table indexes and interpolation weights for temperature and then combining three bi-linear interpolations of third and fourth dimensions of a 4D table respectively. The *kernel_3* in the performance evaluation Sect. 3.1 reflects this code-optimization technique.

```
1  !$OMP TARGET TEAMS DISTRIBUTE
2  DO k = 1, n
3    // Computing 1
4    !$OMP PARALLEL DO SIMD
5    DO j = 1, m
6      // Computing 2
7    END DO
8  END DO
```
Listing 1.1. Pattern-1 of optimizable hierarchical parallelism.

```
1  !$OMP TARGET TEAMS DISTRIBUTE PARALLEL
         DO SIMD COLLAPSE(2)
2  DO k = 1, n
3    DO j = 1, m
4      // Computing 1
5      // Computing 2
6    END DO
7  END DO
```
Listing 1.2. Optimized hierarchical parallelism

```
1  !$OMP TARGET TEAMS DISTRIBUTE MAP
      ...
2  DO k = 1, n
3    // Computing 1
4    DO j = 1, p
5      // Computing 2
6    END DO
7    !$OMP PARALLEL DO SIMD
8    DO i = 1, m
9      // Computing 3
10   END DO
11 END DO
```
Listing 1.3. Pattern-2 of optimizable hierarchical parallelism.

```
1  !$OMP TARGET DATA MAP
2  !$OMP TARGET TEAMS DISTRIBUTE PARALLEL
         DO SIMD COLLAPSE(2)
3  DO k = 1, n
4    DO j = 1, p
5      // Computing 2
6    END DO
7  END DO
8  !$OMP TARGET TEAMS DISTRIBUTE PARALLEL
         DO SIMD COLLAPSE(2)
9  DO k = 1, n
10   DO i = 1, m
11     // Computing 1
12     // Computing 3
13   END DO
14 END DO
```
Listing 1.4. Optimized hierarchical parallelism.

B. Parameter tuning: Here, we mainly consider the size of worker threads used in GPU accelerators which influence the code performance. Even though compilers have features for auto-tuning these parameters [16,43], manual settings can often help to confirm the optimum value of team size `thread_limit` and number of teams `num_teams`. Intel `oneapi-icpx` compiler uses 32 as the default team size, but we noticed that some kernels require bigger team size for the best performance (e.g., 128).

Intel Systems' Based Optimization: In this section, we discuss optimizations made based on Intel architecture, mainly focusing on the Aurora HPC system being built at Argonne National Laboratory, and OneAPI compiler-suite, focusing on Fortran and OpenMP compilers.

A. Configuration of Memory Pool: Through our experiment, we discovered untapped performance gains in compiler configuration via setting a runtime environment variable for tuning memory pool usage. Controlling device memory using `Level Zero` specifications will help to tune the performance. The `LIBOMPTARGET_LEVEL_ZERO_MEMORY_POOL`, an OpenMP offload environment variable for `Level Zero` offload plugin is used to control memory pool configurations. Memory pool configurations are being used to decide runtime memory size in `Level Zero` which provides system level interface to offload accelerator devices and gives explicit control for high-level runtime APIs and libraries. This reusable memory pool has configurable parameters: *maximum allocation size* in MB supported by the pool, *number of allocations* supported by a single memory block allocated from the Level Zero runtime, and *maximum size of the entire pool* in MB [14].

B. Ahead of Time Compilation: We often used Just-In-Time (JIT) compilation throughout our optimization process, but we noticed a gap between total time and IMEX time for both apps, SSW and Relaxation. The IMEX time represents actual computing time for the implicit-explicit scheme used in Thornado and total time includes overheads like initialization and I/O. We were able to reduce the gap significantly by using Ahead-Of-Time (AOT) compilation instead of JIT. AOT compilation performs pre-compilation that avoids the runtime overhead-time introduced by JIT compilation and also it requires a smaller memory footprint. Further, binaries generated during the AOT compilation will contain the actual assembly code of the platform that was selected at compile time instead of generating intermediate code, SPIR-V on oneAPI [21] and PTX for CUDA [31], that need to be compiled to assembly at runtime using JIT compilation [19]. Hence, the AOT compilation helps to reduce runtime overhead.

C. Concurrent Executions on Multi-Tiles GPU: Thornado is a single MPI-Rank code. It can utilize a GPU to run the entire code's executable unit. A GPU on PVC consists of 2 tiles. To utilize the entire GPU (both tiles), we have to enable implicit communications (`EnableImplicitScaling=1`) between the two tiles inside a GPU to obtain better performance [14]. Based on our experiment, using 2-tiles with enabling implicit communication affects robustness of the app. It also requires a high memory pool configuration and incurs a performance loss. Hence, we decided to use a tile for a unit of execution and we utilize the full GPU by executing two realisations onto two tiles concurrently. Here, two execution units of the app are assigned to two host threads, each runs its task on an assigned GPU-tile. We can expect a higher wall-time than a single run on a tile due to context switching and communication overhead.

3 Performance Evaluation Experiment

The performance of Thornado is evaluated over different heterogeneous systems targeting Intel, AMD, and NVIDIA architectures. We chose a) pre-exascale systems, Summit (V100) [33] and Polaris (A100) [4] for NVIDIA-based systems and b) exascale systems, Frontier (MI250) [32] for AMD-, and Sunspot (PVC) [5] for Intel-based systems. We also used a PVC system, Florentia, provided by Argonne's Joint Laboratory for System Evaluation (JLSE) [3]. The *develop* branch of Thornado source code on GitHub[1] is used for this test. It requires two external packages: HDF5 to handle I/O and the WeakLib library to access pre-computed tabulations of nuclear equations of state and neutrino-matter interaction rates[2]. The compilers used to build the application varies depending on the system: `nvhpc-nvfortran` on Summit and Polaris, `cce-crayftn` on Frontier,

---
[1] https://github.com/endeve/thornado/tree/develop.
[2] https://code.ornl.gov/astro/weaklib-tables.git.

and `intel-ifx` on Sunspot. For each app, we consider two test cases: 1) small - grid size $8 \times 8 \times 8$ and 2) large - grid size $16 \times 16 \times 16$, both test cases use 6 species and 2 quadrature nodes. The SSW sets for 8 energy-elements while Relaxation sets 16. The spatial resolution is doubled in 3D for the large data, also doubling the number of time steps used in the SSW app such that the Courant-Friedrichs-Lewy (CFL) criteria is properly obeyed for both cases.

3.1 Intel Systems

Sunspot, a test-bed for Aurora, was the primary system used for conducting our optimizations and performance evaluation. As previously explained, hierarchical loops are collapsed and split into multiple sets of loop-nests to expose as much instruction-level parallelism as possible. Figure 2 shows speedups obtained by this treatment for 3 distinct kernels for the small problem of the Relaxation app: two types of interpolation, *kernel_1* and *kernel_3*, and computing neutrino-matter interaction rates, *kernel_2*. By removing hierarchical parallelism, *kernel_1* and *kernel_3* obtained 2.72× and 1.93× speedups. Loop-flattening helped *kernel_1* to achieve 3.3× cumulative speedup. For the optimization of *kernel_2*, a) target data transferring is moved out of the loop (Tgt_Offld) and b) the device kernel (Knl_Decompose) is decomposed (obtained 8.97× speedup). Overall, we obtained 5.76× speedup on those three kernels together.

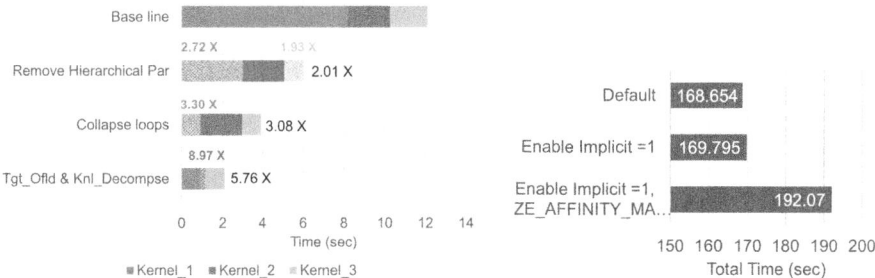

Fig. 2. Kernel-level optimization for the Relaxation app with the small problem size. Here, pattern-filled portions indicate that the relevant optimizations are applied for the specific kernels.

Fig. 3. Effect of using number of tiles with enabling implicit communication for the SSW app on Intel-PVC.

In the following studies, we use two of the memory pool controlling parameters: *maximum allocation size* and *maximum number of allocations*. Using two tiles gave a performance loss due to the cross-tile communication overhead time as described previously. Figure 3 shows this effect clearly. Getting less performance for the default configuration, obviously, requires parameter tuning. Two tiles with enabled implicit communication fails to run for the default configuration as well as for small size of memory pool (e.g., fails for the parameters, maximum allocation size and maximum number of allocations (8,16) and (16,32)). Even though it successfully builds and gives correct results for memory pool size (32,64), it consumes 12% more time compared a single tile's performance. Enabling implicit communication allows for cross-communication between tiles in a GPU and `ZE_AFFINITY_MASK` is used to set which GPUs and tiles are going to be utilized. Here, setting `ZE_AFFINITY_MASK=0` enables the entire use (both tiles) of GPU-0 [14]. Based on this study, we decided to utilize a single tile with an optimum memory pool size to run a Thornado executable. Hence, the memory pool configuration is tuned for both SSW and Relaxation apps to obtain the optimum value for pairs of block size and number of blocks required on a single tile. Figure 4 shows this study. The pool configuration of (16,32) gives 2× speedup for the SSW app compared to the default configuration. The Relaxation app gives improvements for further extension of the mempool size to (32, 64) by 4.8× and (64,128) by 5.2× since it consumes more memory compared to the SSW app. Since we worked on the device kernels, we were able to reduce the wall-time significantly via the optimization steps explained so far. However, there was a big gap that had been maintained between the total execution time and time spent in the primary timestep loop (IMEX), and that was reduced by using AOT compilation. Figure 5 compares the total and IMEX times obtained by JIT and AOT compilations; 2.18× and 1.26× speedups in total time are achieved by AOT compilation for SSW and Relaxation apps respectively.

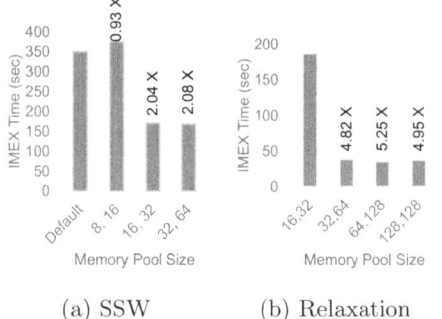
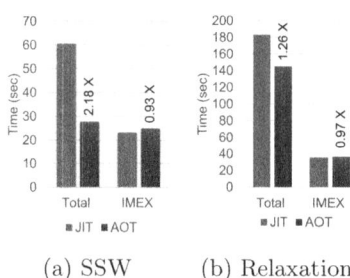

Fig. 4. Tuning memory pool configuration parameters, (maximum allocation size, maximum number of allocations) for the apps, (a) SSW and (b) Relaxation using the small test case on Intel-PVC.

Fig. 5. JIT vs AOT compilations for the apps, (a) SSW and (b) Relaxation using the small test case on Intel-PVC.

The process of porting Thornado to Intel systems began with an internal system. From beginning to now, we achieved 13.45× and 24.77× speedup on IMEX and total times for SSW and 13.87× and 23.57× speedup on IMEX and total times for Relaxation. Kernel-level optimizations, switching compilation from JIT to AOT, tuning memory pool configuration and OpenMP target team sizes, and compiler updates were the notable optimization steps. Specifically, on PVC, we obtained 3.53× and 8.16× speedup on IMEX and total times for SSW, and 3.74× and 14.15× speedup on IMEX and total times for the Relaxation apps.

3.2 Performance Comparisons

We use figure of merit (FOM) [10], Eq. (3) to measure performance across platforms and programming models. Here, nE, $nSpecies$, $nMoments$, $nNodes$, nX, and d are the number of energy elements, number of neutrino species, number of moments, number of quadrature nodes, spatial resolution in each dimension, and number of dimensions respectively.

$$FOM_{app} = DOF * Number of timesteps / IMEX time, \qquad (3)$$

$$DOF = nE * nSpecies * nMoments * nNodes^{(d+1)} * nX^d. \qquad (4)$$

For the performance evaluation of heterogeneous systems, we first wanted to compare performance of the two directive-based parallel programming models—OpenMP and OpenACC—on NVIDIA systems. We tested SSW on Summit (NVIDA-V100) and Polaris (NVIDIA-A100). OpenACC provides better performance due to the fair-support of nvhpc, 1.13× and 1.14× for small and large test-data on V100 and 1.0× and 1.13× on A100, despite tuning the OpenMP implementation. Hence, we decided to use OpenACC on NVIDIA systems for the cross-platform comparisons—it is more fair to compare against the best implementations, regardless of the programming model.

Figure 6 shows FOM-based, cross-platform performance comparisons of the SSW and Relaxation apps on A100, MI250, and PVC, each for two problem sizes, small and large. Based on the hardware architecture, the computation capability of a 2-tile PVC (PVC-2T) is comparable to a 2-GCD MI250 (MI250-2GCD) and to A100 [20,30,32]. Thornado uses one MPI rank per device. Based on our experiments (Fig. 3), we can obtain better performance by choosing a single tile as a device on PVC because of the Thornado-mesh adaptability and internal communication overhead. In order to compare with A100, and to estimate the performance for the entire AMD and Intel devices, we measure performance of 2-GCD on MI250 as well as of 2-tiles on PVC by concurrently running two Thornado executables as described in Sect. 2. For these tests, we use Intel's OneAPI compiler build, *oneapi/eng-compiler/2023.05.15.007* on Sunspot, NVIDIA's *nvhpc/23.3* on Polaris, and Cray's *CCE/15.0.1* on Frontier. MI250-2GCD outperforms A100 for both test-data of the SSW app, and gives 2.81× and 3.03× speedups relative to A100. For the Relaxation app, PVC-2T performs the best, and gives 2.4× and 1.68× speedup for small and large cases relative to A100. However, A100 using two Multi-Process Service (MPS) provides competitive performance with PVC-2T and MI250-2GCD. For the Relaxation app, it gives better performance than MI250-2GCD.

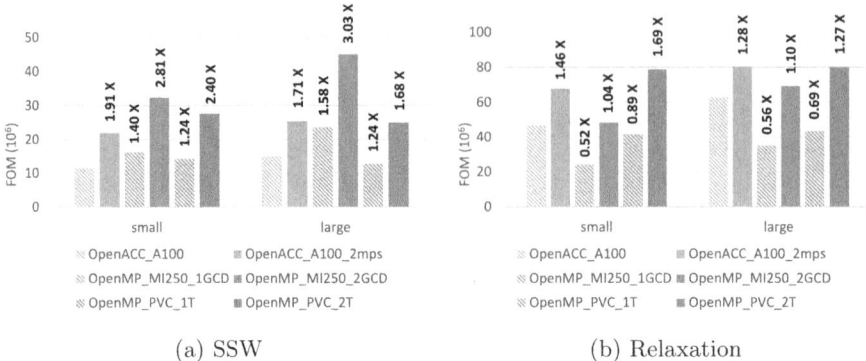

Fig. 6. Performance measurement of the a) SSW and b) Relaxation apps on Intel's PVC, NVIDIA's A100, and AMD's MI250 systems.

3.3 Multi-tasking and Concurrent Execution

This section discusses the concurrent execution of multiple Thornado executable tasks on each system: A100 using NVIDIA's MPS features, PVC using tiles and Compute-Command Streamers (CCS), and MI250 using GCDs. We evaluate performance and task throughput of each system for the small and large test cases of both apps, SSW and Relaxation. Table 1 shows the obtained FOM ($\times 10^6$). On A100, the environment variable CUDA_MPS_ACTIVE_THREAD_PERCENTAGE is set to 50%, 25%, and 12.5% for the runs of 2, 4, and 8 tasks respectively. On PVC, to execute 2, 4, and 8 tasks, we use 2 PVC tiles and 1 (default), 2, and 4 CCSs respectively. The environment variable ZEX_NUMBER_OF_CCS is set to 0:2 and 0:4 to obtain 2 and 4 CCS streamers on PVC. On MI250, we use 2 GCDs for the multi(n)-task execution and run $n/2$ task/GCD. For the SSW app, MI250 shows the better performance and high-throughput, but for the Relaxation app, PVC gives better performance as well as high-throughput. Due to the resource limitation, A100 fails (out of memory usage) for the 4 and 8 tasks for the large test case of Relaxation. For the same reason and the same test case, MI250 fails for the 8 tasks. However, tuning the memory pool size on PVC allowed us to run 4 and 8 tasks for Relaxation-large successfully. We tuned the memory pool configuration parameter from (256,128) (that is identified as an optimum value for 1 task) to (128,128) and (32,32) for 4 and 8 tasks respectively. The tunability of memory pool size on PVC supports to obtain higher task throughput even for bigger test cases.

Table 1. FOM ($\times 10^6$) for The Concurrent Execution of Multi-Tasking Over Cross-Platforms, NC - Not capable due to memory limitation.

App	Test	rank-1			rank-2			rank-4			rank-8		
		A100	MI250	PVC	A100	MI250	PVC	A100	MI250	PVC	A100	MI250	PVC
SSW	small	11.5	16.2	14.3	21.9	32.1	27.6	31.1	48.1	39.2	36.9	59.6	42.3
	large	14.9	23.6	12.7	25.4	45.1	25.0	34.0	60.9	32.6	39.8	71.7	37.3
Relax	small	46.5	24.2	41.6	67.7	48.4	78.8	78.6	57.7	89.6	79.4	64.9	95.4
	large	62.8	35.2	43.4	77.7	69.2	80.2	NC	76.0	88.9	NC	NC	92.3

4 Discussion and Conclusion

In this work, we have successfully ported Fortan-OpenMP code base, Thornado (SSW and Relaxation) on the Intel-based systems Sunspot, an early test-bed system of Aurora and AMD-based Frontier. A series of optimization strategies are applied to the SSW and Relaxation apps: a) kernel-level optimizations, including removal of inter-loop dependencies, loop flattening, and offloading as much of the code as possible to the GPU; b) compiler-level optimizations, including switching from JIT to AOT compilation and tuning thread-affinity parameters; c) system-level optimizations including memory pool parameter-tuning, and obtained 8.16× and 14.15× speedups on Sunspot. Our cross-platform performance comparison study over A100, MI250, and PVC shows that PVC-2T gives the best performance for the Relaxation app, obtaining 1.69× and 1.27× speedups over A100 for the small and large test problems. The MI250-2GCD outperforms for the SSW app by ≈3× for both sizes of the test problems. Concurrent task-execution features of the three systems were examined, and we encountered issues with memory-resource allocation/limitation in the large problem with 4 or more tasks. However, we were able to use custom memory pool configurations on the PVC system to overcome this issue and successfully run multiple tasks for the large problem. This work also helped to improve the systems' respective Fortan-OpenMP compilers by isolating and reporting various compiler bugs, and we identified specific strategies for improving performance with certain compilers (e.g., memory pool tuning).

In conclusion, we demonstrated performance-enhancement strategies using OpenMP-target offloading on a selection of new heterogeneous systems with varied GPU architectures. The study also provided a measure of the performance-portability of the Thornado application with directive-based programming models across different compilers and GPU vendors—specifically, NVIDIA, AMD, and Intel. Furthermore, the study serves as a reminder for the need to include real scientific applications as use-cases for system assessments.

Acknowledgments. This work was supported by the Argonne Leadership Computing Facility, which is a DOE Office of Science User Facility supported under Contract DE-AC02-06CH11357, and by the Exascale Computing Project (17-SC-20-SC), a collaborative effort of two U.S. Department of Energy organizations (Office of Science and the

National Nuclear Security Administration). This research also used resources of the Oak Ridge Leadership Computing Facility at the Oak Ridge National Laboratory, which is supported by the Office of Science of the U.S. Department of Energy under Contract No. DE-AC05-00OR22725. We also gratefully acknowledge the computing resources provided and operated by the Joint Laboratory for System Evaluation (JLSE) at Argonne National Laboratory(http://energy.gov/downloads/doe-public-access-plan).

We extend our gratitude to Shaoping Quan, Dahai Guo, and William Dieter from Intel for their invaluable help and guidance in successfully completing this work. We would also like to thank Colleen Bertoni and Thomas Applencourt from Argonne for their fruitful discussions and timely guidance.

References

1. Almgren, A., et al.: CASTRO: a massively parallel compressible astrophysics simulation code. J. Open Source Softw. **5**(54), 2513 (2020). https://doi.org/10.21105/joss.02513
2. Argonne Leadership Computing Facility: Aurora (2023). https://www.alcf.anl.gov/aurora
3. Argonne Leadership Computing Facility: JLSE (2023). https://www.jlse.anl.gov/hardware-under-development/
4. Argonne Leadership Computing Facility: Polaris (2023). https://docs.alcf.anl.gov/polaris/hardware-overview/machine-overview/
5. Argonne Leadership Computing Facility: Sunspot (2023). https://www.alcf.anl.gov/support-center/aurorasunspot/getting-started-sunspot
6. Ascher, U., Ruuth, S., Spiteri, R.: Implicit-explicit Runge-Kutta methods for time-dependent partial differential equations. Appl. Numer. Math. **25**, 151–167 (1997)
7. Bruenn, S.W., et al.: CHIMERA: a massively parallel code for core-collapse supernova simulations. APJS **248**(1), 11 (2020). https://doi.org/10.3847/1538-4365/ab7aff
8. Cardall, C.Y., Endeve, E., Mezzacappa, A.: Conservative 3+1 general relativistic variable Eddington tensor radiation transport equations. Phys. Rev. D **87**, 103004 (2013)
9. Chapman, B., et al.: Outcomes of OpenMP hackathon: OpenMP application experiences with the offloading model (Part II). In: McIntosh-Smith, S., de Supinski, B.R., Klinkenberg, J. (eds.) IWOMP 2021. LNCS, vol. 12870, pp. 81–95. Springer, Cham (2021). https://doi.org/10.1007/978-3-030-85262-7_6
10. Christlieb, A.J., Guthrey, P.T., Sands, W.A., Thavappiragasm, M.: Parallel algorithms for successive convolution. J. Sci. Comput. **86**, 1–44 (2021)
11. Chu, R., Endeve, E., Hauck, C., Mezzacappa, A.: Realizability-preserving DG-IMEX method for the two-moment model of fermion transport. J. Comput. Phys. **389**, 62–93 (2019)
12. Clauss, P., Altintas, E., Kuhn, M.: Automatic collapsing of non-rectangular loops. In: 2017 IEEE International Parallel and Distributed Processing Symposium (IPDPS), pp. 778–787. IEEE (2017)
13. Cockburn, B., Shu, C.W.: Runge-Kutta discontinuous Galerkin methods for convection-dominated problems. J. Sci. Comput. **16**, 173–261 (2001)
14. Corporation, I.: Developer guide: oneAPI GPU optimization guide (2023). https://www.intel.com/content/www/us/en/docs/oneapi/optimization-guide-gpu/2023-0/overview.html

15. Dubey, A., Weide, K., O'Neal, J., Dhruv, A., Couch, S., Harris, J.A., Klosterman, T., Jain, R., Rudi, J., Messer, B., et al.: Flash-x: a multiphysics simulation software instrument. SoftwareX **19**, 101168 (2022)
16. Georgakoudis, G., Parasyris, K., Liao, C., Beckingsale, D., Gamblin, T., de Supinski, B.: Machine learning-driven adaptive OpenMP for portable performance on heterogeneous systems. arXiv preprint arXiv:2303.08873 (2023)
17. Harris, A.: wlInterpolationModule. https://github.com/starkiller-astro/weaklib/blob/89c2ff3228c37022e74e3bb98290a1c9a52ba93e/Distributions/Library/wlInterpolationModule.F90
18. Harris, J.A., et al.: Exascale models of stellar explosions: quintessential multiphysics simulation. Int. J. High Perform. Comput. Appl. **36**(1), 59–77 (2022)
19. Intel-Corporation: Compilation Flow Overview. https://www.intel.com/content/www/us/en/docs/oneapi/programming-guide/2023-2/compilation-flow-overview.html
20. Intel-Corporation: Intel Data Center GPU Max Series Overview. https://www.intel.com/content/www/us/en/developer/articles/technical/intel-data-center-gpu-max-series-overview.html#gs.25c0bs
21. Intel-Corporation: oneAPI GPU Optimization Guide. https://www.intel.com/content/www/us/en/docs/oneapi/optimization-guide-gpu/2024-0/ahead-of-time-compilation.html
22. Just, O., Obergaulinger, M., Janka, H.T.: A new multidimensional, energy-dependent two-moment transport code for neutrino-hydrodynamics. MNRAS **453**, 3386–3413 (2015)
23. Kuroda, T., Takiwaki, T., Kotake, K.: A new multi-energy neutrino radiation-hydrodynamics code in full general relativity and its application to the gravitational collapse of massive stars. Astrophys. J. Suppl. Ser. **222**(2), 20 (2016). https://doi.org/10.3847/0067-0049/222/2/20
24. Laiu, M.P., Endeve, E., Chu, R., Harris, J.A., Messer, O.E.B.: A DG-IMEX method for two-moment neutrino transport: nonlinear solvers for neutrino-matter coupling*. Astrophys. J. Suppl. Ser. **253**(2), 52 (2021). https://doi.org/10.3847/1538-4365/abe2a8
25. Laiu, M.P., Endeve, E., Harris, J.A., Elledge, Z., Mezzacappa, A.: DG-IMEX method for a two-moment model for radiation transport in the $\mathcal{O}(v/c)$ Limit. arXiv e-prints arXiv:2309.04429 (2023). https://doi.org/10.48550/arXiv.2309.04429
26. Liska, M.T.P., et al.: H-AMR: a new GPU-accelerated GRMHD code for exascale computing with 3D adaptive mesh refinement and local adaptive time stepping. APJS **263**(2), 26 (2022). https://doi.org/10.3847/1538-4365/ac9966
27. Luebke, D.: CUDA: scalable parallel programming for high-performance scientific computing. In: 2008 5th IEEE International Symposium on Biomedical Imaging: From Nano to Macro, pp. 836–838 (2008). https://doi.org/10.1109/ISBI.2008.4541126
28. Martineau, M., McIntosh-Smith, S., Gaudin, W.: Evaluating OpenMP 4.0's effectiveness as a heterogeneous parallel programming model. In: 2016 IEEE International Parallel and Distributed Processing Symposium Workshops (IPDPSW), pp. 338–347 (2016). https://doi.org/10.1109/IPDPSW.2016.70
29. Mei, X., Chu, X.: Dissecting GPU memory hierarchy through microbenchmarking. IEEE Trans. Parallel Distrib. Syst. **28**(1), 72–86 (2016)
30. NVIDIA: NVIDIA Ampere Architecture In-Depth. https://developer.nvidia.com/blog/nvidia-ampere-architecture-in-depth
31. NVIDIA: PTX Compiler APIs. https://docs.nvidia.com/cuda/ptx-compiler-api/index.html

32. Oak Ridge Leadership Computing Facility: Frontier user guide (2023). https://docs.olcf.ornl.gov/systems/frontier_user_guide.html
33. Oak Ridge Leadership Computing Facility: Summit (2023). https://docs.olcf.ornl.gov/systems/summit_user_guide.html
34. Pareschi, L., Russo, G.: Implicit-explicit Runge-Kutta schemes and application to hyperbolic systems with relaxation. J. Sci. Comput. **25**, 129–155 (2005)
35. Pophale, S., et al.: Outcomes of OpenMP hackathon: OpenMP application experiences with the offloading mode. Technical report, Brookhaven National Lab.(BNL), Upton, NY (United States) (2021)
36. Shankar, S., Mösta, P., Brandt, S.R., Haas, R., Schnetter, E., de Graaf, Y.: GRaM-X: a new GPU-accelerated dynamical spacetime GRMHD code for Exascale computing with the Einstein toolkit. Class. Quantum Gravity **40**(20), 205009 (2023). https://doi.org/10.1088/1361-6382/acf2d9
37. Shibata, M., Kiuchi, K., Sekiguchi, Y., Suwa, Y.: Truncated moment formalism for radiation hydrodynamics in numerical relativity. Progress Theoret. Phys. **125**, 1255–1287 (2011)
38. Skinner, M.A., Dolence, J.C., Burrows, A., Radice, D., Vartanyan, D.: FORNAX: a flexible code for Multiphysics astrophysical simulations. ApJS **241**, 7 (2019)
39. Vergara Larrea, V.G., Budiardja, R.D., Gayatri, R., Daley, C., Hernandez, O., Joubert, W.: Experiences in porting mini-applications to OpenACC and OpenMP on heterogeneous systems. Concurrency Comput. Pract. Exper. **32**(20), e5780 (2020)
40. White, C.J., et al.: An extension of the Athena++ code framework for radiation-magnetohydrodynamics in general relativity using a finite-solid-angle discretization. APJ **949**(2), 103 (2023). https://doi.org/10.3847/1538-4357/acc8cf
41. Wibking, B.D., Krumholz, M.R.: QUOKKA: a code for two-moment AMR radiation hydrodynamics on GPUs. MNRAS **512**(1), 1430–1449 (2022). https://doi.org/10.1093/mnras/stac439
42. Wienke, S., Springer, P., Terboven, C., an Mey, D.: OpenACC — first experiences with real-world applications. In: Kaklamanis, C., Papatheodorou, T., Spirakis, P.G. (eds.) Euro-Par 2012. LNCS, vol. 7484, pp. 859–870. Springer, Heidelberg (2012). https://doi.org/10.1007/978-3-642-32820-6_85
43. Wu, X., et al.: ytopt: Autotuning scientific applications for energy efficiency at large scales. arXiv preprint arXiv:2303.16245 (2023)

Event-Based OpenMP Tasks for Time-Sensitive GPU-Accelerated Systems

Cyril Cetre[1,3](✉), Chenle Yu[2,4], Sara Royuela[2], Rémi Barrere[1], Eduardo Quiñones[2], and Damien Gratadour[3]

[1] Thales Research & Technology, Palaiseau, France
cyril.cetre@thalesgroup.com, remi.barrere@thalesgroup.com
[2] Barcelona Supercomputing Center, Barcelona, Spain
{chenle.yu,sara.royuela,eduardo.quinones}@bsc.es
[3] LESIA, Observatoire de Paris, Université PSL, CNRS, Sorbonne Université, Université de Paris, 5 place Jules Janssen, 92195 Meudon, France
damien.gratadour@obspm.fr
[4] Universitat Politècnica de Catalunya, Barcelona, Spain

Abstract. The throughput-centric design of GPUs poses challenges when integrating them into time-sensitive applications. Nevertheless, modern GPU architectures and software have recently evolved, making it possible to minimize overheads and interference along the critical path through advanced mechanisms, such as GPU graphs, while sustaining high throughput. However, GPU vendors provide programming ecosystems specific to their products, raising concerns about code portability. Hence, there is a need for a hardware-agnostic API capable of managing time-sensitive GPU-accelerated pipelines. In this context, we propose integrating event-based synchronizations into the high-level OpenMP programming model to, in combination with GPU graphs, notably reduce interference and overheads over the critical path. This work showcases how this combination offers significant performance improvements and time consistency. We also enable portability across several vendor ecosystems and demonstrate our work on a set of representative applications for cyber-physical systems. According to our experiments, we measured a maximum jitter below 20 µs, representing less than 5% of time variation.

Keywords: Time-sensitive systems · GPU · High-performance computing · OpenMP · CUDA · ROCm

1 Introduction

Advanced Cyber-Physical Systems (CPS) are required to support increasingly complex specifications with ever tighter deadlines. Typically composed of sensors, actuators, data transfer devices, and computing hardware, their elaboration represents a significant challenge for many application domains in academia and industry. An illustrative CPS example is the astronomical Adaptive Optics (AO) system [14], in which the algorithms in charge of processing input data from sensors require significant computing power with minimal and consistent response time. AO Real-Time Controllers (RTC) like the upcoming Extremely Large Telescope (ELT) are integrating GPUs to sustain the 1.7 TB/s of required single precision memory bandwidth with a 285 µs time budget [10].

However, the modular nature of AO RTCs necessitates a software solution that can accommodate flexibility with even more complex computing pipelines in heterogeneous environments. In addition, deployed solutions may remain used for decades and maintained by researchers who are not necessarily experts in heterogeneous programming. Therefore, there is a strong need for an API that allows for (1) ensuring reliability and consistent response time, (2) avoiding dependency on specific hardware configurations, and (3) minimum learning effort.

OpenMP, a high-level directive-based programming model supporting GPU acceleration, is an excellent candidate to address these needs. Its use allows developers to integrate accelerator-agnostic code, greatly enhancing productivity through portability and modularity. However, adopting such an approach usually leads to lower performance compared to native GPU APIs, and OpenMP also lacks several critical features to enable time-sensitive GPU computations within complex CPS. This paper addresses the previously mentioned through the following contributions:

1. An extension to the OpenMP specification of event-based synchronizations to support the release of host and target tasks based on events, while still fulfilling dependencies.
2. An extension of the OpenMP taskgraph to CUDA graph framework [24] to create CUDA graphs including the proposed event-based activation of tasks and so make graphs more suitable for real-time applications.
3. An extension to the same framework to generate HIP graphs for AMD GPUs and so increase the portability of the framework.
4. An evaluation of the proposed extension to OpenMP and its implementation that analyzes the response time variability in CUDA and ROCm ecosystems. The study uses complex pipelines coming from Adaptive Optics (AO) [11] and Adaptive Beamforming (ABF) [6].

2 Background

This section briefly presents the components of our framework and its intended applicability, i.e., the graph execution model, the current mechanisms in OpenMP for event-based synchronization, and the requirements of real-time CPS.

GPU Graphs. Introduced along with CUDA 10 in 2018, the CUDA graph features [18] allow for wrapping multiple interdependent kernels as a single execution unit, requiring only one submission onto a CUDA stream to launch all inner kernels. AMD released a similar feature, namely HIP Graph [1], in 2021. The graph programming paradigm reduces kernel submission overhead, a crucial aspect for short kernels. However, the intricacies of exposing parallelism with the stream-capturing method and the tedious and error-prone nature of the explicit graph API render the implementation of CUDA graphs complex, especially when the number of graph nodes (kernels) and edges (dependencies) increases.

Host Taskgraphs. Graph-based execution has shown its benefits in reducing offloading overheads, and this paradigm has also been introduced in modern and portable programming languages like Kokkos [23] and SYCL [17] to enable a record and replay mechanism that reduces the overhead of task orchestration. OpenMP is also working towards introducing this paradigm based on a proposal that augments the API with the taskgraph directive [25] to expose the region of code that can be represented as a Task Dependency Graph (TDG). Furthermore, the LLVM compilation framework already offers a prototype implementation for this feature [8] in its upstream main branch. Finally, further proposals improve the interoperability between OpenMP and CUDA by statically transforming the OpenMP TDG into a CUDA graph for optimized programmability (from the former) and performance (from the latter).

OpenMP Detachable Tasks. The OpenMP specification provides event-based execution through the detach(event) clause, which ties the completion of a task to the fulfillment of a given event, and the *omp_fulfill_event(event)* runtime routine, which implements the fulfillment of an event. These features are useful, for example, to allow the interoperability of OpenMP with other languages, like CUDA, HIP and MPI. In particular, a common use case involves an OpenMP task waiting for completion until a foreign library executes a specific callback function (e.g., data transmission completed), as shown in Listing 1.1[1].

Listing 1.1. OpenMP example of event-based task synchronization

```
void callback(hipStream_t stream, hipError_t status, void *data)
{ omp_fulfill_event((omp_event_t *) data); }

void task_detach_example() {
  omp_event_t *hip_event;
  #pragma omp task detach(hip_event)    // task A
  {
    do_something();
    hipMemcpyAsync(dst, src, nbytes, hipMemcpyDeviceToHost, stream);
    hipStreamAddCallback(stream, callback, hip_event, 0);
  }
  #pragma omp task                       // task B
  do_something_else();
  #pragma omp taskwait
}
```

CPS Specifications. Fig. 1 exemplifies the AO CPS used in this paper. This use case receives an image that triggers a timer and the execution of a matrix pre-processing computation, which in turn triggers a matrix-based computation when it completes. AO requires a memory bandwidth of at least 1700 GB/s, achievable only by a few top-end GPU accelerators. In addition, the pipeline must constantly adapt to changing operational conditions through repeated re-configurations to maintain optimal performance. Given these specifications, to provide an agnostic solution to a wide range of similar time-sensitive CPS, this work considers the following constraints:

---

[1] OpenMP detachable task example extracted from https://indico.euro-fusion.org/event/688/attachments/854/2752/OpenMP_Webinar_5_2021-05-25.pdf.

- **Time sensitivity**: Target GPU-accelerated systems with critical time constraints and short deadlines.
- **Productivity**: Offer a straightforward approach to express intricate synchronization mechanisms with mainstream tools and concepts that minimize the development time and cost.
- **Maintainability**: Avoid dependency with specific hardware or ecosystem.
- **Modularity/flexibility**: Facilitate on-the-fly modifications on the pipeline, like incorporating new stages or responsive system halts.

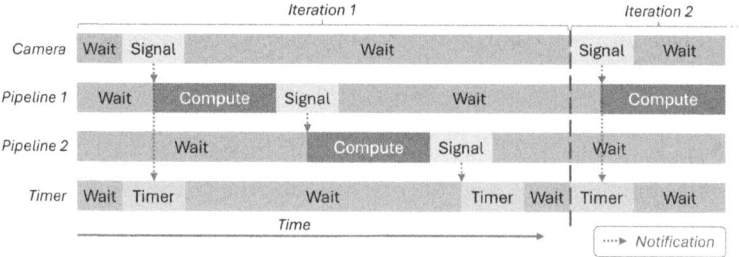

Fig. 1. Adaptive Optics (AO) pipeline.

3 Related Work

The CUDA ecosystem's closed nature complicates predicting and certifying the behavior of time-sensitive applications. Several studies work towards unveiling architecture and scheduler specificities to understand GPU behavior in discrete accelerators [16,19] and embedded platforms [2,4]. While these approaches pave the way to real-time GPU scheduling, more is needed to support them on critical systems. Examples include *persistent kernels* [13,22], which can reduce GPU latency at the cost of maintainability, and *busy-wait kernels*, first proposed by F. Ferreira et al. [12] and further explored by C. Cetre et al. [5], to mitigate the drawbacks above while maintaining latency specifications. Orthogonal to these efforts, our work aims to exploit the graph execution paradigm available on modern GPUs to further optimize the kernel submission and scheduling overhead.

Event-based synchronization among tasks has long been supported in safety-critical systems and embedded systems, for instance, by Ada language for the former and TinyGALS [9] for the latter. However, these solutions become insufficient when applied on High Performance Computing applications due to different system characteristics. Hence, there is a need to introduce a model, suitable for HPC systems, that includes event-based synchronization mechanism.

High level programming APIs, like OpenMP, provide an interesting bedrock to build such a mechanism because it already defines a task synchronization method, although limited, through events.

Accordingly, we plan to extend the existing event-based model for task launches. Furthermore, since the OpenMP's accelerator model improves productivity at the cost of performance [15], which is crucial for real-time applications such as Adaptive Optics applications, we plan to couple event-based launches with the taskgraph framework [25], to deliver a programming model that allows to conveniently define GPU graphs synchronized with external events.

4 Event-Based Task Release with OpenMP

Contrary to the *allow-completion event* created by the `detach` clause that affects task completion, our work introduces a new mechanism that specifies the beginning of task execution. The proposition, along with its implementation overview, is detailed in the following of this section.

4.1 Proposed Extension to the OpenMP API

The new clause `attach(event)` attached to the `task` and `target` constructs describes a new restriction affecting task releases. More specifically, tasks defined with the `attach` clause will only begin the execution of their task region once their associated events are fulfilled. In order to fulfill such an event, we propose a new OpenMP directive, namely `fulfill_event`, including clauses to define host (`cpu_notify`) or device (`gpu_notify`) synchronization. Table 1 summarizes the proposed extension with brief descriptions.

Table 1. Extensions (in bold) proposed to the OpenMP API.

Directive	Associated clause	Description
task	**attach(event)**	Defer the execution of the task until the **event** is fulfilled
target nowait		Create a target task that will initiate its execution once the **event** is fulfilled
fulfill_event	**cpu_notify(event)**	Release **event** for host task waiting on it
	gpu_notify(event)	Release **event** for target task waiting on it

Syntax and Semantics. Listing 1.2 illustrates the proposal with an example that generates four interdependent target tasks, two of which are synchronized with events. The corresponding TDG is shown in Fig. 2. Upon the encountering of a `attach(event)` clause, the implementation creates a new *allow-launch event* and connects it to the beginning of the execution of the associated task region. Furthermore, the implementation updates the original *event-handle* to represent that *allow-launch event*. The generated task can only start executing its associated structured block when the *allow-launch event* is fulfilled. The *allow-launch event* is fulfilled when another thread encounters the `fulfill_event` directive with either the `cpu_notify` or `gpu_notify` clauses taking the *event-handle* corresponding to the *allow-launch event* as the argument. Once fulfilled, the *allow-launch event* will be destroyed and the *event-handle* in the argument will become disassociated from any event.

Listing 1.2. Event-based task release proposal.

```
1  // In a thread: tasks depending on events
2  int dep1, dep2, dep3, event1, event2;
3  void tdg_computation() {
4  #pragma omp target nowait   \
5      depend(out:dep1) attach(event1)
6  { /* task1 */ }
7  #pragma omp target nowait   \
8      depend(in:dep1) depend(out:dep2)
9  { /* task2 */ }
10 #pragma omp target nowait   \
11     depend(out:dep3) attach(event2)
12 { /* task3 */ }
13 #pragma omp target nowait   \
14     depend(in:dep2,dep3)
15 { /* task4 */ }
16 }
17 // In a separate thread: release events
18 void notify() {
19 #pragma fulfill_event gpu_notify(event1)
20 #pragma fulfill_event gpu_notify(event2)
21 }
```

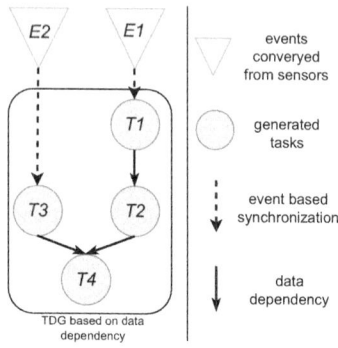

Fig. 2. TDG with events.

The Choice of a Directive Instead of a Routine. The existing *allow-completion event* is fulfilled through calling omp_fulfill_event, an OpenMP runtime routine. Similarly, we could define a new routine function that fulfills an *allow-launch event*. However, the possible lowering opportunities of the graph of execution (through the OpenMP taskgraph in our case) are hindered when using runtime routines, as these have a fixed implementation in each runtime system. Instead, a directive enables implementing lowering options depending on the targeted system. The lowering phase of this work is described in Sect. 4.3, which details the interaction of the fulfill_event construct and the gpu_notify and cpu_notify clauses with the taskgraph framework.

Current Limitations. In the current implementation, to satisfy the tight timing requirements of real-time applications, threads executing a task whose *allow-launch event* is not fulfilled are set to spin actively in an infinite loop while waiting (i.e., busy wait). However, this behavior can be modified to satisfy other requirements. For instance, a blocking wait mechanism could be used to prevent these threads from consuming CPU cycles when the implementation does not target hard real-time use cases.

4.2 Interactions with the Taskgraph Framework

The new event allows OpenMP tasks to be conveniently synchronized with external sensors, such as a camera. However, due to the restrictive timing requirements of real-time CPS, it is needed to minimize the runtime overhead, primarily related to task management, as it typically represents the main overhead in task programs [20,21]. The taskgraph framework [25] is a compelling method to mitigate such cost as it does not incur most task orchestrating operations when replaying.

Event with Taskgraph in OpenMP Runtime. Once the taskgraph is built for a region, replaying such taskgraph omits the user code within the corresponding region. Consequently, the `attach(event)` clause is not executed, and new events will not be created. As a solution, we record the tasks with their associated events, so that the fulfillment of such events still releases the corresponding tasks.

Event with Taskgraph in Foreign Runtime. GPU-accelerated real-time applications often have their device kernels tailored to the underlying GPU. The kernels automatically generated by the LLVM compiler may not be sufficiently optimized to fulfill the real-time requirements. Therefore, we leverage the device taskgraph approach proposed by C. Yu et al. [24], which enables to generate CUDA graphs through OpenMP directives using existing CUDA kernels. The device taskgraph framework creates kernel nodes for `target nowait` constructs and CUDA host nodes for `task` directives. By integrating `allow-launch events` as new CUDA graph nodes into the graph, we can further reduce the synchronization cost. Consequently, in this work, we solely focus on using the new event with taskgraph in foreign runtime.

4.3 Implementation in LLVM

Based on LLVM 15, our framework implementation in the compiler includes front-end modifications, middle-end IR transformations, and runtime support. Following, we give an overview of the implementation in the OpenMP context and then in a foreign context interacting with another runtime, such as CUDA.

Implementation in the OpenMP Context. The compiler front-end emits a runtime function call, namely `__kmpc_task_allow_launch_event`, when encountering a task with the `attach(event)` clause. The runtime function associates the created task with the event. As a result, when the task has its input data dependencies satisfied, it also evaluates whether its associated event is fulfilled before executing. For the `fulfill_event` directive, the `cpu_notify` is used to notify the OpenMP runtime while the `gpu_notify` clause is effective in foreign contexts, i.e., in GPU graphs. Hence, when the taskgraph is managed by the OpenMP runtime, host and target tasks are all orchestrated from the host library. Consequently, the fulfillment of an `allow-launch` event through the runtime function `__kmpc_fulfill_launch_event` can synchronize both host and target tasks.

Implementation in Foreign Contexts. To generate a CUDA graph with event synchronization, we are based on the implementation of taskgraphs proposed by C. Yu et al. [24]. Figure 3 shows an overview of the complete compilation process, including our alterations. This CUDA graph generation can be summarized to:

Step1. An analysis pass on the LLVM IR of the OpenMP program determines the task instances and their corresponding arguments through inspecting the task constructing runtime calls (e.g., *__kmpc_omp_target_task_alloc*).

Step2.1. A transformation pass takes the analysis result and transforms, or inserts calls to the CUDA runtime in the LLVM IR file at the right places, e.g., replacing host-to-device copies with *cudaMemcpy* calls. The figure represents the output file as *augmented LLVM file*.

Step2.2. Along with the transformation pass, a CUDA file is generated from scratch, noted in the figure as *genGraph.cu*. Based on the information gathered in the analysis pass, the file builds the CUDA graph by calling CUDA graph API functions (e.g., *cudaGraphAddKernelNode*).

Step3. Link the object files compiled from the *augmented LLVM file* and the *genGraph.cu* files to produce the final binary.

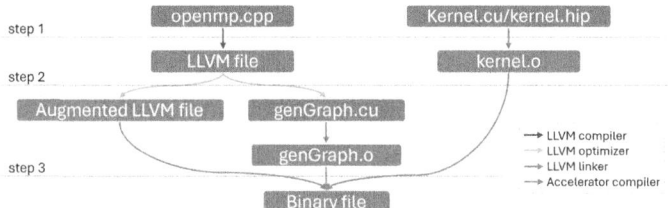

Fig. 3. Compilation steps of the GPU graph generation.

To incorporate event-based synchronization into the *genGraph.cu* file, the following additional transformations are performed:

1. Upon encountering the `attach` clause for the first time, two kernels exclusively used for synchronization are created and inserted in the generated CUDA file. One represents the active wait on the associated event (referred to as *BusyWaitKernel*), and the other is to notify the fulfillment of it (referred to as *FulfillingKernel*).
2. For each *attach* clause, two graph nodes are created: one containing the encapsulated task (referred to as *TaskNode*), and the other with *BusyWaitKernel* (referred to as *BusyWaitNode*).
3. All input dependencies of *TaskNode* are transferred to the *BusyWaitNode*.
4. A dependency is created from *BusyWaitNode* to the *TaskNode*, ensuring that the synchronization kernel finishes before the encapsulated task can start.

Additionally, the `fulfill_event` and the `gpu_notify` clause remain independent from the taskgraph, producing the following on the LLVM IR:

1. Create or retrieve a stream for the GPU notification (it must be a different stream from the one launching the GPU graph).
2. Insert the *FulfillingKernel* to such a stream so that the *BusyWaitNode* can be released.

4.4 Generation of HIP Graph

This work extends LLVM to support HIP graphs for AMD GPUs from OpenMP to support a broader range of GPUs. Targeting AMD devices can be done effortlessly by the user, who just provides an additional flag at the compilation time, namely *-hip-tdg*, to carry the following modifications to generate a HIP graph:

1. The *augmented LLVM file* in Fig. 3 is modified accordingly so that the inserted CUDA calls (data allocation and transfers from host to device and conversely) are transformed to HIP API calls.
2. The *genGraph.cu* file is translated to HIP C++ through the *hipify* script.
3. Similarly, the final binary is created by linking the object files compiled from kernel code, HIP Graph C++ file, and the *augmented LLVM file*.

Regarding step 2, it is possible to enhance the LLVM framework to generate HIP C++ directly, without translating it from CUDA. This approach could lead to a more robust implementation for AMD devices and will be addressed in future work.

5 Evaluating the Proposed OpenMP Extension

Our experiments measure the response time and time variability of real-time CPSs. The response time includes all possible interrupts, overheads, and external events. For each application tested, we evaluate three implementations: (1) the *Regular CUDA/HIP Graph*, which relies on CUDA/HIP graphs with active wait kernels for synchronizing computations and serves as the reference implementation because, although it requires more effort from the user, it typically provides the best performance; (2) *OpenMP CUDA/HIP Graph with GPU Sync.*, which uses GPU graphs generated from the proposed taskgraph lowering to CUDA graphs, including the new event synchronization; and (3) *OpenMP CUDA/HIP Graph with CPU Sync.*, which uses the taskgraph framework to generate a GPU graph but leaves the synchronizations to the CPU processes, i.e., the `fulfill_event gpu_notify` directive makes a CPU process to submit the *FulfillingKernel* to the GPU instead of translating it to a graph node.

The metrics used in the experiments are: (i) the *Mean Execution Time* (MET), (ii) the *Maximum Measured Execution Time* (MMET), and (iii) the *Max Jitter* (i.e., $MMET - MET$). The first two evaluate the response time and the last assesses the time variability. The measurements are obtained on a server with the configuration shown in Table 2. The applications are launched on isolated CPU threads through the *isolcpus* kernel boot command line.

Table 2. Environmental setup.

OS	Ubuntu 22.04 (w/o real-time patch)
Linux kernel	5.15.0-75
CPU	Intel Xeon 5220
CUDA ver.	12.0
ROCm ver.	5.6.0
NVIDIA GPU	A100 80GB
AMD GPU	MI100

Two use cases are selected:

An Adaptive Optics (AO) real-time controller, which reproduces all the steps from data acquisition to the output array [11]. As described in Fig. 1, this application combines two computational Pipeline Units (PU): a pixel processing unit that takes as input the raw data from wavefront sensor cameras and processes the pixels with a series of simple arithmetic kernels before sending the processed pixels to the second PU. The latter PU performs linear algebra operations, particularly matrix-vector multiplications, to produce a command as a vector sent to the deformable mirror actuators associated with a physical component, typically a telescope.

An Adaptive Beam Forming (ABF) algorithm, used in various fields, including wireless communications, radar/sonar systems, and medical imaging. It can leverage the throughput provided by the GPU to improve the quality of the received signal [3,6,7]. ABF uses weights and phases to combine signals from multiple sensors and build spatial beams by lowering signals from other directions. Building beams require high bandwidth data acquisition, low latency, and, lastly, high computing power to form and produce signals that would be unusable without ABF. The implementation used in our experimentation has one PU, which takes incoming signals as input and outputs the reconstructed signal through a combination of several arithmetic and linear algebra kernels.

These applications are typically measured in microseconds; therefore, we include a timer PU within the pipeline to obtain an accurate yet non-intrusive time measurement. This timer PU submits CUDA/HIP events to the computation stream to set an iteration's start and end points. The numbers reported in this section result from executing one million iterations.

5.1 Adaptive Optics Application

Figure 4 shows the results obtained with the AO application using CUDA (in Fig. 4a) and HIP (in Fig. 4b). The reference implementation with vanilla CUDA/HIP graphs gives the best results with a maximum jitter of 16 µs (520 µs MET and 536 µs MMET) with CUDA and 11 µs (430 µs MET, 441 µs MMET) with HIP. Our method, i.e., OpenMP GPU graph with event synchronization, achieves an identical 16 µs max. jitter (538 µs MET and 554 µs MMET) with CUDA, and slightly higher max. jitter of 21 µs (443 µs MET and 464 µs MMET) with HIP, both increasing around 15 µs the average execution time. Finally, the third method using the CPU synchronization strategy showed the largest execution times and a max. jitter of 28 µs (562 µs MET and 590 µs MMET) with CUDA and 33 µs (478 µs MET and 511 µs MMET) with HIP.

The CPU synchronization strategy showed the most significant response time and lower stability. Although the maximum jitter of the third implementation is the largest, it can still be considered by the target specification as the maximum jitter is smaller than 10% of MET. However, this high jitter shows that even if the involved CPU threads are thoroughly isolated, such an approach is more

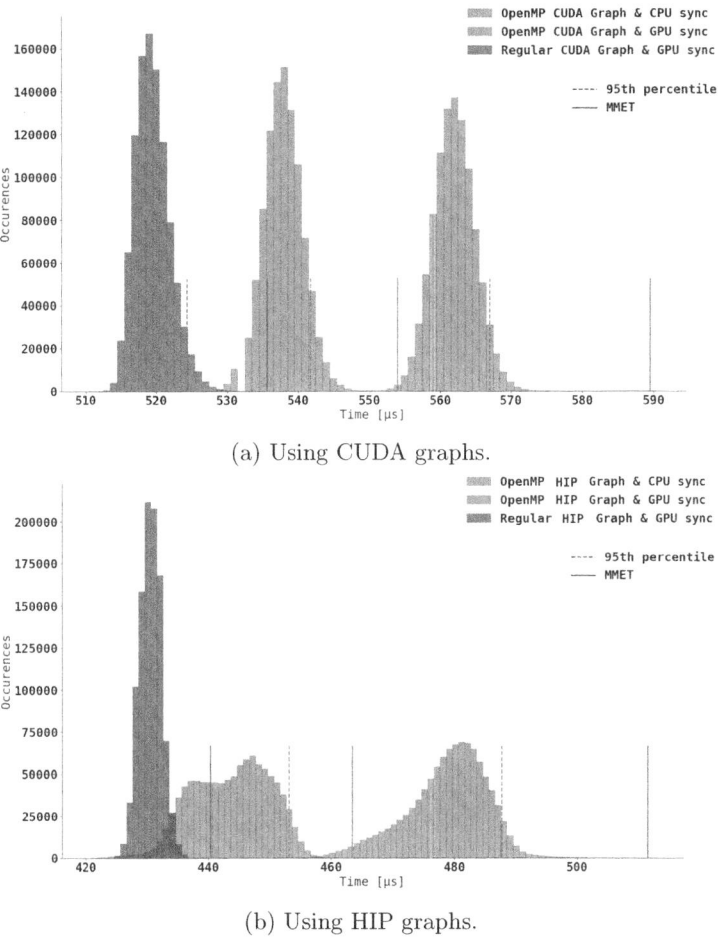

Fig. 4. Occurrences of different response time of the AO application.

prone to be impacted by interrupts. Over the long term, this method is more likely to miss the application deadline, which makes it more challenging to meet our target specifications.

Our approach with OpenMP GPU Graphs delivered competitive mean execution times and jitters compared to the native CUDA/HIP implementation while maintaining a simple, directive-based programming style. This method benefits from event synchronization and GPU graphs, combining time sensitivity with productivity and maintainability. Furthermore, real-life AO and ABF applications accommodate dozens of PUs, making writing manually CUDA/HIP graphs challenging and invalidating the implementation with CPU synchronization as the jitter scales with the number of synchronizations.

5.2 Adaptive Beam Forming Application

Tables 3a and 3b present the results obtained with the ABF application. Similar to the AO application, the native CUDA/HIP implementations showed the best performance with the shortest MET. The proposed method, OpenMP CUDA/HIP graph with event synchronization, only introduces an overhead of about 10 µs compared to the native implementation (a MET of 520 µs vs. 515 µs for CUDA, and 551 µs vs. 540 µs for HIP). Whereas with the CPU synchronization, this overhead is 18 µs for CUDA and 39 µs on AMD GPUs. Again, real-life ABF applications contain multiple computing PUs, making our solution more valuable, as it provides a convenient way to define an efficient and consistent execution pattern.

Table 3. Metrics for the ABF application.

Metrics (µs)	MET	MMET	Max jitter
CUDA busy-wait	515	523	8
OpenMP CUDA graph with GPU Sync.	520	525	5
OpenMP CUDA graph with CPU Sync.	533	550	17

(a) Using CUDA graphs.

Metrics (µs)	MET	MMET	Max jitter
HIP busy-wait	540	555	15
OpenMP HIP Graph with GPU Sync.	551	564	13
OpenMP HIP Graph with CPU Sync.	579	598	19

(b) Using HIP graphs

6 Conclusion

This paper extends the OpenMP support for event-based synchronization with an *allow-launch event* through a new directive and a series of clauses detailed in Table 1. Combining with an enhancement of an existing taskgraph implementation [24,25], we create a framework that is capable of statically generating CUDA and HIP graphs containing synchronizing kernels out of an OpenMP code. These extensions enable the use of OpenMP in domains nowadays requiring HPC capabilities and real-time behaviour, from the presented adaptive optics and adaptive beamforming applications, to other domains like autonomous mobility, including automotive, railway and avionics, among others.

Although our experiments show that such graphs are particularly suitable for real-time applications, the current framework cannot be scaled dynamically due to the intrinsic, static nature of the taskgraph framework. In the future, we plan to adopt a new proposal for dynamically recording GPU graphs [26] to satisfy on-the-fly modifications required by some CPSs. Additionally, for the CUDA ecosystem, the introduction of device-launched graphs in CUDA 12 and conditional nodes in CUDA 12.3 could further enhance the flexibility of our work.

Acknowledgements. This work is supported by the RisingStars project, under the Marie Skłodowska-Curie grant agreement No 873120 from the European Union's Horizon 2020 research and innovation programme. This work is co-financed by the ASCENDER project of the UNICO I+D Cloud program that has MINECO and the EU-Next Generation EU as financing entities, within the framework of the PRTR and the MRR. This work is also partly supported by the HiPERT project, with reference PID2023-148117NA-I00, financed by MCIU/AEI/10.13039/501100011033/ FEDER, UE.

References

1. AMD: HIP documentation (2024). https://rocm.docs.amd.com/projects/HIP/en/latest/
2. Amert, T., Otterness, N., Yang, M., Anderson, J.H., Smith, F.D.: GPU scheduling on the NVIDIA TX2: hidden details revealed. In: 2017 IEEE Real-Time Systems Symposium (RTSS), pp. 104–115 (2017). https://doi.org/10.1109/RTSS.2017.00017
3. Barrere, R., Lenormand, E., Bui, D., Lee, E.A., Shaver, C., Tripakis, S.: An introduction to the pthales domain of Ptolemy II. Technical report UCB/EECS-2011-32, EECS Department, University of California, Berkeley (2011). http://www2.eecs.berkeley.edu/Pubs/TechRpts/2011/EECS-2011-32.html
4. Capodieci, N., Cavicchioli, R., Olmedo, I.S., Solieri, M., Bertogna, M.: Contending memory in heterogeneous SoCs: Evolution in NVIDIA tegra embedded platforms. In: 2020 IEEE 26th International Conference on Embedded and Real-Time Computing Systems and Applications (RTCSA), pp. 1–10 (2020). https://doi.org/10.1109/RTCSA50079.2020.9203722
5. Cetre, C., Ferreira, F., Sevin, A., Barrere, R., Gratadour, D.: Real-time high performance computing using a Jetson Xavier AGX. In: 11th European Congress Embedded Real Time System (ERTS2022). Toulouse, France (2022). https://hal.science/hal-03693764
6. Chen, J., Chen, J., Min, H., Wang, X.: Real-time embedded implementation of adaptive beamforming for medical ultrasound imaging. In: 2016 Sixth International Conference on Instrumentation & Measurement, Computer, Communication and Control (IMCCC), pp. 356–360 (2016). https://doi.org/10.1109/IMCCC.2016.66
7. Chen, J., Yu, A.C.H., So, H.K.H.: Design considerations of real-time adaptive beamformer for medical ultrasound research using FPGA and GPU. In: 2012 International Conference on Field-Programmable Technology, pp. 198–205 (2012). https://doi.org/10.1109/FPT.2012.6412134
8. Chenle Yu, A.M.: Task record and replay mechanism in LLVM (2023). https://reviews.llvm.org/D146642
9. Cheong, E., Liebman, J., Liu, J., Zhao, F.: TinyGALS: a programming model for event-driven embedded systems. In: Proceedings of the 2003 ACM Symposium on Applied Computing, pp. 698–704. SAC 2003, Association for Computing Machinery, New York, NY, USA (2003). https://doi.org/10.1145/952532.952668
10. Clénet, Y., et al.: MICADO-MAORY SCAO Preliminary design, development plan & calibration strategies. In: Adaptive Optics for Extremely Large Telescopes conference, 6th edn. Québec, Canada (2020). https://hal.science/hal-03078430
11. Ferreira, F., Bernard, J., Sevin, A., Doucet, N., Gratadour, D.: Cosmic: a real-time platform for signal processing pipelines. In: 2022 IEEE Workshop on Signal Processing Systems (SiPS), pp. 1–6 (2022). https://doi.org/10.1109/SiPS55645.2022.9919251

12. Ferreira, F., et al.: Hard real-time core software of the AO RTC COSMIC platform: architecture and performance, p. 172 (2020). https://doi.org/10.1117/12.2561244
13. Gupta, K., Stuart, J.A., Owens, J.D.: A study of persistent threads style GPU programming for GPGPU workloads. In: 2012 Innovative Parallel Computing (InPar), pp. 1–14 (2012). https://doi.org/10.1109/InPar.2012.6339596
14. Guyon, O.: Extreme adaptive optics. Ann. Rev. Astron. Astrophys. **56**, 315–355 (2018)
15. Khalilov, M., Timoveev, A.: Performance analysis of CUDA, OpenACC and OpenMP programming models on TESLA V100 GPU. In: Journal of Physics: Conference Series, vol. 1740, p. 012056. IOP Publishing (2021)
16. Li, H., Yu, D., Kumar, A., Tu, Y.C.: Performance modeling in CUDA streams - a means for high-throughput data processing. In: 2014 IEEE International Conference on Big Data (Big Data), pp. 301–310 (2014). https://doi.org/10.1109/BigData.2014.7004245
17. Ltd, C.S.: SYCL Graphs (2024). https://codeplay.com/portal/blogs/2024/01/22/sycl-graphs
18. NVIDIA: CUDA 10 Features Revealed: Turing, CUDA Graphs, and More (2018). https://developer.nvidia.com/blog/cuda-10-features-revealed/
19. Olmedo, I.S., Capodieci, N., Martinez, J.L., Marongiu, A., Bertogna, M.: Dissecting the CUDA scheduling hierarchy: a performance and predictability perspective. In: 2020 IEEE Real-Time and Embedded Technology and Applications Symposium (RTAS), pp. 213–225 (2020). https://doi.org/10.1109/RTAS48715.2020.000-5
20. Podobas, A., Karlsson, S.: Towards unifying OpenMP under the task-parallel paradigm. In: Maruyama, N., de Supinski, B.R., Wahib, M. (eds.) IWOMP 2016. LNCS, vol. 9903, pp. 116–129. Springer, Cham (2016). https://doi.org/10.1007/978-3-319-45550-1_9
21. Rico, A., Sánchez Barrera, I., Joao, J.A., Randall, J., Casas, M., Moretó, M.: On the benefits of tasking with OpenMP. In: Fan, X., de Supinski, B.R., Sinnen, O., Giacaman, N. (eds.) IWOMP 2019. LNCS, vol. 11718, pp. 217–230. Springer, Cham (2019). https://doi.org/10.1007/978-3-030-28596-8_15
22. Todd, A.: Improving real-time performance with CUDA persistent threads (CuPer) on the Jetson TX2. Concurrent Real-Time White Paper (2018)
23. Trott, C.R., et al.: Kokkos 3: Programming model extensions for the exascale era. IEEE Trans. Parallel Distrib. Syst. **33**(4), 805–817 (2021)
24. Yu, C., Royuela, S., Quiñones, E.: OpenMP to CUDA graphs: a compiler-based transformation to enhance the programmability of NVIDIA devices. In: Proceedings of the 23th International Workshop on Software and Compilers for Embedded Systems, p. 42-47. SCOPES 2020, Association for Computing Machinery (2020)
25. Yu, C., Royuela, S., Quiões, E.: Taskgraph: a low contention OpenMP tasking framework. IEEE Transactions on Parallel and Distributed Systems (2023)
26. Yu, C., Royuela, S., Quiñones, E.: Enhancing heterogeneous computing through OpenMP and GPU graph. In: 53rd International Conference on Parallel Processing (2024). https://doi.org/10.1145/3673038.3673050

Open Access This chapter is licensed under the terms of the Creative Commons Attribution 4.0 International License (http://creativecommons.org/licenses/by/4.0/), which permits use, sharing, adaptation, distribution and reproduction in any medium or format, as long as you give appropriate credit to the original author(s) and the source, provide a link to the Creative Commons license and indicate if changes were made.

The images or other third party material in this chapter are included in the chapter's Creative Commons license, unless indicated otherwise in a credit line to the material. If material is not included in the chapter's Creative Commons license and your intended use is not permitted by statutory regulation or exceeds the permitted use, you will need to obtain permission directly from the copyright holder.

Targeting More Devices

Integrating Multi-FPGA Acceleration to OpenMP Distributed Computing

Pedro Henrique Rosso[1]([✉])[iD], Lucian Petrica[4][iD], Nusrat Jahan Lisa[1][iD], Marcio Pereira[1][iD], Sandro Rigo[1][iD], Hervé Yviquel[1][iD], Vanderlei Bonato[2][iD], Emilio Francesquini[3][iD], and Guido Araujo[1][iD]

[1] Universidade Estadual de Campinas (UNICAMP), Campinas, Brazil
{pedro.rosso,guido}@ic.unicamp.br
[2] Universidade de São Paulo (USP), São Carlos, Brazil
[3] Universidade Federal do ABC (UFABC), Santo André, Brazil
[4] Advanced Micro Devices (AMD), Dublin, Ireland

Abstract. Designing high-performance scientific applications has become a time-consuming and complex task that requires developers to master multiple frameworks and toolchains. Although re-configurability and energy efficiency make FPGA a powerful accelerator, efficiently integrating multiple FPGAs into a distributed cluster is a complex and cumbersome task. Such complexity grows considerably when applications require partitioning execution among CPUs, GPUs, and FPGAs. This paper introduces FPGA offloading support to OpenMP cluster (OMPC), an OpenMP-only framework capable of transparently offloading computation across nodes in a cluster, which reduces developer effort and time to solution. In addition, OMPC enables true heterogeneity by allowing the programmer to assign program kernels to the most appropriate architecture (CPUs, GPUs, or FPGA), depending on their workload characteristics. This is achieved by adding only a few lines of standard OpenMP code to the application. The resulting framework was applied to the heterogeneous acceleration of an image recoloring application. Experimental results demonstrate speed-ups gains using different acceleration arrangements with CPU, GPU and FPGA. Measurements using Halstead metrics show that the proposed framework is faster to program. Furthermore, the solution enables transparently offloading OMPC communication tasks to multiple FPGAs, which results in speed-ups of up to 1.41x over the default communication mechanism (Message Passing Interface - MPI) on Task Bench, a synthetic benchmark for task parallelism.

Keywords: Distributed Computing · FPGA Acceleration · Heterogeneous Computing

1 Introduction

With Dennard scaling declining [15,23], the use of accelerators like GPUs and FPGAs has become essential for improving performance in HPC workloads.

FPGAs offer a flexible fabric of computational and data movement hardware components, enabling tailored data flow and custom-precision computation. They exhibit enhanced performance and energy efficiency across various applications [26,34,36], and outperform GPUs in certain specialized domains [35]. Accelerated FPGA application design is now accessible through major cloud services [6,10].

While FPGAs are powerful accelerators, programming them is highly complex, especially in distributed environments, as depicted in Fig. 1(a). Domain expert developers are expected to be proficient in programming languages, distributed computing frameworks, parallel programming, and FPGA acceleration, which is often impractical. To tackle these challenges, this paper proposes a framework to simplify the tool stack complexity for FPGA acceleration, illustrated in Fig. 1(b). The proposed framework extends OMPC [37], an OpenMP plugin that enables distributed computation through OpenMP standard directives, while leveraging MPI for efficient internode communication.

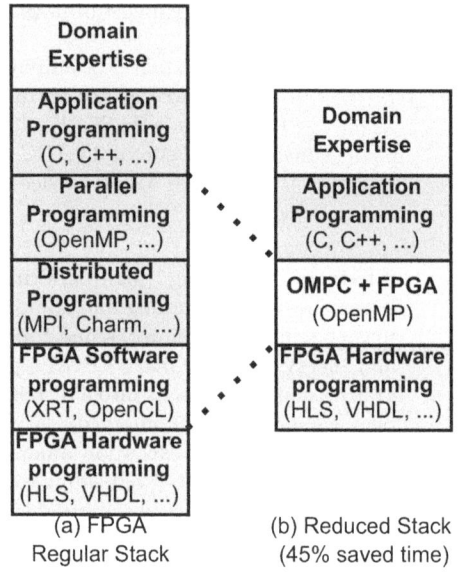

Fig. 1. (a) Regular FPGA acceleration tool stack. (b) FPGA-aware OMPC stack.

The proposed OMPC-based approach simplifies computation distribution and abstracts FPGA intricacies from programmers. It requires pre-designed FPGA kernels, which can be crafted separately by FPGA engineers. The framework significantly reduces the time needed to adapt applications for FPGA acceleration, for instance, experiments showed 45% reduction in programming time based on Halstead Metrics [18].

To implement this framework, this approach extends OMPC with FPGA acceleration. With FPGA-aware OMPC, users can add a few lines of standard OpenMP code [28] to declare FPGA kernels as alternatives to CPU kernels, enabling FPGA-accelerated, distributed, and heterogeneous applications.

Communication efficiency is critical in distributed environments, particularly when handling terabytes of data, which becomes more challenging with accelerators due to the frequent requirement for host-accelerator memory synchronization. FPGA-aware OMPC leverages the Alveo Collective Communication Library (ACCL) [20] to enable direct communication between interconnected FPGAs, thereby eliminating the need for manual data movement and abstracting away most FPGA complexities for developers.

This paper has the following contributions:

- An approach that reduces the amount of time spent to integrate FPGA kernels into an application.
- A fully abstracted mechanism to integrate FPGAs in a distributed environment.
- Integration of transparent direct FPGA-to-FPGA communication.
- A validation mechanism that seemingly switches between CPU and FPGA kernels at application compile time.

2 Background

2.1 FPGA Overview

Field-programmable gate arrays (FPGAs) are integrated circuits comprising reconfigurable logic blocks (Look-Up Tables), registers (Flip-flops), DSP slices, BRAM, and interconnecting signal switching nodes. They offer maximum re-implementation flexibility to meet specific application requirements, being especially suited for applications with a pipeline flow and typically results in low energy consumption (especially when compared to other accelerators, like GPUs).

FPGA Kernels are computational structures written using hardware description languages (e.g., VHDL) or C/C++, that are compiled into FPGA bitstreams capable of reconfiguring the FPGA fabric. The *FPGA host code* is the software part used to manage the FPGA boards, configuration, data synchronization, and kernel execution. It can be written using vendor-specific APIs (*e.g.,* AMD XRT) or open-source APIs (*e.g.,* OpenCL). Application control can become complex if multiple co-executing kernels exist, possibly on multiple FPGA boards.

For real-world scientific applications scaling beyond a single node, synchronization and data movement between FPGAs across a network are necessary. While GPU ecosystems offer robust developer tools like GPU-aware MPI and GPU-specific collective communication libraries (e.g., NCCL and RCCL), FPGA-aware MPI tools like ACCL are emerging but still complex. This paper aims to leverage such tools while abstracting their usage complexities from developers.

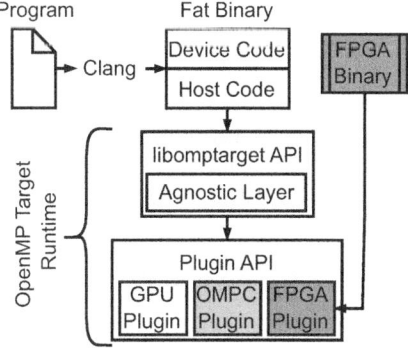

Fig. 2. Overview of the OpenMP Target architecture.

2.2 OpenMP Target Offloading

OpenMP is currently the dominant parallel programming abstraction [22]. Target offloading is a task-based paradigm that standardizes offloading computation to accelerators (e.g., GPUs) in OpenMP.

```
1 void array_sum_hls(int *A, int *B, int *C, int N);
2 #pragma omp declare variant(array_sum_hls) match(device={arch(alveo)})
3 void array_sum(int *A, int *B, int *C, int N);
```

Listing 1. Declaring FPGA kernels with variants.

```
1 #pragma omp target map(to: A[:N], B[:N]) map(from: C[:N]) nowait
2 array_sum(A, B, C, N);
```

Listing 2. Example of target task using OpenMP.

Figure 2 illustrates the components involved in the OpenMP target offloading [7] within the LLVM infrastructure [25]. An OpenMP annotated program is compiled with LLVM's Clang compiler, resulting in a fat binary encompassing both the host code (application) and the device code (accelerator code, *i.e.,* target directives). Depending on the architecture, an OpenMP runtime can translate device code into an architecture-specific implementation through plugin implementations.

Offloading to the device is managed by the OpenMP Target Runtime library, which can be divided into two main blocks: the *agnostic layer* and the *plugins*. The former is responsible for data mapping and execution, while the latter handles target-specific operations like allocation and execution.

This work leverages OMPC [37], which proposes a plugin that extends OpenMP to enable distributed computation across the cluster nodes, and proposes an FPGA plugin that manages the FPGA acceleration part.

3 OMPC FPGA Extension

As discussed before, Fig. 1 illustrates how challenging the development process can be, particularly for developers who are not specialists in this domain. Therefore, expecting them to be skilled in every tool and framework in the stack is not practical. Considering these challenges, next sections elaborate how this work proposes using OpenMP as a bridge to mitigate this complexity.

3.1 FPGA Plugin

Plugins are the way to implement execution blocks for specific devices (such as GPUs or FPGAs). Figure 2 shows the FPGA plugin in the OpenMP Target architecture (blue boxes). Since the proposed approach separates the hardware design from the software development, the FPGA bitstream is fed into the FPGA plugin instead of being present in the Fat Binary as the other devices do.

The implementation uses AMD native Xilinx runtime (XRT) library APIs. It enables bitstream downloading, kernel execution, and data management across single or multiple FPGAs. Although this project targeted Alveo FPGAs, which deliver the best performance-per-energy for HPC and Big Data workloads according to AMD [3], it supports any AMD device compatible with XRT.

A cornerstone of the FPGA plugin is its adoption of the *declare variant* directive, a concept introduced recently in the OpenMP standard 5.0 [29]. Listing 1 demonstrates the use of the directive in the proposed methodology. This directive receives a symbol (*array_sum_hls*) as an alternative to the succeeding declared symbol (*array_sum*). Compiling the application with *-fopenmp-targets=alveo* satisfies the condition in the *match* clause, therefore, delegating the task to the FPGA each time the corresponding CPU kernel is called in a target task during the run time (like show in Listing 2). That way, developers do not need to change the code anywhere else.

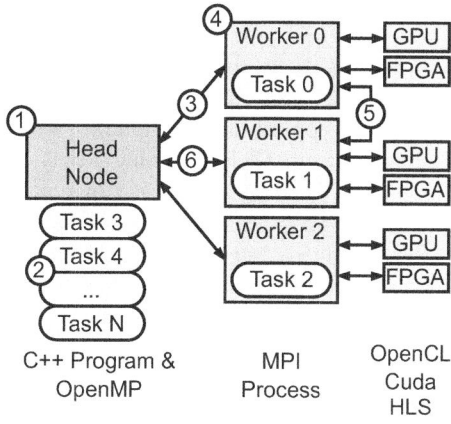

Fig. 3. Execution flow of OMPC runtime.

That mechanism also proves to be advantageous for application developers, allowing them to assess potential performance gains from different acceleration kernels, and for hardware designers, as a validation of in-progress FPGA kernels, enabling easy comparison of results obtained with FPGA and CPU kernels.

3.2 Integration with OMPC

To address real-world applications demanding for distributed computing, this framework leverages OMPC [37]. OMPC provides an MPI plugin (highlighted in green in Fig. 2) that abstracts distributed computing from the application developer, requiring only OpenMP to program applications in clusters.

OMPC was proposed for CPU execution and GPU kernels embedded in CPU tasks. By integrating the FPGA plugin with OMPC, the proposed methodology adds an extra accelerator to OMPC heterogeneous execution. Within this framework, OMPC would oversee computation distribution while specialized tasks are delegated to the respective plugins. By default, OMPC will take care of the communication between nodes using MPI.

Both the FPGA and OMPC plugins are implemented as OpenMP Target plugins and can work standalone. In this work, rather than the OpenMP Target Runtime directly invoking FPGA plugin operations, OMPC coordinates them. This coordination seamlessly extends distributed computing to the FPGA plugin, as depicted in Fig. 3. The OMPC head node executes the application ①, generating a task graph ② and delegates tasks to the workers ③. When necessary, the workers offload tasks to the GPU or FPGA ④. Communication can occur between nodes ⑤ and with the head node ⑥.

3.3 Accelerating Communication

The inter-workers and host-worker communications showed in Fig. 3 represent the default communication engine, which is derived from OMPC (using MPI). In large and distributed applications, with multiple nodes and devices, communication tends to become the bottleneck, which is especially true in accelerated computing due to Amdahl's law. This bottleneck grows even larger for FPGA-accelerated applications, stemming from the absence of an FPGA-aware MPI implementation. Often, there is a need to synchronize data between the FPGA and host memory (*staging*), before employing MPI for data movement.

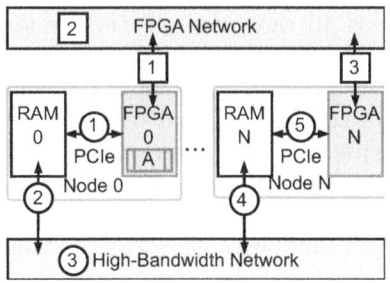

Fig. 4. Distributed architecture of the FPGA-aware OMPC, showing the available communication paths to transfer buffers in different FPGAs on different worker nodes.

Figure 4 depicts two communication pathways for FPGAs. One method involves communication via the FPGA's hosts (illustrated by the circles' path). While the other, involves a direct FPGA-to-FPGA communication (represented by the squares' path), that leverages FPGA-implemented networking blocks and I/Os, a distinctive feature of FPGAs.

In the communication method illustrated by the circles in Fig. 4, data transfer between FPGAs requires an initial transfer from FPGA to host memory via PCIe ①. Steps ②, ③, and ④ involve data movement through an Ethernet interface, typically utilizing high-bandwidth networks. The process concludes with data transmission back to the FPGA via PCIe ⑤, mirroring the initial step. Steps ① and ⑤ are called *staging*. This represents the default mechanism for communication in the proposed integration.

Upon transferring the communication backend from OMPC (MPI) to the FPGA plugin, communication occurs directly between FPGAs. Examining the squares' route in Fig. 4, data interchange between FPGAs uses a dedicated switch. This switch is directly tethered to each FPGA via QSFP28 ports, channeling data from the source FPGA [1] through the dedicated switch [2] to the recipient FPGA [3]. This mechanism sidesteps the staging operations observed in the other method. It is worth noting that hosts and FPGAs can share the same network switches, given FPGAs' compatibility with standard Ethernet.

For communication between FPGAs, the system leverages ACCL [20], an MPI-like FPGA communication library that implements collective operations such as broadcast, as well as regular sends and receives. Currently, this approach employs only *send* and *receive* operations, which will be extended to collective operations in the future. When ACCL FPGA kernels are build with the user FPGA kernels in the same FPGA bitstream, the plugin handles all data movement between the FPGAs through ACCL using the FPGA's QSFP28 ports and the Ethernet network. ACCL is directly used by FPGA Plugin, shown in Fig. 2.

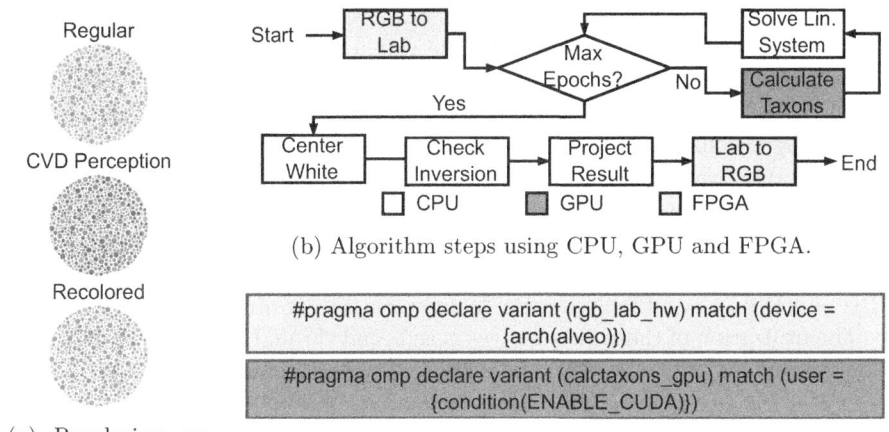

Fig. 5. Image recoloring application results (a), algorithm steps (b), and variants declaration for FPGA (green) and GPU (blue) (c). (Color figure online)

4 Exploring Heterogeneity

Extending OMPC with FPGA execution support enables the framework to execute applications in a heterogeneous environment. As discussed before, OMPC also enables GPU kernel execution by embedding GPU calls into CPU tasks. Therefore, OMPC can run applications accelerated by GPUs and FPGAs simultaneously. This section showcases this capability.

To showcase the potential of heterogeneity, this study utilizes an application designed for Color Vision Deficiency (CVD) [31]. It addresses the needs of dichromats—individuals with a particular form of CVD characterized by anomalies in one type of cone cells. These anomalies result in a two-dimensional color perception instead of the typical three-dimensional perception (like RGB). Employing dimensionality reduction using Elastic Maps [17], the application recalibrates images for dichromats, mapping colors from a 3D space to the 2D plane dichromats perceive. This ensures dichromats view images adjusted to the hues they are capable of discerning. Recoloring aids those with CVD in distinguishing colors, such as in scientific images, addressing a hereditary deficiency which affects approximately 1 in 12 men [4].

Figure 5(a) demonstrates the recoloring algorithm. The *Regular Image*, seen as the *CVD Simulation* by individuals with protanomaly dichromacy, is mapped to the *Recolored Image*. Figure 5(b) illustrates the pipeline stages of the recoloring algorithm, encompassing RGB/Lab color space transformations, elastic map approximation, and map projection. It also highlights one possible arrangement of kernel acceleration, with kernels in CPU, FPGA and GPU.

Analysis of the pipeline suggests that the *Calculate Taxons* followed by both *RGB/Lab* conversions are the three pipeline stages that share mostly of the

CVD's application execution time. Therefore, the best kernels to be optimized by accelerators. To show the capability of this framework, variants of the three kernels were developed for both FPGA and GPU.

The FPGA variants are implemented using HLS, compiled with vendor tools and having the final binary feed to the application (like Fig. 2 suggests). The GPU variants are implemented using CUDA, and embedded in CPU kernels (working as CPU tasks for OpenMP). It is not in the scope of this work to fully study and optimize the implementation of kernels on the FPGA or GPU. Instead, the objective is to show heterogeneous capabilities and how users can put CPU, GPU and FPGA together using the framework to test different arrangements.

The utilization of these alternatives is achieved through *variants*, as discussed in Sect. 3.1. This streamlined transition to heterogeneous acceleration, as demonstrated in Fig. 5(c), simplifies the exploration of various acceleration strategies tailored to the application's needs.

5 Experimental Results

This section presents a comprehensive evaluation of the proposed framework. It first delves into heterogeneous computing experiments in Sect. 5.1 and then discusses a set of experiments highlighting communication performance improvements in Sect. 5.2. The OMPC FPGA implementation [1] and the experimental artifacts [2] are open source and available to the community through the corresponding repositories.

5.1 Heterogeneous Computing

The CVD application was used to showcase heterogeneity. Evaluations were performed for the algorithm using CPU, CPU + GPU, CPU + FPGA and CPU + FPGA + GPU. The experiments were performed in a cluster where the compute nodes are equipped with Xeon Silver 4108 CPU @ 1.80 GHz CPUs, AMD Alveo U55c FPGA boards, NVIDIA Tesla P100 GPUs and are connected through 1 Gbps Ethernet links. The baseline for the experiments is the CVD's OMPC-based implementation that utilizes only CPU kernels (internally parallelized with OpenMP). The distributed approach comprises in using one node for CPU, one for FPGA and another for GPU.

The CPU version of the recoloring algorithm (parallelized with OpenMP) is used as baseline for comparison with three arrangements: (a) GPU acceleration targeting the three selected kernels; (b) FPGA acceleration targeting the three selected kernels; and (c) combining FPGA acceleration for the color conversion kernels with GPU acceleration for the taxons calculation. Figure 6 shows the speed-up comparing the arrangements. The best arrangement selection was using CPU + GPU, especially for larger images. The CPU + FPGA acceleration shows less speed than GPU or GPU and FPGA combined. Meanwhile, the CPU + FPGA + GPU version performs better for small images than the other arrangements. These results show that being able to quickly set up and arrange

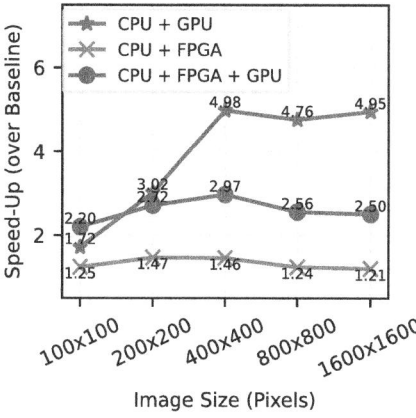 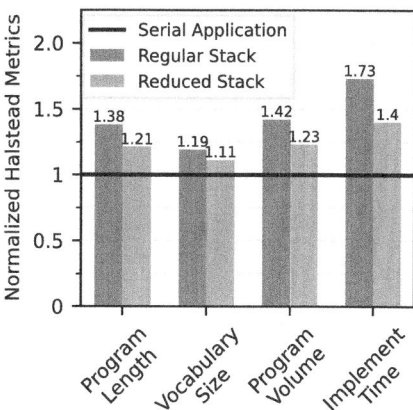

Fig. 6. Speed-up obtained for GPU, FPGA and GPU+FPGA acceleration.

Fig. 7. Normalized Halstead metrics analysis.

different selections is important and provides an easy path to define the best approach according to the application details and constraints.

The Halstead Metrics [18] consist of a set of software engineering metrics designed to quantify the complexity of code implementation. These metrics are derived from the counts of operands and operators in a codebase. Figure 7 shows the comparison of the implementation of the CVD application comparing the two stacks presented in Fig. 1, both regarding the CPU implementation of the application. The metrics are calculated based on the number of operands and operators found in the implementation. In particular, the metrics reveal that employing *reduced stacks* (OMPC + FPGA) can decrease the coding effort by approximately 45% compared to using the *regular stack*. For instance, the effort required to transform the serial version of the application into one that is distributed and accelerated by FPGA and GPU (using the *regular stack*) is reduced from 41 h to 22 h using the *reduced stack*. It is important to notice that these numbers may change depending on the size and implementation complexity of the serial application.

Figure 8 breaks down runtime for each version, showing each accelerator time and staging operations, as well as time spent in communication. In the baseline mostly of the time is spent on CPU computation. The integration with GPU shows that the acceleration reduces the percentage of CPU, making the communication time more visible (which should be similar to the baseline). The FPGA approach shows that for larger images, the FPGA starts to saturate and occupy mostly of the computation time compared to the CPU time. For the heterogeneous approach, time spent on CPU computation is more evident than FPGA or GPU, on the other hand, communication occupies the major part of the application make span, specially on large images. Meaning that communication become the current bottleneck in that approach. Breaking down the runtime execution helps to identify the current bottlenecks for each approach.

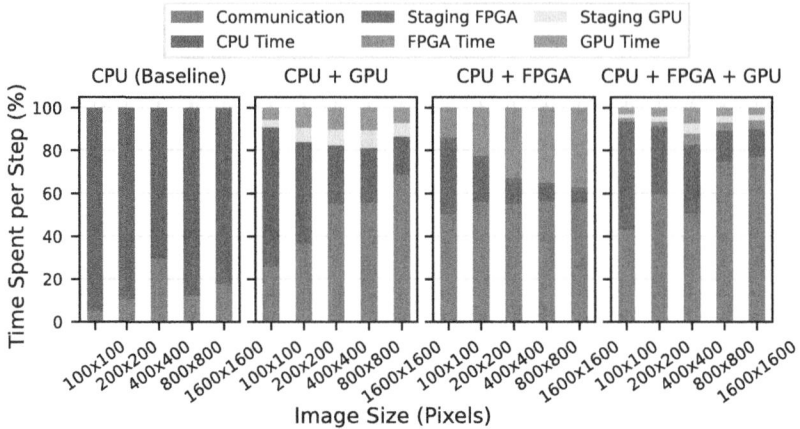

Fig. 8. Algorithm runtime decomposition.

5.2 Communication Acceleration

As discussed in Sect. 3.3, communication can be a major issue in distributed computing. This section evaluates communication acceleration using experiments conducted with the Task Bench benchmark tool [32]. The computation part was implemented as an FPGA kernel, which was combined with an existing version of OMPC, adding FPGA variants to the benchmark kernels. Task Bench facilitates comparison between kernel types and communication patterns. For these experiments, an FPGA compute-bound kernel was used with varying communication patterns (*Tree*, *FFT*, and *All-to-All*), described in Fig. 9(a). These choices were based on the communication weights: *Tree* (1 buffer transfer per task), *FFT* (average of 2.17 buffer transfers per task), and *All-to-All* (average of 9 buffer transfers per task). Buffer sizes were fixed at 4 MB while varying the computation performed by the FPGA kernel.

Experiments were conducted on the AMD heterogeneous accelerated compute cluster (HACC) at ETH Zurich [5] comprising high-end servers (*e.g.*, AMD EPYC CPUs) with various re-configurable acceleration cards and AMD GPUs linked via a high-speed network switch. The experiments were evaluated on nine servers, each equipped with one Alveo U55c card and two 100 Gbps interfaces connected to a 100 Gbps switch, across an average of 10 runs.

Communication performance was compared between two backends: *Baseline* using OMPC (MPI) and *ACCL* leveraging the accelerated collective communication library (discussed in Sect. 3.3). A network efficiency roofline model [9] was used for comparison, where the results were normalized against a non-communication experiment to isolate overheads. The Communication Arithmetic Intensity (CAI) metric was used to control the experiments, based on FLOPS to bytes transferred ratio. The effective bandwidth roof is 79.5 Gbps.

Figure 9(b) shows performance across communication patterns. For higher CAIs, both options perform similarly due to increased computation, while for

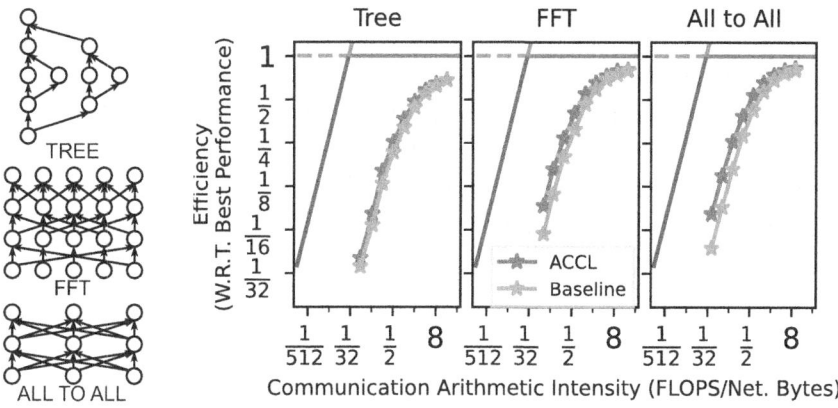

(a) Evaluated Comm. patterns. (b) Network efficiency roofline when varying the Computing Arithmetic Intensity.

Fig. 9. Communication acceleration results

lower CAIs, ACCL demonstrates advantages. ACCL achieved effective bandwidths of 13.1 Gbps, 19.6 Gbps, and 33.4 Gbps, while the baseline achieved 10.8 Gbps, 15.3 Gbps, and 23.6 Gbps for *Tree*, *FFT*, and *All-to-All*, respectively. ACCL consistently outperforms the baseline when application is communication-bounded. In summary, ACCL offers up to 1.41× higher network bandwidth than baseline for the most communication-intensive *All-to-All* pattern and tend toward 1× as communication diminishes relative to computation. These results advocate ACCL's effectiveness in boosting FPGA-accelerated distributed computing communication.

6 Related Work

FPGA acceleration, known for its low latency, reprogramming capabilities, and energy efficiency, is gaining traction. Research aims at optimizing computing kernels, simplifying development, and creating specialized solutions. This work aims to generalize FPGA usage by enabling the integration of existing kernels into diverse applications.

Early works have encompassed offloading entire OpenMP programs to FPGAs, accelerating kernels, and synthesizing the sequential portion in soft cores on the FPGA [12,13,30]. In contrast, this approach concentrates on offloading kernels to FPGA while preserving the sequential portion on CPUs for faster execution. This approach provides enhanced developer flexibility and adopts a distributed architecture.

Other works have concentrated on supporting CPU+FPGA single-node systems, restricting the use of other accelerators [21,24,27,33]. These studies integrate the vendor compiler into the compilation flow to generate FPGA code and manage FPGA execution. In contrast, the proposed approach allows for the use of multiple accelerators and introduces distributed FPGA acceleration, maintaining a clear separation between hardware design and software development, giving the developer more flexibility.

Some approaches have focused on single-node FPGA acceleration, targeting Zynq Xilinx boards and utilizing FPGA resources to run their runtime on FPGA [8,16]. These efforts are based on OmpSs [14], which offers extensions to the OpenMP standard. In contrast, OmpSs@cloudFPGA [19] aims at distributed FPGAs in cloud environments, also utilizing FPGA space and supporting MPI-like explicit FPGA-to-FPGA messages. Unlike previous OmpSs-based approaches, this approach provides transparent FPGA-to-FPGA communication, hiding it from users, and enables communication through FPGA hosts when direct communication is unavailable. Additionally, it complies with the OpenMP standard, while providing distributed acceleration.

All previously cited works require developers to integrate FPGA kernels into the OpenMP code and employ an HLS compiler to generate FPGA code. In contrast, this approach utilizes pre-built bitstreams, allowing developers to utilize (or generate) bitstreams to execute their applications. This flexibility also enables the utilization of HDL-designed kernels.

Some works, like this proposal, propose an OpenMP plugin to facilitate FPGA utilization. While a previous work target cloud FPGAs [11], focus on offloading to single-node FPGAs, this approach stands out for its distributed acceleration feature. And unlike that approach, it doesn't require additional FPGA resources beyond the application itself to run the framework. Focusing on the offloading to multiple FPGAs [28], other work also use variants to configure FPGA kernels for distributed interconnected FPGAs. Alternatively, this approach is more flexible regarding the system configuration as well as enables communication for non-interconnected FPGAs.

Unlike any other work, this approach facilitates multiple configurations of FPGAs in a cluster, allowing FPGAs to execute different bitstreams. Such flexibility can be essential for certain applications [38].

7 Conclusions

This paper presents a framework capable of offloading and executing kernels in multiple FPGAs in parallel through OpenMP directives. This framework was integrated with OMPC [37] to ease distributed computing acceleration with FPGAs. Developers can plug FPGA kernels into their corresponding distributed applications with only two lines of code: (a) Declaring the kernel; and (b) Defining it as a variant of an existing method, which makes FPGA programming much easier than before, reducing the time to implement distributed FPGA acceleration by 45%.

Results show that the proposed framework provides an easy path for heterogeneous computation. Experimental results show that one can easily test different acceleration arrangements to identify the best selection for a real-world application using GPUs and FPGAs depending on the application inputs. Leveraging ACCL [20], experimental results showed up to 41.5% more network bandwidth when using ACCL, while being likely equal to the default communication backend for the worst-case scenarios. For future work, the plan is to improve scheduling of the generated tasks, enable support for data streaming between FPGA kernels and turn the communication into non-blocking versions, providing parallel handling of communications. Remote and direct access to memory (RDMA/DMA) are topics that could provide optimizations to the framework, therefore should be tackled in future works.

Acknowledgment. The authors are grateful to Fundação de Amparo à Pesquisa do Estado de São Paulo (FAPESP) by the grant support 2021/09355-2. This project was also partially funded by Petrobras (under grant 2018/00347-4), and AMD under the Heterogeneous Accelerated Compute Clusters (HACC) program.

References

1. OpenMP Cluster - FPGA Artifacts. https://gitlab.com/phrosso/researchartifacts/-/tree/master
2. OpenMP Cluster - FPGA Repository. https://gitlab.com/ompcluster/llvm-project/-/tree/fpga/alveo-plugin
3. Accelerating sensor signal processing with the Alveo U55C card (2022). https://www.xilinx.com/content/dam/xilinx/publications/solution-briefs/sensor-signal-processing-solution-brief.pdf. Accessed 03 Nov 2023
4. Color blindness (2023). https://www.nei.nih.gov/learn-about-eye-health/eye-conditions-and-diseases/color-blindness. Accessed 26 Oct 2023
5. HACC ETH Zurich Cluster (2023). https://www.amd-haccs.io/ethz.html. Accessed 03 Nov 2023
6. Amazon Web Services: Amazon EC2 F1 instances (2019). https://aws.amazon.com/ec2/instance-types/f1. Accessed 26 Oct 2023
7. Antao, S.F., et al.: Offloading support for OpenMP in clang and LLVM. In: 2016 Third Workshop on the LLVM Compiler Infrastructure in HPC (LLVM-HPC), pp. 1–11 (2016). https://doi.org/10.1109/LLVM-HPC.2016.006
8. Bosch, J., et al.: Application acceleration on fpgas with ompss@ fpga. In: 2018 International Conference on Field-Programmable Technology (FPT), pp. 70–77. IEEE (2018)
9. Cardwell, D., Song, F.: An extended roofline model with communication-awareness for distributed-memory HPC systems. In: Proceedings of the International Conference on High Performance Computing in Asia-Pacific Region, pp. 26–35 (2019)
10. Caulfield, A.M., et al.: A cloud-scale acceleration architecture. In: 2016 49th Annual IEEE/ACM International Symposium on Microarchitecture (MICRO), pp. 1–13 (2016). https://doi.org/10.1109/MICRO.2016.7783710
11. Ceissler, C., Nepomuceno, R., Pereira, M., Araujo, G.: Automatic offloading of cluster accelerators. In: 2018 IEEE 26th Annual International Symposium on Field-Programmable Custom Computing Machines (FCCM), pp. 224–224. IEEE (2018)
12. Choi, J., Brown, S., Anderson, J.: From software threads to parallel hardware in high-level synthesis for FPGAs. In: 2013 International Conference on Field-Programmable Technology (FPT), pp. 270–277. IEEE (2013)

13. Cilardo, A., Gallo, L., Mazzeo, A., Mazzocca, N.: Efficient and scalable OpenMP-based system-level design. In: 2013 Design, Automation & Test in Europe Conference & Exhibition (DATE), pp. 988–991. IEEE (2013)
14. Duran, A., et al.: Ompss: a proposal for programming heterogeneous multi-core architectures. Parallel Process. Lett. **21**(02), 173–193 (2011)
15. Esmaeilzadeh, H., Blem, E., Sankaralingam, R.S.A.K., Burger, D.: Retrospective: dark silicon and the end of multicore scaling
16. Filgueras, A., et al.: OmpSs@ Zynq all-programmable SoC ecosystem. In: Proceedings of the 2014 ACM/SIGDA International Symposium on Field-Programmable Gate Arrays, pp. 137–146 (2014)
17. Gorban, A.N., Zinovyev, A.Y.: Elastic maps and nets for approximating principal manifolds and their application to microarray data visualization. In: Gorban, A.N., Kégl, B., Wunsch, D.C., Zinovyev, A.Y. (eds.) Principal Manifolds for Data Visualization and Dimension Reduction. LNCSE, vol. 58, pp. 96–130. Springer, Heidelberg (2008). https://doi.org/10.1007/978-3-540-73750-6_4
18. Halstead, M.H.: Elements of Software Science (Operating and programming systems series). Elsevier Science Inc. (1977)
19. de Haro, J.M., et al.: OmpSs@ cloudFPGA: an FPGA task-based programming model with message passing. In: 2022 IEEE International Parallel and Distributed Processing Symposium (IPDPS), pp. 828–838. IEEE (2022)
20. He, Z., Parravicini, D., Petrica, L., O'Brien, K., Alonso, G., Blott, M.: ACCL: FPGA-accelerated collectives over 100 Gbps TCP-IP. In: 2021 IEEE/ACM International Workshop on Heterogeneous High-Performance Reconfigurable Computing (H2RC), pp. 33–43 (2021). https://doi.org/10.1109/H2RC54759.2021.00009
21. Huthmann, J., Sommer, L., Podobas, A., Koch, A., Sano, K.: OpenMP device offloading to FPGAs using the Nymble infrastructure. In: Milfeld, K., de Supinski, B.R., Koesterke, L., Klinkenberg, J. (eds.) IWOMP 2020. LNCS, vol. 12295, pp. 265–279. Springer, Cham (2020). https://doi.org/10.1007/978-3-030-58144-2_17
22. Kadosh, T., Hasabnis, N., Mattson, T., Pinter, Y., Oren, G.: Quantifying OpenMP: statistical insights into usage and adoption. arXiv preprint arXiv:2308.08002 (2023)
23. Kanduri, A., Rahmani, A.M., Liljeberg, P., Hemani, A., Jantsch, A., Tenhunen, H.: A perspective on dark silicon. In: Rahmani, A.M., Liljeberg, P., Hemani, A., Jantsch, A., Tenhunen, H. (eds.) The Dark Side of Silicon, pp. 3–20. Springer, Cham (2017). https://doi.org/10.1007/978-3-319-31596-6_1
24. Knaust, M., Mayer, F., Steinke, T.: OpenMP to FPGA offloading prototype using OpenCL SDK. In: 2019 IEEE International Parallel and Distributed Processing Symposium Workshops (IPDPSW), pp. 387–390. IEEE (2019)
25. Lattner, C., Adve, V.: LLVM: a compilation framework for lifelong program analysis & transformation. In: International Symposium on Code Generation and Optimization, 2004. CGO 2004, pp. 75–86 (2004). https://doi.org/10.1109/CGO.2004.1281665
26. Lielāmurs, E., Cvetkovs, A., Novickis, R., Ozols, K.: Infrared image pre-processing and IR/RGB registration with FPGA implementation. Electronics **12**(4), 882 (2023)
27. Mayer, F., Brandner, J., Hellmann, M., Schwarzer, J., Philippsen, M.: The ORKA-HPC compiler—practical OpenMP for FPGAs. In: Li, X., Chandrasekaran, S. (eds.) LCPC 2021. LNCS, vol. 13181, pp. 83–97. Springer, Cham (2022). https://doi.org/10.1007/978-3-030-99372-6_6
28. Nepomuceno, R., Sterle, R., Valarini, G., Pereira, M., Yviquel, H., Araujo, G.: Enabling openMP task parallelism on multi-FPGAs. In: 2021 IEEE 29th Annual

International Symposium on Field-Programmable Custom Computing Machines (FCCM), pp. 260–260. IEEE (2021)
29. Pennycook, S.J., Sewall, J.D., Duran, A.: Supporting function variants in OpenMP. In: de Supinski, B.R., Valero-Lara, P., Martorell, X., Mateo Bellido, S., Labarta, J. (eds.) IWOMP 2018. LNCS, vol. 11128, pp. 128–142. Springer, Cham (2018). https://doi.org/10.1007/978-3-319-98521-3_9
30. Podobas, A., Brorsson, M.: Empowering openMP with automatically generated hardware. In: 2016 International Conference on Embedded Computer Systems: Architectures, Modeling and Simulation (SAMOS), pp. 245–252. IEEE (2016)
31. Rosso, P.H.D.F.: Recoloração de imagens para dicromatas baseada em mapas elásticos (2018). https://repositorio.ufsc.br/handle/123456789/192338. Accessed 26 Oct 2023
32. Slaughter, E., et al.: Task bench: a parameterized benchmark for evaluating parallel runtime performance. In: SC20: International Conference for High Performance Computing, Networking, Storage and Analysis, pp. 1–15. IEEE (2020)
33. Sommer, L., Korinth, J., Koch, A.: OpenMP device offloading to FPGA accelerators. In: 2017 IEEE 28th International Conference on Application-specific Systems, Architectures and Processors (ASAP), pp. 201–205. IEEE (2017)
34. Strickland, M.: FPGA accelerated HPC and data analytics. In: 2018 International Conference on Field-Programmable Technology (FPT), pp. 21–21 (2018). https://doi.org/10.1109/FPT.2018.00009
35. Xuan, L., Un, K.F., Lam, C.S., Martins, R.P.: An FPGA-based energy-efficient reconfigurable depthwise separable convolution accelerator for image recognition. IEEE Trans. Circuits Syst. II Express Briefs **69**(10), 4003–4007 (2022)
36. Young, A.R., Miniskar, N.R., Liu, F., Blokland, W., Vetter, J.S.: Adrastea: an efficient FPGA design environment for heterogeneous scientific computing and machine learning. In: Doug, K., Al, G., Pophale, S., Liu, H., Parete-Koon, S. (eds.) SMC 2022. CCIS, vol. 1690, pp. 227–243. Springer, Cham (2023). https://doi.org/10.1007/978-3-031-23606-8_14
37. Yviquel, H., et al.: The OpenMP cluster programming model. In: Workshop Proceedings of the 51st International Conference on Parallel Processing, pp. 1–11 (2022)
38. Zhu, Y., He, Z., Jiang, W., Zeng, K., Zhou, J., Alonso, G.: Distributed recommendation inference on FPGA clusters. In: 2021 31st International Conference on Field-Programmable Logic and Applications (FPL), pp. 279–285. IEEE (2021)

Towards a Scalable and Efficient PGAS-Based Distributed OpenMP

Baodi Shan[1(✉)], Mauricio Araya-Polo[2], and Barbara Chapman[1]

[1] Stony Brook University, Stony Brook, NY 11794, USA
{baodi.shan,barbara.chapman}@stonybrook.edu
[2] TotalEnergies EP Research & Technology US, LLC, Houston, TX 77002, USA

Abstract. MPI+X has been the *de facto* standard for distributed memory parallel programming. It is widely used primarily as an explicit two-sided communication model, which often leads to complex and error-prone code. Alternatively, PGAS model utilizes efficient one-sided communication and more intuitive communication primitives. In this paper, we present a novel approach that integrates PGAS concepts into the OpenMP programming model, leveraging the LLVM compiler infrastructure and the GASNet-EX communication library. Our model addresses the complexity associated with traditional MPI+OpenMP programming models while ensuring excellent performance and scalability. We evaluate our approach using a set of micro-benchmarks and application kernels on two distinct platforms: Ookami from Stony Brook University and NERSC Perlmutter. The results demonstrate that DiOMP achieves superior bandwidth and lower latency compared to MPI+OpenMP, up to 25% higher bandwidth and down to 45% on latency. DiOMP offers a promising alternative to the traditional MPI+OpenMP hybrid programming model, towards providing a more productive and efficient way to develop high-performance parallel applications for distributed memory systems.

Keywords: PGAS · MPI · OpenMP · Distributed Computing

1 Introduction

HPC systems continue to grow in size and complexity, pushing legacy programming models to their limits. Developers of numerical simulation applications must adapt to this reality. Fortunately, alternative programming models and productivity frameworks are available and continually evolving to provide necessary support. Currently and for most of the last decade, MPI+X is the mainstream paradigm for distributed cluster programming models, where X can be OpenMP, OpenACC, CUDA, RAJA or Kokkos, etc. [3,7,21]. However, there is an increasing need for alternatives to MPI+X that are more flexible and less complex. One such alternative is the PGAS (Partitioned Global Address Space) programming model, which is gaining momentum. Notable PGAS models such as UPC++, OpenSHMEM, and Legion and languages such as Chapel are reaching larger developer audiences.

OpenMP is rapidly evolving from a traditional CPU-based and shared-memory programming model to one that includes task-based programming and accelerator-based offloading capabilities. Therefore, we aim to leverage the power of PGAS to extend OpenMP to operate in distributed environments. To that end, we propose the PGAS-based Distributed OpenMP (**DiOMP**). DiOMP's main contributions are:

Enhanced Scalability and Improved Performance: DiOMP boosts performance and scalability for distributed applications by allowing efficient data sharing across nodes without the overhead of traditional message-passing.

Simplified Communication in the PGAS Model: DiOMP exploits the PGAS model direct operations on global memory addresses, which reduces the complexities of message matching and buffer management commonly found in MPI. In the PGAS framework, communication operations like reading and writing remote data are conducted directly via global addresses, without the need for additional management of communication domains.

Simplified Memory Management: By extending native OpenMP statements, such as `omp_alloc()`, this model simplifies the allocation and management of memory. Compared to MPI RMA, this approach avoids the complexities and overhead associated with creating and destroying MPI windows.

Excellent Extensibility through Activate Message: Active Messages is a communication mechanism that reduces latency and overhead by directly executing a handler function upon message arrival, ensuring efficient and immediate processing. This guarantees the extensibility of DiOMP, in the current version of DiOMP, `ompx_lock()` is implemented using Active Messages. In future versions, Active Messages will play a crucial role in handling task dependencies within DiOMP by allowing for dynamic and responsive communication patterns.

2 Background

2.1 OpenMP

OpenMP [11] is one the main standard for shared-memory parallelism in HPC. It provides a straightforward and flexible interface for developers to create parallel applications by exploiting the capabilities of multi-core processors and shared memory systems. Current versions of OpenMP support the task-based programming model, for instance, OpenMP 4.0 introduced task dependencies, allowing programmers to specify dependencies between tasks and enabling the runtime system to automatically manage the execution order based on these dependencies. With the introduction of version 4.0, OpenMP also expanded its capabilities to include device offloading [17], enabling code execution on accelerators without requiring users to develop device-specific kernels using vendor-specific APIs.

2.2 The PGAS Model

PGAS stand for Partitioned Global Address Space programming model. In contrast to the message-passing model (MPI), the PGAS programming model [19] utilizes a globally accessible memory space that is divided among the basic units distributed across one or more nodes.

PGAS models offer a uniform view of distributed memory objects and enable high-performance access to remote memory through direct operations such as reads (**get**s) and writes (**put**s). Point-to-point communication in the PGAS model is one-sided, requiring active participation only from the initiating unit. This decouples communication and synchronization, allowing the target unit's computation to continue uninterrupted during data exchanges.

Many distributed and parallel computing programming languages and libraries feature the PGAS model, including OpenSHMEM, Legion, UPC++, DASH, Chapel, and OpenUH Co-Array Fortran. In the programming languages and libraries that have adopted PGAS, some use MPI as their communication framework, such as DASH, while others utilize UCX, such as OpenSHMEM. But the de-facto communication standard targeted by portable PGAS system is GASNet API. Current and historical GASNet clients include: UPC++ [1], Cray Chapel [4], Legion [2], OpenUH Co-Array Fortran [5], OpenSHMEM Reference implementation [14], Omni XcalableMP [10], and several miscellaneous projects.

2.3 Related Work

The idea of executing OpenMP programs within distributed architectures has been extensively explored in scholarly research. The concept of Remote OpenMP offloading, as introduced by Patel and Doerfert [12], together with subsequent enhancements [8,18] and practical implementations, has demonstrated considerable promise for facilitating OpenMP target offloading to remote devices. Nonetheless, as noted in reference [8], the scalability of such remote offloading is sub-par when compared with conventional hybrid MPI+OpenMP methodologies. In a similar line of analysis, the OpenMP Cluster developed by Yviquel et al. [20], which also focuses on OpenMP target offloading, conceptualizes remote nodes as a computational resource for OpenMP targets. Another path to distributed directive-based programming approach is by combining XMP and YML [13].

3 Design of PGAS-Based Distributed OpenMP

PGAS-based Distributed OpenMP is developed based on LLVM/OpenMP and utilizes GASNet-EX as the underlying communication middleware. In this section, we will sequentially introduce the memory management model of our PGAS-based approach, point-to-point communication, collective communication, and the synchronization mechanisms, as well as the role and future potential of GASNet-EX Active Message in these mechanisms.

3.1 Memory Management

In the PGAS layer, we use process (*rank*) as the main unit for memory management and communication. The memory region of each rank is divided into private memory and global memory, adhering to the PGAS paradigm guidelines. The memory management model is illustrated in Fig. 1. Due to the segment constraints imposed by the communication middleware GASNet-EX, the memory space related to communication must reside within the segment previously allocated via `gex_Segment_Attach()`. To address this requirement, we introduce aligned global memory and unaligned global memory. The allocation of aligned global memory needs the involvement of all ranks, with each rank acquiring an equal size of global memory, which is then placed at the front of their respective segments.

The segments attached by GASNet-EX do not support address alignment, meaning that GASNet-EX cannot guarantee identical address ranges across different ranks' segments. Therefore, PGAS-based distributed OpenMP uses virtual address alignment. Virtual address alignment operates as follows: although the actual memory addresses assigned to each rank during the allocation of aligned global memory may differ, the runtime system maintains a specific mapping that provides a virtually aligned address space. Thus, when a rank intends to transfer data to other ranks, it can simply utilize its own memory address to obtain the corresponding memory addresses of the other ranks.

As for non-aligned global memory, which is global memory that can be created by individual or some ranks. This type of memory is allocated at the end of the segment in a limited manner. This memory does not receive virtual address mapping, as the process is invisible to ranks that do not participate in this portion of the memory allocation. Non-aligned global memory is particularly suitable for storing and retrieving specific or temporary data.

Whether using aligned or non-aligned global memory, developers utilizing DiOMP can easily allocate global memory by invoking the `omp_alloc()` function, which is part of the OpenMP standard. DiOMP is equipped with specially designed allocators for allocating data in the global space. In addition to supporting standard **C** function from OpenMP, we have also provided a **C++** allocation function with template support, enabling developers to allocate memory for specific data type or data structure.

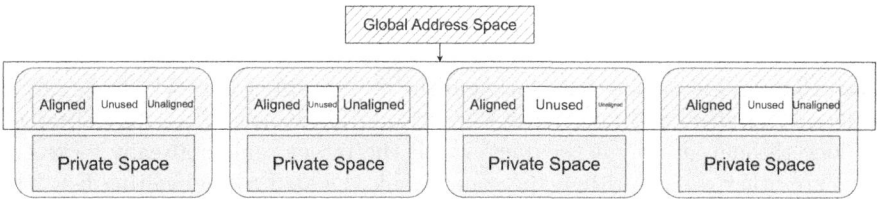

Fig. 1. Memory management model of the DiOMP. Each node has its own private space (green) and a shared global space (striped), with the global space further divided into aligned space (orange) and unaligned space (red). The white parts represent unused (unallocated) memory space. (Color figure online)

3.2 Point-to-Point and Collective Communication

DiOMP incorporates two fundamental communication paradigms: point-to-point and collective communication. These paradigms enhance data exchange and synchronization across different ranks, facilitating efficient parallel computing.

```
void ompx_get(void *dst, int rank, void *src, size_t nbytes);
void ompx_put(int rank, void *dst, void *src, size_t nbytes);
```

Listing 1. Point-to-point APIs for PGAS-based Distributed OpenMP

Point-to-point communication leverages one-sided communication primitives, including put and get[1]. This method enables ranks to directly access each other's memory without needing explicit coordination, thus reducing synchronization overhead and allowing computation and communication to overlap. These operations could utilize a virtual address alignment mechanism to seamlessly map between local and remote memory spaces. Listing 1 shows the APIs for point-to-point communication in DiOMP. Collective communication, on the other hand, requires all ranks to participate in data exchange or synchronization. DiOMP supports various collective operations like barrier, broadcast, and reduction, which are optimized based on the network topology and hardware capabilities. These operations help in the efficient distribution and aggregation of data, supporting common parallel programming patterns. Together, these communication strategies provide a robust framework in PGAS-based Distributed OpenMP.

3.3 Synchronization Mechanisms and Active Messages

DiOMP based on GASNet-EX offers a variety of synchronization mechanisms, including ompx_barrier(), ompx_waitRMA(), and ompx_lock(). Among these, the implementations of barrier and waitRMA are based on the native interfaces of GASNet-EX, while ompx_lock() utilizes the Active Message mechanism of GASNet-EX. We will use ompx_lock() as a case study to demonstrate the significant role that Active Message plays in our model.

The primary function of ompx_lock() is to ensure that a specific rank has exclusive access to the shared memory space of a target rank by establishing a lock. This process is facilitated by several dedicated GASNet-EX active message handlers. When one rank (source rank) wants to lock another rank (target rank), it starts by sending an active message. The source rank then waits for a reply to see if it got the lock. Meanwhile, the target rank checks this request and manages a list of all ranks waiting for a lock, along with a lock status indicator. If no other rank is waiting for a lock and the target rank is not locked, the target rank will lock itself and inform the source rank that it has successfully obtained the lock through a reply active message. If the target rank is already locked or there are other ranks waiting, the source rank is added to the waiting list. The

---

[1] The model and framework proposed in this paper are currently limited to the proof of concept stage, and the function names are provisional.

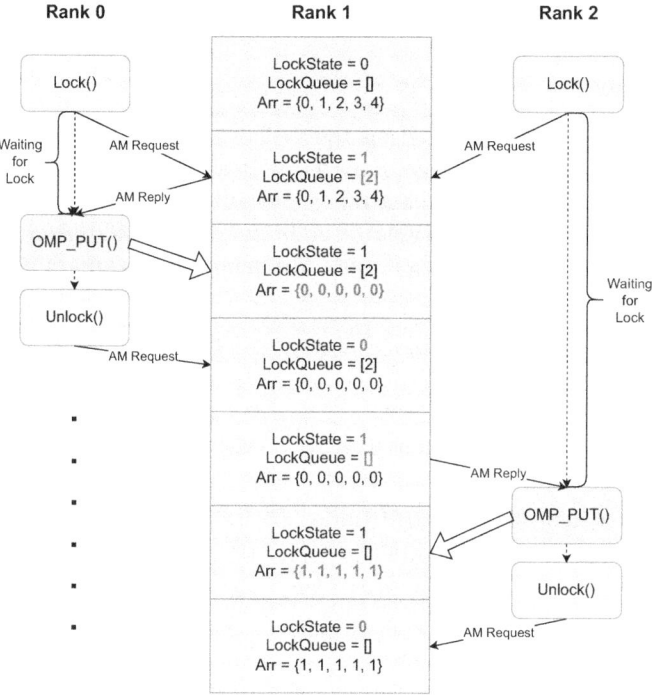

Fig. 2. The workflow of the ompx_lock() and ompx_unlock() based on Active Messages in the presence of contention.

source rank must then wait its turn until it is at the front of the list and the target rank is unlocked.

Each active message handler in GASNet-EX possesses a unique token, which means the rank queue stores these tokens, each embodying information about its corresponding source rank. This mechanism ensures that every request is uniquely identified and correctly processed. In cases where the lock cannot be immediately granted, the target rank does not idle. Instead, it monitors the rank queue and only responds once the locking rank issues an unlock active message. This efficient management prevents unnecessary delays and optimizes resource use. Figure 2 illustrates the process where rank0 and rank2 simultaneously initiate lock requests and put data on rank1.

Building upon this, we have also introduced the ompx_lockt() function, which is an extension of ompx_lock() that provides thread-level locking. This function implements both thread-level and process-level locking, making it extremely useful in mixed thread and process programming scenarios, such as when inter-rank communication occurs within an omp parallel for region.

In the future, we plan to further expand the role of active message within DiOMP, particularly in handling OpenMP task dependencies. Active message is expected to play a crucial role in this context.

4 Evaluation

4.1 Experimental Setup

The experiments were conducted on the Ookami system at Stony Brook University and the Perlmutter supercomputer at Lawrence Berkeley National Laboratory. Refer to Table 1 for the hardware and software specifications of the systems. We performed micro-benchmarks on both systems and tested weak scaling matrix multiplication and strong scaling Minimod [9] benchmark on Ookami.

Table 1. Hardware and software configuration of the experimental platforms

	Ookami	Perlmutter
CPUs	Fujitsu A64FX	AMD EPYC 7763 * 2
CPU cores	48	64
Memory	32 GB HBM2	512 GB DDR4
Interconnect	InfiniBand HDR	HPE Slingshot-11
MPI	MVAPICH 2.3.7	Cray MPICH 8.1.28
GASNet-EX	GASNet-2023.9.0	

4.2 Micro-benchmarks

We conducted micro benchmark tests on Ookami and Perlmutter platforms to evaluate the performance of DiOMP in terms of bandwidth and latency.

The bandwidth tests using large message sizes showed that DiOMP achieved higher peak bandwidth and sustained higher throughput compared to MPI on both platforms (Fig. 3 and Fig. 4). As the message size increases, DiOMP-based implementation achieves peak bandwidth earlier than MPI. This can be attributed to the efficient utilization of the underlying interconnect through the GASNet-EX communication layer.

The latency tests using small message sizes demonstrated that DiOMP consistently demonstrates lower latency compared to MPI on both Ookami and Perlmutter (Fig. 5 and Fig. 6). The reduction in latency is up to 45%. The lower latency of DiOMP is a result of its lightweight one-sided communication model, which eliminates the overhead associated with explicit message matching and synchronization in MPI. Notice that the performance of mpi_put and mpi_get on Perlmutter is consistent but apart, it has been previously reported [6].

These findings suggest that DiOMP is a promising alternative for high-performance inter-node communication in parallel applications.

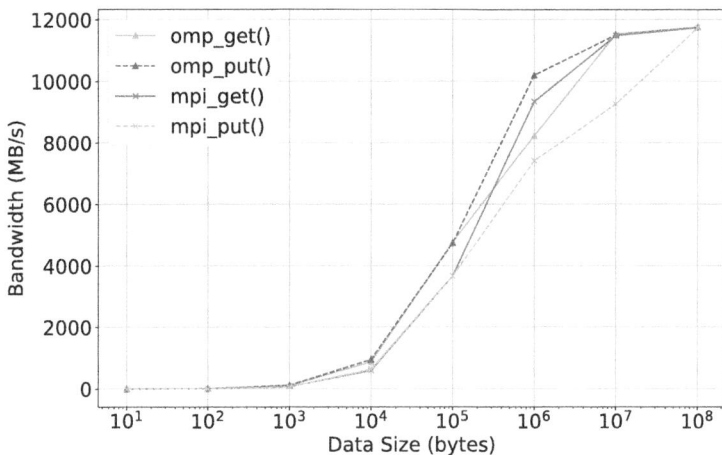

Fig. 3. Micro-benchmark for bandwidth on Ookami

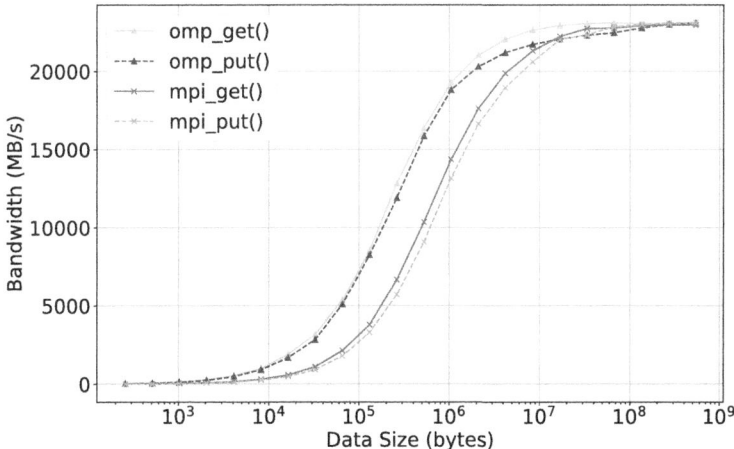

Fig. 4. Micro-benchmark for bandwidth on Perlmutter. Notice that for messages of size 10^6, PGAS+OpenMP outperforms MPI+OpenMP by 25%.

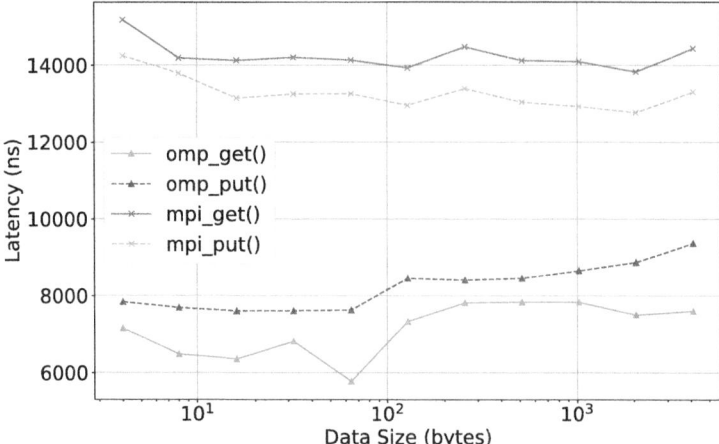

Fig. 5. Micro-benchmark for latency on Ookami. Notice that PGAS+OpenMP latency across message sizes is in average 45% lower then MPI+OpenMP.

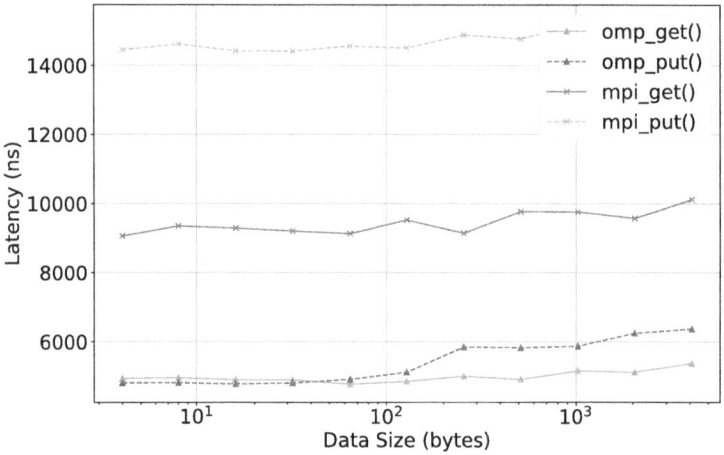

Fig. 6. Micro-benchmark for latency on Perlmutter.

4.3 Weak Scaling-Matrix Multiplication

We subsequently evaluate the ring exchange communication pattern using a mini-application that implements Cannon's algorithm to perform square matrix multiplication, resulting in the product $C = A \times B$. Both the MPI version and the DiOMP version of the mini-app incorporate an additional bLoCk stripe for matrix B, enabling the overlap of computation and communication. In this miniapp, as the number of ranks increases, the size of the matrix and the volume of data transferred also increase. In this test, the matrix size is $500 \times 500 \times$ ranks number, resulting in a linear increase in computational load. Due to the ring communication pattern employed, the volume of communication increases in squares. Figure 7 presents the results of matrix multiplication on the Ookami system using both DiOMP and MPI+OpenMP.

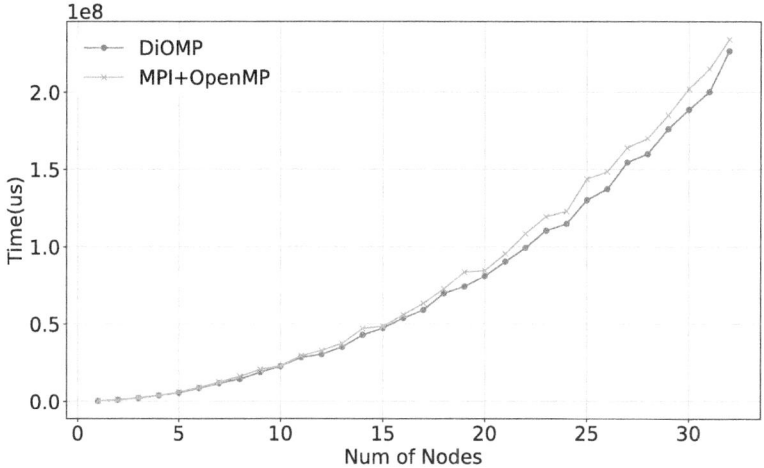

Fig. 7. Matrix Multiplication on Ookami

4.4 Strong Scaling-Minimod

Table 2. Lines of code of MPI+OpenMP verus PGAS+OpenMP

Programming Model	Lines of Code
MPI+OpenMP	26
PGAS+OpenMP	14

Minimod [9] is a proxy application designed to simulate the propagation of waves through subsurface models by solving the wave equation in its finite difference discretized form. In this study, we utilize one of the kernels included in Minimod, specifically the acoustic isotropic propagator in a constant-density domain [15].

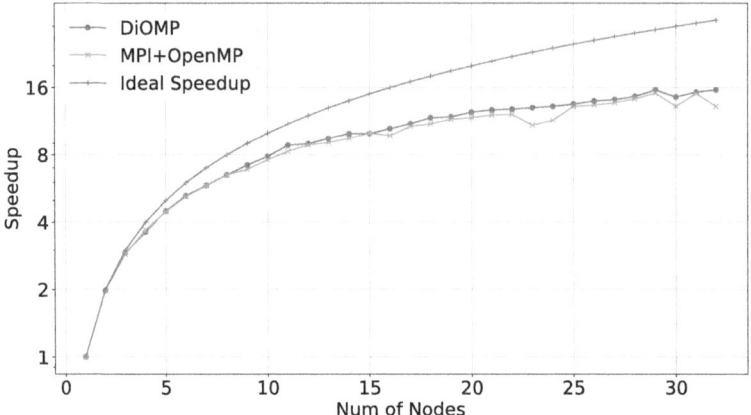

Fig. 8. Minimod on Ookami

Minimod supports multi-device OpenMP offloading using `target` regions encapsulated within OpenMP tasks and exhibits strong-scaling characteristics [16]. We ported the multi-GPU version of Minimod to versions using MPI+OpenMP and DiOMP. In these versions, the original GPUs device numbers are treated as ranks, with data exchanges being handled through PGAS or MPI. Remarkably, the MPI+ OpenMP version LoCs required for communication are significantly larger than those for the DiOMP version as shown in Listing 2 and Listing 3. In Listing 2, since MPI uses two-sided communication, both the sender and receiver need to be involved in the data transmission process, in order to minimize the waiting time, we set up `MPI_Request` arrays for both sides of the transmission to ensure the synchronization of information. In Listing 3, since DiOMP uses windowless one-sided communication, the data sender only needs to put the data to the target rank. The `ompx_waitALLRMA` will wait for all data to be received completely before executing the code below. The specific values can be referenced in Table 2. For tests in Fig. 8, the grid size is 1000^3 and 1000 time steps. We conducted evaluations on the Ookami system using 1 to 32 nodes. Figure 8 shows the results of Minimod running on Ookami using both DiOMP and MPI+OpenMP versions. We observed excellent strong scalability. It is clear that in the majority of cases, DiOMP demonstrated either comparable or superior performance to MPI+OpenMP.

```
1  MPI_Request requests[4*nranks];
2  int req_cnts[nranks];
3  memset(req_cnts, 0, nranks*sizeof(int));
4  for (int r=0; r<nranks; r++) {
5      RANK_XMIN_XMAX(r,gxmin,gxmax);
6      if (rank == r) {
7          if (r != 0) {
8              rc = MPI_Isend(..., &requests[req_cnts[r]++]);
9          }
10         if (r != nranks-1) {
11             rc = MPI_Isend(..., &requests[req_cnts[r]++]);
12         }
13     }
14     if (rank == r-1) {
15         rc = MPI_Irecv(..., &requests[req_cnts[r]++]);
16     }
17     if (rank == r+1) {
18         rc = MPI_Irecv(..., &requests[req_cnts[r]++]);
19 }}
20 for (int r=0; r<nranks; r++) {
21     if (req_cnts[r] > 0) {
22         MPI_Waitall(req_cnts[r], requests,
23             MPI_STATUSES_IGNORE);
24 }}
```

Listing 2. Minimod - MPI

```
1  for (int r = 0; r < nranks; ++r) {
2      llint gxmin, gxmax;
3      RANK_XMIN_XMAX(r,gxmin,gxmax);
4      if (r != 0) {
5          if(rank == r){
6              ompx_put(...);
7      }}
8      if (r != nranks-1) {
9          if(rank == r){
10             ompx_put(...);
11 }}}
12 ompx_waitALLRMA();
```

Listing 3. Minimod - DiOMP

5 Conclusion and Future Work

In conclusion, this paper introduces **DiOMP**, an extension of OpenMP utilizing the PGAS distributed model. DiOMP leverages LLVM/OpenMP and GASNet-EX to offer a portable, scalable, and high-performance solution for parallel programming across diverse architectures. We hope that DiOMP can become an important extension of OpenMP and eventually become part of the OpenMP specification. Based on the current experimental results, DiOMP achieves competitive performance against the legacy MPI+X approach. The PGAS-based Distributed OpenMP model has the potential to replace the traditional MPI+OpenMP hybrid programming approach in many scenarios.

Looking ahead, we aim to further expand the usability of DiOMP, particularly with respect to OpenMP target offloading, including support for accelerators like GPUs, and managing OpenMP task dependencies through active message. We also intend to apply the PGAS-based Distributed OpenMP model to real-world scientific applications and study its productivity and performance in comparison with other PGAS approaches and the MPI+OpenMP hybrid model.

Acknowledgements. We would like to thank TotalEnergies E&P Research and Technologies US for their support of this work. Our gratitude also extends to Alice Koniges from the University of Hawaii for providing access to the NERSC Perlmutter system.

Additionally, we acknowledge to thank Stony Brook Research Computing and Cyberinfrastructure, and the Institute for Advanced Computational Science at Stony Brook University for access to the innovative high-performance Ookami computing system, which was made possible by a $5M National Science Foundation grant (#1927880). This research also used resources of the National Energy Research Scientific Computing Center, which is supported by the Office of Science of the U.S. Department of Energy under Contract No. DE-AC02-05CH11231.

References

1. Bachan, J., et al.: UPC++: a high-performance communication framework for asynchronous computation. In: 2019 IEEE International Parallel and Distributed Processing Symposium, IPDPS 2019, Rio de Janeiro, Brazil, May 20–24, 2019, pp. 963–973. IEEE (2019). https://doi.org/10.1109/IPDPS.2019.00104
2. Bauer, M.: Legion: programming distributed heterogeneous architectures with logical regions. Ph.D. thesis, Stanford University, USA (2014). https://searchworks.stanford.edu/view/10701368
3. Biswas, B., Ghosh, S.K., Ghosh, A.: A novel intuitionistic-near fuzzy sets based image fusion approach: development on hybrid MPI+OpenMP parallel model. Multim. Tools Appl. **81**(21), 29699–29730 (2022). https://doi.org/10.1007/S11042-022-12333-0
4. Callahan, D., Chamberlain, B.L., Zima, H.P.: The cascade high productivity language. In: 9th International Workshop on High-Level Programming Models and Supportive Environments (HIPS 2004), 26 April 2004, Santa Fe, NM, USA, pp. 52–60. IEEE Computer Society (2004). https://doi.org/10.1109/HIPS.2004.10002, https://doi.ieeecomputersociety.org/10.1109/HIPS.2004.10002

5. Eachempati, D., Jun, H.J., Chapman, B.M.: An open-source compiler and runtime implementation for coarray fortran. In: Moreira, J.E., Iancu, C., Saraswat, V.A. (eds.) Proceedings of the Fourth Conference on Partitioned Global Address Space Programming Model, PGAS 2010, New York, NY, USA, October 12-15, 2010, p. 13. ACM (2010). https://doi.org/10.1145/2020373.2020386
6. Hargrove, P.H., Bonachea, D.: GASNet-EX performance improvements due to specialization for the Cray Aries network (2018). https://doi.org/10.25344/S44S38, https://www.osti.gov/biblio/1481769
7. Khuvis, S., Tomko, K., Hashmi, J.M., Panda, D.K.: Exploring hybrid MPI+Kokkos tasks programming model. In: 3rd IEEE/ACM Annual Parallel Applications Workshop: Alternatives To MPI+X, PAW-ATM@SC 2020, Atlanta, GA, USA, November 12, 2020, pp. 66–73. IEEE (2020). https://doi.org/10.1109/PAWATM51920.2020.00011
8. Lu, W., et al.: Towards efficient remote OpenMP offloading. In: Klemm, M., de Supinski, B.R., Klinkenberg, J., Neth, B. (eds.) IWOMP 2022. LNCS, vol. 13527, pp. 17–31. Springer, Cham (2022). https://doi.org/10.1007/978-3-031-15922-0_2
9. Meng, J., Atle, A., Calandra, H., Araya-Polo, M.: Minimod: a finite difference solver for seismic modeling. arXiv (2020). https://arxiv.org/abs/2007.06048
10. Murai, H., Nakao, M., Iwashita, H., Sato, M.: Preliminary performance evaluation of coarray-based implementation of fiber miniapp suite using XcalableMP PGAS language. In: Proceedings of the Second Annual PGAS Applications Workshop. PAW17, Association for Computing Machinery, New York, NY, USA (2017). https://doi.org/10.1145/3144779.3144780
11. OpenMP Architecture Review Board: OpenMP Application Programming Interface (2018). https://www.openmp.org/wp-content/uploads/OpenMP-API-Specification-5.0.pdf. version 5.0
12. Patel, A., Doerfert, J.: Remote OpenMP offloading. In: Varbanescu, A.L., Bhatele, A., Luszczek, P., Marc, B. (eds.) ISC High Performance 2022. LNCS, vol. 13289, pp. 315–333. Springer, Cham (2022). https://doi.org/10.1007/978-3-031-07312-0_16
13. Petiton, S., Sato, M., Emad, N., Calvin, C., Tsuji, M., Dandouna, M.: Multi level programming paradigm for extreme computing. In: SNA+ MC 2013-Joint International Conference on Supercomputing in Nuclear Applications+ Monte Carlo, p. 04305. EDP Sciences (2014)
14. Pophale, S., Nanjegowda, R., Curtis, T., Chapman, B., Jin, H., Poole, S., Kuehn, J.: OpenSHMEM performance and potential: a NPB experimental study. In: Proceedings of the 6th Conference on Partitioned Global Address Space Programming Models (PGAS 2012) (2012)
15. Qawasmeh, A., Hugues, M.R., Calandra, H., Chapman, B.M.: Performance portability in reverse time migration and seismic modelling via OpenACC. Int. J. High Perform. Comput. Appl. **31**(5), 422–440 (2017). https://doi.org/10.1177/1094342016675678
16. Raut, E., Meng, J., Araya-Polo, M., Chapman, B.: Evaluating performance of OpenMP tasks in a seismic stencil application. In: Milfeld, K., de Supinski, B.R., Koesterke, L., Klinkenberg, J. (eds.) IWOMP 2020. LNCS, vol. 12295, pp. 67–81. Springer, Cham (2020). https://doi.org/10.1007/978-3-030-58144-2_5
17. Shan, B., Araya-Polo, M.: Evaluation of programming models and performance for stencil computation on current GPU architectures (2024). https://arxiv.org/abs/2404.04441

18. Shan, B., Araya-Polo, M., Malik, A.M., Chapman, B.M.: MPI-based remote OpenMP offloading: a more efficient and easy-to-use implementation. In: Chen, Q., Huang, Z., Si, M. (eds.) Proceedings of the 14th International Workshop on Programming Models and Applications for Multicores and Manycores, PMAM@PPoPP 2023, Montreal, QC, Canada, 25 February 2023–1 March 2023, pp. 50–59. ACM (2023). https://doi.org/10.1145/3582514.3582519
19. Yelick, K., et al.: Productivity and performance using partitioned global address space languages. In: Proceedings of the 2007 International Workshop on Parallel Symbolic Computation, pp. 24–32. PASCO 2007, Association for Computing Machinery, New York, NY, USA (2007). https://doi.org/10.1145/1278177.1278183
20. Yviquel, H., et al.: The OpenMP cluster programming model. In: 51st International Conference on Parallel Processing Workshop Proceedings (ICPP Workshops 22) (2022)
21. Zhang, X., Guo, X., Weng, Y., Zhang, X., Lu, Y., Zhao, Z.: Hybrid MPI and CUDA paralleled finite volume unstructured CFD simulations on a multi-GPU system. Future Gener. Comput. Syst. **139**, 1–16 (2023). https://doi.org/10.1016/J.FUTURE.2022.09.005

Multilayer Multipurpose Caches for OpenMP Target Regions on FPGAs

Julian Brandner[(✉)], Florian Mayer, and Michael Philippsen

Friedrich-Alexander Universität Erlangen-Nürnberg (FAU)
Programming Systems Group, Erlangen, Germany
{julian.brandner,florian.andrefranc.mayer,michael.philippsen}@fau.de

Abstract. Multipurpose caches can improve the throughput between the FPGA's memory and the hardware that is generated when offloading OpenMP target regions. We discuss and evaluate the weaknesses (and also advantages) of different cacheing techniques in this context. Our OpenMP-to-FPGA compiler fully automatically combines and inserts them as a multilayer cache to get the best of all worlds. We evaluate on a diverse benchmark and achieve an average speedup of 3.65, outperforming 1-layer caches both in terms of runtime and resilience.

Keywords: FPGA · OpenMP · hardware cache · target offloading

1 Introduction

When offloading OpenMP target regions to FPGAs to harvest their potential for computational tasks [12,15,18,21], the latency between the FPGA's reprogrammable logic and its onboard DDR memory often limits the achievable performance. All the caches that were added to the FPGA hardware to solve this problem without relying on manual code rewrites or domain specific optimizations have their specific weaknesses. Our OpenMP-to-FPGA compiler can freely insert three of these types of caches when generating FPGA hardware for OpenMP target regions. It combines them into multilayer caches, similar to those found in modern CPU designs. The resulting multilayer caches bundle the benefits of all their components while reducing their individual weaknesses.

The first of the covered techniques, a source code level cache based on dataflow ideas, works well in other FPGA domains [6], but relies on static assumptions and often prevents the use of fast memory bursts. To the best of our knowledge we are the first to use it automatically for OpenMP offloading. The second technique, a read-only cache directly embedded into the bus adapter of the generated hardware block, is part of the Xilinx Vitis toolset [32]. We are the first to publish a comparative evaluation of its performance. This cache has high demands on the FPGA hardware. The third technique, a highly optimized cache block in a separate kernel [4], it is quite slow even for cache hits. Our contribution is the combination of the three types of caches to in multilayer cacheing hierarchies. Both the compiler [25] and the benchmarks [5] are publicly available.

After a sketch of the compiler's offloading workflow, Sect. 2 summarizes the cacheing types. Section 3 adds multilayer caches to OpenMP and shows how we implemented them. Section 4 evaluates the cacheing techniques both in isolation and in combination. Before we conclude, Sect. 5 discusses related work.

2 State of the Art

2.1 OpenMP-to-FPGA Compilation

All the published OpenMP-to-FPGA compilers create both a host binary and an FPGA bitstream from a given OpenMP program [12,15,18,21]. For the host binary, they cut the target regions from the source code and replace them with code that handles the data shipments between the host and the FPGA and also launches the computations on the FPGA. To generate the FPGA hardware, they feed the target regions into a high level synthesis (HLS) tool that creates one hardware block (kernel) per target region. They embed those kernels in a low-level platform (LLP) that holds pre-built blocks like a PCI controller, a DDR memory interface, etc. The host binary interacts with the LLP (e.g., via PIC Express) to store/load data directly into/from the FPGAs on-board DDR or to launch the kernels. The kernels process the data in the DDR and signal their completion through the LLP to the host side. The main bottleneck of this design is the bus connection between the kernels and the DDR memory since due to the FPGA's low clock rates (compared to CPUs) the protocol is slow.

In typical HLS development, the developer would solve this issue by manually optimizing the code by fine-tuning HLS pragmas and synthesis settings. This is infeasible in OpenMP development as the required optimization are highly platform dependent and require HLS features that are normally not exposed to the OpenMP code. This necessitates a solution that can be automatically applied to arbitrary code. Our multipurpose cacheing is such a solution.

2.2 Dataflow Cache

Brignone et al. [6] use the `dataflow` pragma of the Vitis HLS to synthesize a kernel with two concurrent hardware blocks with FIFO channels between them. One block holds the user code, the other serves as cache hardware, see Fig. 1(a). The user block waits at a FIFO until the requested data is available.

To use this cache the programmer has to manually restructure the code. First, a C++ library must be included that provides a class for which the HLS synthesizes fast FPGA RAM resources. Second, the programmer has to put all the code into one single work function that receives a reference to the cache as a parameter. There also needs to be a wrapper function labeled with the `dataflow` pragma that instantiates the cache and calls the work function. Third, to redirect the data accesses in the user code to use the FIFO channels, the programmer must replace them with calls of member functions of the cache class that hold the FIFO operations. For convenience, the library overloads the square bracket

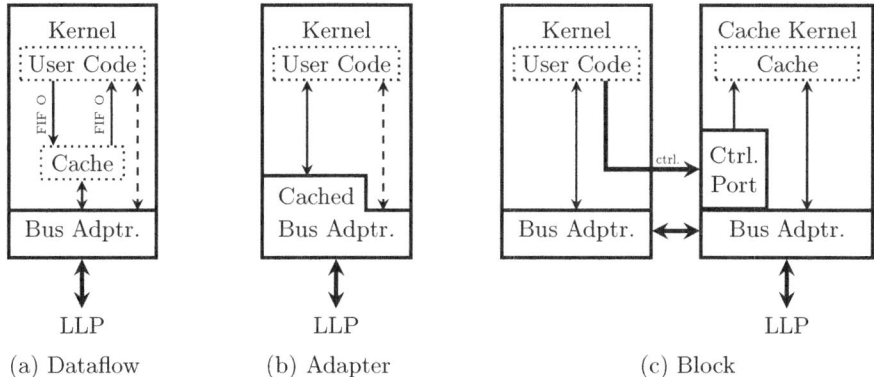

Fig. 1. Three cacheing techniques. Legend: single/double-headed arrows are uni/bi-directional connections; thin/bold arrows are internal/bus connection; dashed arrows are optional bypass capabilities.

operator so that most of the array accesses can remain untouched. Only those that copy pointers, use address arithmetics, etc. need rewrites. When done, the work function must call the stop function of the cache class that sends a stop request to the cache and terminates the dataflow region. The cache implements a write-back policy. Changes written into a cache line only propagate to the DDR memory when the line is evicted, or the cache is stopped or flushed.

Strengths: a) Since both the cache and the user code reside in the kernel the latency between a request on a FIFO and the response is low. b) The member functions for accessing the cache are built in a way that results in well-performing hardware pipelines, when used from within a loop. This matters as memory intensive algorithms tend to spend most of their time in such loops. c) The programmer can leave arrays uncached that do not have much reuse. Requests for them bypass the cache and do not replace any cached data of other arrays.

Weaknesses: a) A dataflow cache only works for OpenMP target codes with arrays of statically known sizes as this is a requirement of the provided class. b) It restricts compiler optimizations as instead of array accesses the user code calls (overloaded) functions. Especially when the user code works on consecutive memory addresses the optimizer misses any potential for fast memory bursts.

2.3 Adapter Cache

As shown in Fig. 1(b), version 2023.2 of the Xilinx Vitis [31] can synthesize a multipurpose cache per array seamlessly into the bus adapter that ties the user kernel to the LLP. Programmers do not need to restructure their codes at all.

Strengths: a) This cache is easy to use. b) It has a low latency as user code and cache live in the same kernel. As the cache resides in the bus adapter cache hits are fast. c) Arrays with little reuse can remain uncached. Accessing them bypasses the caches of other arrays.

Weaknesses: a) At the time of writing the cache is read-only. The target region may not write to a cached array. b) There is no way to manually clear the cache. While it is in a clean state when the kernel starts, there is no way to guarantee that changes that other concurrent kernels do to shared data ever become visible. c) Adapter caches are direct mapped caches in which a segment of the memory address bits determines the exact cache line the data will occupy. Since such caches cannot store data from two addresses with the same segment of address bits, unfavorable data access patterns may cause high miss rates. d) In the interest of fast accesses, the FPGA synthesis implements the cache with hardware demanding registers and LUT resources, instead of RAM slices.

2.4 Block Cache

In an earlier publication [4] we accelerated OpenMP target regions with a highly optimized standard write-back cache block that resides in a separate kernel and has its bus adapters connected to each user kernel, see Fig. 1(c). Our OpenMP-to-FPGA compiler [15] automatically inserts into the HLS input the code that clears and flushes the cache. This code uses an additional control port that is connected to the control interface of the cache hardware. The compiler also overwrites some bus input lines during LLP generation to enable the cache.

Strengths: a) The cache block is optimized for small resource demands. b) There is only one cache block regardless of the number of user kernels. This keeps the cost low. c) As the compiler adds the cache it does not lose the ability to exploit pipelinig or memory bursts for performance gains.

Weaknesses: a) Since the cache is connected via a standard bus interface, its protocol restricts performance, even for cache hits. b) As there is no way to bypass the cache, accesses to arrays that do not exhibit reuse pass through the cache and potentially cause slowdowns when they replace more useful content.

3 Approach

In a previous work [4] we already added the option to use a block cache to our OpenMP-to-FPGA compiler. This section shows how we added the other two cache types and made all of them composable into multilayer caches. Note that while the block cache affects all memory accesses from all kernels and is hence enabled by a global compiler flag, the other two cache types can be engaged on a per-array basis with new clauses directly at the OpenMP target region. With the compiler flag and the two clauses the programmer can select multilayer caches.

3.1 Dataflow Cache Integration

To make the dataflow caches easy to use for OpenMP programmers, our compiler's code transformation does (most of) the necessary code restructurings. Listing 1 holds an example. The programmer just adds the orka-translate clause and specifies dataflow for the array v (in bold in the code). See the

Listing 1. Transformation for a **dataflow** and an adapter cache.

```
int* v = // ...
#pragma omp target map (tofrom: v[0:N]) \
    orka_translate(v_cache: "dataflow:<parameters>") \
    orka_translate(v_cache: "vitis:<parameters>")
{
    v[0]++;
}
```

⇓

```
typedef v_cache_t DaCH::cache<parameters>
void work(v_cache_t& v){
    v.start(); // clear
    v[0]++;    // unchanged
    v.stop();  // flush and stop cache
}
void wrapper(int* v){
    #pragma HLS dataflow
    v_cache_t v_cache(v); // cache instantiation
    work(v_cache);
}
void topLevel(int* v){
    #pragma HLS cache <parameters>
    // control logic for block cache (if needed)
    wrapper(v);
}
```

documentation [25] for the parameters that specify the settings and behavior of the cache. The transformation includes the C++ library DaCH, declares the v_cache, moves the content of the OpenMP target region to a work function that also contains the surrounding explicit cache clear/flush operations, and it calls this work function from a generated wrapper, which also contains the HLS dataflow pragma and instantiates the cache according to the user-provided parameters. Note that the v[0]++ in the original user code remains unchanged.

3.2 Adapter Cache Integration

For an adapter cache the programmer adds the orka_translate clause with the vitis attribute to an OpenMP target region (underlined in Listing 1). Our compiler just adds the Vitis HLS cache pragma to the topLevel function of the kernel. The parameters of the orka_translate clause that control the length of the cache lines as well as the number of lines are passed on to the HLS cache pragma. The Xilinx HLS tool does the rest.

3.3 Composability Notes

Multilayer Cache Architecture. There are $2^3 = 8$ ways to switch on one or more of the three cache types. Figure 1 illustrated the designs with just one type of cache. For the multilayer cache hierarchy there is only one technically possible ordering, shown in Fig. 2 for all three types of caches. Closest to the user code is the dataflow cache that then attaches to the cached bus adapter that in turn uses the cache block in a separate kernel. From this three-layer cache the design of the two-layer caches is obvious.

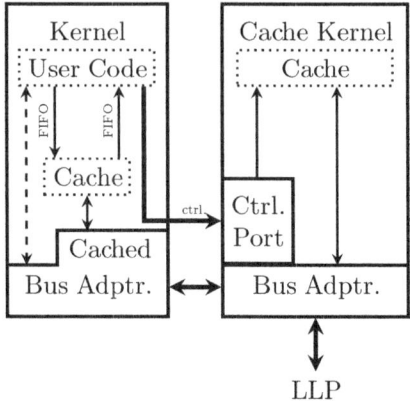

Fig. 2. 3-layer cache. Legend as in Fig. 1.

Code Transformation Rationale. We constructed the code transformation for the dataflow cache so that it can be composed with an additional block cache. The key idea here is the split into a topLevel function without the dataflow pragma and a wrapper function with the pragma that instructs the HLS to parallelize all constructs within its body, i.e., that later runs the cache instantiation and the work function concurrently. The split is needed as the topLevel function must not have a dataflow pragma since the cache controlling functions of the block cache must not run concurrently (as this would yield unsynthesizable code or even undefined behavior).

Clearing and Flushing. Before an outlined OpenMP target region with an added cache may run on the FPGA, the cache(s) need to be cleared as otherwise the kernel may not see the data that the host has shipped to the FPGA's DDR. If the compiler can statically prove that there can never be another kernel working in parallel on the same array, it suffices to invalidate all lines of all caches. Otherwise all cached writes need to be flushed before invalidation so that they do not get lost. Note, that since the dataflow cache is never shared, there is never the need for flushing before an invalidation. After the execution of the user code any written data needs to be flushed from the cache(s) to the DDR memory so that the host can access the results. In a cache hierarchy the cache closest to the user code needs to be flushed first, so that changes propagate along the cache hierarchy until they reach the DDR memory. Note, that the read-only adapter cache cannot be flushed.

Sizing Restrictions. There are some restrictions for multilayer caches with both an adapter cache and a block cache. An adapter cache always has a port width of the size of a cache line. While wider ports increase the memory bandwidth, block caches typically have an upper limit on the width of the incoming connections that they support. The width of an adapter cache line can therefore not be larger than the limit of the block cache (512 Bit in our case).

3.4 Implementation Details

We integrated the cacheing techniques into the Orka OpenMP-to-FPGA compiler [15] that is publicly available [25]. Our system targets the Xilinx FPGA ecosystem and uses the Vitis HLS and Vivado v2023.2 to generate the hardware. The host CPU (Intel Core i7-4770) connects to our FPGA board (AMD Virtex UltraScale+ FPGA VCU118 Evaluation Kit) via PCI Express.

The dataflow cache by Brignone et al. [6] is the authors' original implementation. We moved the interfaces to a new namespace to avoid name collisions. For the adapter cache we used the Vitis 2023.2 implementation [32] and left the default implementation settings unchanged. We described the block cache in an earlier paper [4]. As its core it uses the LogiCORE System Cache [30].

4 Evaluation

4.1 Benchmark Set

To evaluate the three cacheing techniques and the multilayer caches we use a diverse benchmark set (see Table 1) consisting of a matrix multiplication [6,10,13,20,26], a bitonic sort [6,8,13,27], the Lucas-Kanade optical flow [2,13], a 2D convolution (Filter) [3,6,10,19,23], the Levenshtein distance [7,33], the 3D stencil code 19p3d from the Adept benchmarks [17], and the Knapsack problem [11,22]. The rationale for this set is as follows: (a) other authors also use these benchmarks to evaluate their FPGA compilations, (b) 19p3d represents all Adept stencils as their fixed stencil-shaped access patterns showed similar cache behaviors in preliminary studies, (c) all benchmarks reuse data, which is the required for a cache to work, (d) they vary in the number of arrays that exhibit reuse (column *reused arrays*), and (e) there are benchmarks that write to those arrays (*write cache*). We used textbook or open source implementations and modified the codes in two ways. (a) We wrapped their computationally intensive parts in target regions with or without the respective `orka_translate` clauses. (b) To be able to measure various problem sizes (*memory demand*) for the dataflow caches we needed to resize the array declarations to be large enough for the largest tested problem size. This does not falsify our results, as at runtime the kernel (and thus the cache) does not use the excess space.

From all the possible $2^3 = 8$ cache hierarchies (one of which is the baseline without any cache), we generated all the reasonable ones. For the 3 benchmarks that write to caches there are $2^2 = 4$ versions as the read-only adapter cache

Table 1. Benchmark Set.

Benchmark	Reused Arrays	Write Cache	Memory Demand (KB)
Matrix Multiplication	2		12–3146
Bitonic Sort	1	X	1–524
Lucas-Kanade	2		10–10486
Filter	2		17–4196
Levenshtein Distance	3	X	4–10496
Adept 19p3d	1		2–262
Knapsack	3	X	4–1052

Table 2. Speedups that caches/cache hierarchies achieve. Problem size: ∼64 KB. No adapter caches (n.a.) for benchmarks that write to a cached array.

Benchmark	Dataflow	Adapter	Block	Dataflow + Block	Adapter + Block
Matrix Multiplication	2.32	4.17	2.20	**3.05**	**4.50**
Bitonic Sort	5.15	n.a.	1.62	**5.67**	n.a.
Lucas-Kanade	4.34	4.34	1.98	*4.34*	*4.34*
Filter	2.56	2.88	1.72	*2.58*	*2.91*
Levenshtein Distance	3.12	n.a.	1.84	**3.43**	n.a.
Adept 19p3d	1.65	3.98	2.00	**2.26**	*3.70*
Knapsack	2.54	n.a.	1.91	**3.40**	n.a.

cannot be used. For the other 4 benchmarks we dropped those 2 (of 8) versions that include both a dataflow and an adapter cache due to the bad performance of this combination. Multilayer caches always aim to place a small and fast cache close to the user code and a larger but slower cache further away. That way they gain the performance of the faster cache most of the time, but can rely on the larger cache, when the smaller one has a cache miss. The dropped combination would have the slower (see Sect. 4.2) but cheaper (see Sect. 4.3) dataflow cache closer to the user code and would have both the bad performance of the dataflow cache and the high costs of the adapter cache.

For the generated versions, the dataflow/adapter caches hold 16 KiByte in 32 Byte lines. For some benchmarks, larger dataflow caches would need more than 2 h of HLS or larger adapter caches would not fit into our FPGA (see Sect. 4.3). The block cache [4] uses 256 KiByte in 4-way associative 64 Byte lines.

We measured the wall-clock time spent in target regions, i.e., excluding the data shipments between the host and the FPGA. The kernel frequency was 100 MHz, except for Lucas-Kanade and Filter, which we had to run at 70/50 MHz respectively, as some of their versions failed to achieve timing closure. The different frequency does not affect our results qualitatively, as the kernels and the bus components that create the memory bottleneck both run with the same frequency. In a given time budget for the evaluation it was impossible to search for a frequency that works for all benchmarks and all versions.

4.2 Runtime Effects of Multilayer Caches

To start, let us discuss the runtime for a problem size of around 64 KB of DDR memory per benchmark (see Table 2). This is the largest selectable size for all benchmarks that does not cause any of the single layer caches to thrash.

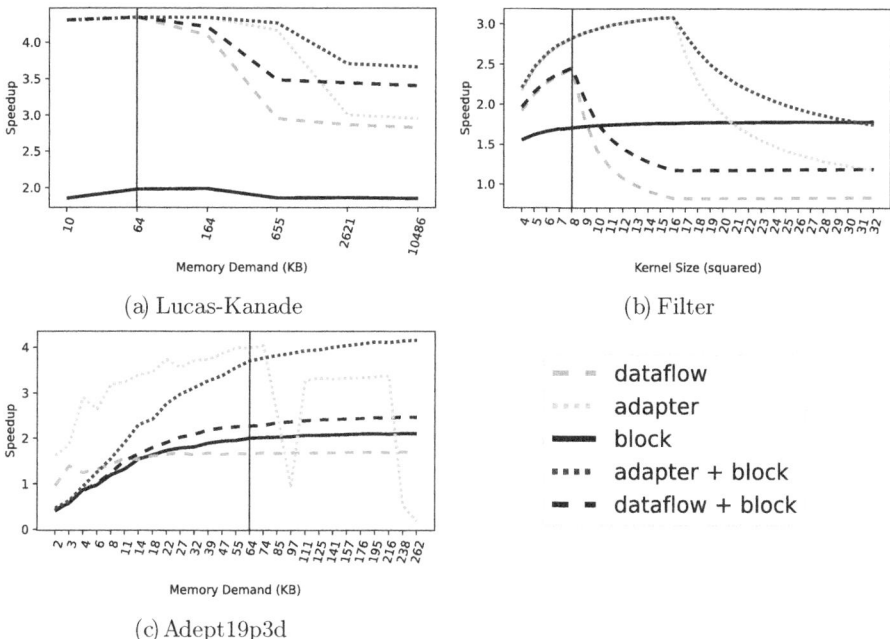

Fig. 3. Performance of three benchmarks for increasing problem sizes. The vertical line indicates the problem size shown in Table 2.

There are two takeaways from the speedup numbers. First, all three 1-layer caches boost performance.[1] Both the dataflow and the adapter cache (that both reside in the user kernel) outperform the larger yet slower block cache. Even though they are considerably smaller, they still catch most of the data reuse (e.g., Matrix Multiplication has a hit-rate of 96.96%[2]). However, between benchmarks there are variations on how well the two cache types perform. While in general the adapter cache has the smaller latency for cache hits, the dataflow cache can often hide most of its latency by means of pipelines that handle concurrently overlapping cache accesses. But if the loop in the user code holds too many cache accesses or if it has a low trip count, then the pipeline cannot amortize its length through concurrent accesses. See the underlined numbers in Table 2. Here the 1-layer adapter cache achieves better speedups than a dataflow cache.

---

[1] The performance results differ from the numbers Brignone et al. report for the baseline and the dataflow cache [6]. They handpick the ideal cache configuration for each of their benchmarks and manually optimize the HLS code for maximal hit-rates and throughput. Neither can (our) compiler do this type of optimization automatically, nor can an average OpenMP developer do this due to a lack of HLS experience.

[2] The hitrates were only obtainable for the dataflow cache. Obtaining them for the block cache would require an extensive restructuring of the LLP and the adapter cache does not offer any interface to read them.

The second main takeaway is that for most of the benchmarks and for this problem size, adding a block cache to a dataflow or to an adapter cache improves performance (bold numbers in Table 2) because the much larger block cache catches the reuses that the smaller cache misses. Adding a block cache always retains the relative order that 1-level dataflow/adapter caches achieve.

Let us now discuss the *italic* numbers where adding a block cache does not yield an additional speedup boost, at least for our fixed problem size. The first good news is that in general adding a block cache does not hurt performance. However, there is one problematic scenario: If all memory accesses in the user code have a strong spatial locality but also a limited reuse, an added block cache can slightly damp the speedup that the smaller first-level caches gain. In this case because of the access pattern the smaller cache catches every cacheable reuse. Thus, the second-level block cache has a low hit-rate. But as the amount of reuses is limited, the smaller cache still exhibits a high enough miss-rate, to make the performance overhead of the block cache matter. As Table 2 shows, in our benchmark set only Adept 19p3d suffers from this damping effect, that reduces the achievable speedup from 3.98 to 3.70, i.e., by 7%. The second good news is that the multilayer caches become advantageous for larger problem sizes as Fig. 3 demonstrates. For Lucas-Kanade (see Fig. 3(a)), the dataflow and the adapter cache achieve a speedup of 4.34 for the 64 KB problem size (vertical line). As soon as for growing problems the hit-rate starts to drop (from 99.99% to 91.63%) the 1-layer caches only achieve smaller speedups. With an added block cache the speedups stay up and are better than what a 1-layer cache can achieve. The lower the hit-rate of the first cache layer is, the more an added block cache boosts performance. Figure 3(b) shows a similar effect for Filter. Note that, as the size of the filtering kernel matters more than the total memory demand (including the to-be-filtered picture data) there is a different x-axis. Figure 3(c) differs from the other two benchmarks as there is no sharp edge when the dataflow and adapter cache fill up. The reason is that the memory locality of Adept 19p3d is mostly static across all problem sizes. While the impact of an added block cache started to kick in just at that edge in the other benchmarks, its beneficial effects gradually grow with the problem size here until the multilayer cache achieves better speedups than the 1-layer caches. Note that in this benchmark one can also see the effects of unfavorable access patterns that cause the 1-layer adapter cache to suffer. At a memory demand of around 85 KB the memory accesses start to align badly with the direct mapped cache lines, leading to premature replacement and thus thrashing. This effect is reflected in steep drop in performance of the affected cache in Fig. 3(c). Again, the block cache mitigates this effect.

4.3 Resource Utilization

Table 3 shows the resource costs (look-up tables (LUTs), registers, and RAM) of the three 1-layer caches, measured by subtracting the resource consumption of the baseline from the ones of the different cache configurations. None of the caches uses digital signal processors (DSPs). (Note, that adding a cache may

Table 3. Resource cost of the caches. Absolute numbers and fraction of the FPGA's size (in parentheses).

Cache	Size	LUTs		Registers		RAM Blocks	
Dataflow	16 KiB	5928	(0.5%)	9316	(0.4%)	10.5	(0.5%)
Adapter	16 KiB	34932	(19.8%)	290577	(12.3%)	0	(0.0%)
Block	256 KiB	7882	(0.7%)	0	(0.0%)	70	(3.2%)

replace other hardware components and hence lead to a more economical bitstream. An example is the 0 register cost in Table 3).

The key insights from Table 3 are: First, the dataflow cache is cheapest with respect to LUTs and RAM. The block cache is cheaper relative to its size. The resource demands of both are neglectable on a sizable FPGA, as they take up below 1% of the available resources (except for the block cache that takes up 3.2% of the RAM). Second, the adapter cache uses considerably more resources than the other two, especially w.r.t. LUTs and registers and is thus hardly useful for smaller FPGA boards, especially since one such cache is required per cached array. As the cost of multilayer caches is the sum of the respective costs, the combination of a dataflow and a block cache creates a cheap yet well performing and resilient multilayer cache. For the adapter cache an additional block cache layer may mitigate its high cost: As thrashing caused by an undersized cache has less impact on multilayer caches, the user may use a smaller adapter cache to reduce the cost.

5 Related Work

There are three main ways to improve the throughput between the FPGA's DDR memory and the kernel generated for the offloaded OpenMP target regions: (a) by adding some kind of cacheing, (b) by optimizing the code structure in the target region to allow the HLS to generate faster hardware, or (c) by improving FPGA cache architectures.

Adding Some Kind of Caching. This paper discussed three cache types and their strengths and weaknesses. Our approach is unique as we can fully automatically include them, both alone or as a composed multilayer cache, into the generated FPGA hardware. A few more 1-layer caches have been proposed for FPGAs. Below we cover why we could not include them in our work. Nevertheless, from the experience gained here, it seems reasonable that turning them into a multilayer cache by adding a (larger) block cache may also boost performance.

We could not include a cache by Cheng et al. [9] which relies on expensive consistency hardware and special interconnect circuitry that generic HLS tools cannot deal with. For each so-called hotspot area (found by runtime monitoring in the offloaded code) they build a cache close to the computation. We only study cache types that do not require a hotspot analysis and that a standard

HLS can deal with. While we achieve speedups on codes typical for FPGA, they evaluate SPEC2006 CPU codes [28] which are hard to compare.

Adler et al. [1] generate a cache around user-supplied FPGA hardware that is written in the Bluespec language (which is incompatible with OpenMP). To connect the caches to the user code, their platform employs an expensive ring network with a bus snooping protocol. We could not include their work as it is neither an off-the-shelf IP block nor an includable source code library. As Winterstein et al. [29] also rely on the same platform, we could not include their work either, even though conceptually we could deal with their C code input. Moreover, they are constrained to pointer-chasing algorithms instead of our general OpenMP target regions.

Putnam et al. [26] place custom FPGA caches between automatically selected data structures and memory regions. Their approach requires both a custom HLS and a special hardware platform that provides a single unified address space for the CPU and the FPGA. We cannot include their work because of these special requirements. In contrast, we can accelerate kernels on any system that uses a PCIe-attached FPGA and for us a standard HLS toolchain suffices.

Ma et al. [13] manually replace some array accesses in the source code with calls to C++-library functions that implement cache behaviour and use simple inline caches. We excluded their work because it is even more restrictive and has more weaknesses than the dataflow cache. Moreover, their library functions can only deal with arrays that the code either only reads from or writes to.

To the best of our knowledge, except from us, only Brignone et al. [6] consider a multilayer cache on FPGAs. They manually insert into the user codes the inline caches from Ma et al. as a first cache layer and connect this to a second cache layer that consists of a set of deep FIFOs (the dataflow cache, see Sect. 2.2). Both layers require that the developer rewrites the code before passing it on to the HLS. They achieve excellent speedups when they handpick the parameters of the cache stages for each benchmark and when they manually tile the loops in the benchmark codes. In contrast, our compiler automatically builds and inserts a multilayer cache without manual work when it picks their dataflow cache as the first cache layer.

Optimizing the Code for Hardware Synthesis. As the quality of the hardware that the HLS generates depends on the structure of the input code, there is research [16,17,24] that applies source-level optimizations to improve the throughput (without adding caches). Publications in this area are restricted to certain types of problem domains and to specific data access patterns (e.g., stencils). As they in general only employ simple buffers, they are orthogonal to our hardware multilayer caches that also help to expedite accesses that do not fit the strict constraints of the optimized access patterns.

Improving FPGA Cache Architectures. FPGA cache architectures must meet a different set of constraints compared to caches that are used in GPUs or CPUs, because a FPGA clocks at a much lower frequency. As we make use of cache IPs as building blocks, research on them [10,14] is orthogonal to our work. We would benefit from cache architecture improvements.

6 Conclusion

We integrated three different cacheing techniques into the hardware that the Orka OpenMP-to-FPGA compiler generates form OpenMP target regions. Our compiler automatically inserts them as composable building blocks. On a diverse benchmark a multilayer cache speeds up a no-cache baseline by 3.65 on average, which is 8.5% more than what kernel-integrated 1-layer caches achieve, even on a problem size that is friendly to them because of almost perfect hit-rates. On the one hand, the multilayer cache is resilient as adding a block cache as a second layer does not slow down performance in these situations. On the other hand, the benefits of the multilayer cache grow for larger problem sizes. The additional hardware cost of the second cache layer are neglectable.

Acknowledgments. We acknowledge the financial support by the Federal Ministry of Education and Research of Germany for the ORKA-HPC project (01IH17003A).

This work has also benefitted from the last author's Research Stay at Schloss Dagstuhl in June 2024 (seminar 24259).

References

1. Adler, M., Fleming, K.E., Parashar, A., Pellauer, M., Emer, J.: Leap scratchpads: automatic memory and cache management for reconfigurable logic. In: Proceedings of International Symposium on Field Programmable Gate Arrays (FPGA 2011), pp. 25–28. Monterey, CA (2011). https://doi.org/10.1145/1950413.1950421
2. Blachut, K., Kryjak, T.: Real-time efficient FPGA implementation of the multi-scale Lucas-Kanade and Horn-Schunck optical flow algorithms for a 4k video stream. Sensors **22**(13), 5017–5049 (2022). https://doi.org/10.3390/s22135017, https://www.mdpi.com/1424-8220/22/13/5017. Accessed 18 July 2024
3. Brandner, J., Mayer, F., Philippsen, M.: Reducing OpenMP to FPGA round-trip times with predictive modelling. In: Klemm, M., de Supinski, B.R., Klinkenberg, J., Neth, B. (eds.) IWOMP 2022. LNCS, vol. 13527, pp. 94–108. Springer, Cham (2022). https://doi.org/10.1007/978-3-031-15922-0_7
4. Brandner, J., Mayer, F., Philippsen, M.: Multipurpose cacheing to accelerate OpenMP target regions on FPGAs. In: McIntosh-Smith, S., Klemm, M., de Supinski, B.R., Deakin, T., Klinkenberg, J. (eds.) IWOMP 2023. LNCS, vol. 14114, pp. 147–162. Springer, Cham (2023). https://doi.org/10.1007/978-3-031-40744-4_10
5. Brandner, J., Mayer, F., Philippsen, M.: Dataset for: "Multilayer multipurpose caches for OpenMP target regions on FPGAs" (2024). https://doi.org/10.5281/zenodo.12755510
6. Brignone, G., Usman Jamal, M., Lazarescu, M.T., Lavagno, L.: Array-specific dataflow caches for high-level synthesis of memory-intensive algorithms on FPGAs. IEEE Access **10**, 118858–118877 (2022). https://doi.org/10.1109/ACCESS.2022.3219868
7. Castells-Rufas, D., et al.: OpenCL-based FPGA accelerator for semi-global approximate string matching using diagonal bit-vectors. In: Proceedings of International Conference on Field Programmable Logic and Applications (FPL 2021), pp. 174–178. Dresden, Germany (2021). https://doi.org/10.1109/FPL53798.2021.00036

8. Chen, R., Siriyal, S., Prasanna, V.: Energy and memory efficient mapping of bitonic sorting on FPGA. In: Proceedings of International Symposium on Field Programmable Gate Arrays (FPGA 2015), pp. 240–249. Monterey, CA (2015). https://doi.org/10.1145/2684746.2689068
9. Cheng, S., Lin, M., Liu, H.J., Scott, S., Wawrzynek, J.: Exploiting memory-level parallelism in reconfigurable accelerators. In: Proceedings of International Symposium on Field-Programmable Custom Computing Machines (FCCM 2012), pp. 157–160. Toronto, Canada (2012). https://doi.org/10.1109/FCCM.2012.35
10. Choi, J., Nam, K., Canis, A., Anderson, J., Brown, S., Czajkowski, T.: Impact of cache architecture and interface on performance and area of FPGA-based processor/parallel-accelerator systems. In: Proc. International Symposium on Field-Programmable Custom Computing Machines (FCCM 2012), pp. 17–24. Toronto, Canada (2012). https://doi.org/10.1109/FCCM.2012.13
11. Escobar, F.A., Kolar, A., Harb, N., Vinci Dos Santos, F., Valderrama, C.: Scalable shared-memory architecture to solve the knapsack 0/1 problem. Microprocess. Microsyst. **50**(3), 189–201 (2017). https://doi.org/10.1016/j.micpro.2017.04.001
12. Huthmann, J., Sommer, L., Podobas, A., Koch, A., Sano, K.: OpenMP device offloading to FPGAs using the Nymble infrastructure. In: Milfeld, K., de Supinski, B.R., Koesterke, L., Klinkenberg, J. (eds.) IWOMP 2020. LNCS, vol. 12295, pp. 265–279. Springer, Cham (2020). https://doi.org/10.1007/978-3-030-58144-2_17
13. Ma, L., Lavagno, L., Lazarescu, M.T., Arif, A.: Acceleration by inline cache for memory-intensive algorithms on FPGA via high-level synthesis. IEEE Access **5**, 18953–18974 (2017). https://doi.org/10.1109/ACCESS.2017.2750923
14. Matthews, E., Doyle, N.C., Shannon, L.: Design space exploration of L1 data caches for FPGA-based multiprocessor systems. In: Proceedings of International Symposium on Field Programmable Gate Arrays (FPGA 2015), pp. 156–159. Monterey, CA (2015). https://doi.org/10.1145/2684746.2689083
15. Mayer, F., Brandner, J., Hellmann, M., Schwarzer, J., Philippsen, M.: The ORKA-HPC compiler—practical OpenMP for FPGAs. In: Li, X., Chandrasekaran, S. (eds.) LCPC 2021. LNCS, vol. 13181, pp. 83–97. Springer, Cham (2022). https://doi.org/10.1007/978-3-030-99372-6_6
16. Mayer, F., Brandner, J., Philippsen, M.: Employing polyhedral methods to reduce data movement in FPGA stencil codes. In: Mendis, C., Rauchwerger, L. (eds.) LCPC 2022. LNCS, vol. 13829, pp. 47–63. Springer, Cham (2022). https://doi.org/10.1007/978-3-031-31445-2_4
17. Mayer, F., Brandner, J., Philippsen, M.: Employing polyhedral methods to optimize stencils on FPGAs with stencil-specific caches, data reuse, and wide data bursts. In: 14th International Workshop Polyhedral Compilation Techniques (IMPACT 2024). Munich, Germany (2024). https://doi.org/10.48550/arXiv.2401.13645
18. Mayer, F., Knaust, M., Philippsen, M.: OpenMP on FPGAs—a survey. In: Fan, X., de Supinski, B.R., Sinnen, O., Giacaman, N. (eds.) IWOMP 2019. LNCS, vol. 11718, pp. 94–108. Springer, Cham (2019). https://doi.org/10.1007/978-3-030-28596-8_7
19. Meher, P.K., Chandrasekaran, S., Amira, A.: FPGA realization of FIR filters by efficient and flexible systolization using distributed arithmetic. IEEE Trans. Signal Process. **56**(7), 3009–3017 (2008). https://doi.org/10.1109/TSP.2007.914926
20. Moss, D.J., et al.: A customizable matrix multiplication framework for the Intel HARPv2 Xeon+FPGA platform: a deep learning case study. In: Proceedings of International Symposium on Field Programmable Gate Arrays (FPGA 2018), pp. 107–116. Monterey, CA (2018). https://doi.org/10.1145/3174243.3174258

21. Nepomuceno, R., Sterle, R., Valarini, G., Pereira, M., Yviquel, H., Araujo, G.: Enabling OpenMP task parallelism on Multi-FPGAs. arXiv:2103.10573 [cs.DC] (2021). https://doi.org/10.1109/FCCM51124.2021.00047
22. Nibbelink, K., Rajopadhye, S., McConnell, R.: 0/1 knapsack on hardware: a complete solution. In: Proceedings of International Conference on on Application-specific Systems, Architectures and Processors (ASAP 2007), pp. 160–167. Montréal, Canada (2007). https://doi.org/10.1109/ASAP.2007.4429974
23. Park, S.Y., Meher, P.K.: Efficient FPGA and ASIC realizations of a DA-based reconfigurable FIR digital filter. IEEE Trans. Circuits and Syst. II: Express Briefs **61**(7), 511–515 (2014). https://doi.org/10.1109/TCSII.2014.2324418
24. Pouchet, L.N., Zhang, P., Sadayappan, P., Cong, J.: Polyhedral-based data reuse optimization for configurable computing. In: Proceedings of International Symposium on Field Programmable Gate Arrays (FPGA 2013), pp. 29–38. Montery, CA (2013)
25. Programming Systems Group, Friedrich-Alexander Universität Erlangen-Nürnberg: Orka Compiler Distribution. https://cs2-gitlab.cs.fau.de/orka/orkadistro/-/tags/MultilayerCacheReproduction. Accessed 18 July 2024
26. Putnam, A., et al.: Performance and power of cache-based reconfigurable computing. SIGARCH Comput. Archit. News **37**(3), 395–405 (2009). https://doi.org/10.1145/1555815.1555804
27. Sklyarov, V., Skliarova, I.: High-performance implementation of regular and easily scalable sorting networks on an FPGA. Microprocess. Microsyst. **38**(5), 470–484 (2014). https://doi.org/10.1016/j.micpro.2014.03.003
28. SPEC: SPEC CPU 2006. https://www.spec.org/cpu2006/. Accessed 18 July 2024
29. Winterstein, F., Fleming, K., Yang, H.J., Wickerson, J., Constantinides, G.: Custom-sized caches in application-specific memory hierarchies. In: Proceedings of International Conference on Field Programmable Technology (FPT 2015), pp. 144–151. Queenstown, New Zealand (2015). https://doi.org/10.1109/FPT.2015.7393141
30. Xilinx (AMD): System Cache LogiCORE IP Product Guide. https://docs.amd.com/r/en-US/pg118-system-cache. Accessed 18 July 18 2024
31. Xilinx (AMD): Xilinx Vitis HLS. https://www.xilinx.com/products/design-tools/vitis/vitis-hls.html. Accessed 18 July 2024
32. Xilinx (AMD): Xilinx Vitis PRAGMA HLS CACHE Documentation. https://docs.amd.com/r/en-US/ug1399-vitis hls/pragma-HLS-cache. Accessed 18 July 2024
33. Yoshimi, M., Nishikawa, Y., Miki, M., Hiroyasu, T., Amano, H., Mencer, O.: A performance evaluation of CUBE: one-dimensional 512 FPGA cluster. In: Sirisuk, P., Morgan, F., El-Ghazawi, T., Amano, H. (eds.) ARC 2010. LNCS, vol. 5992, pp. 372–381. Springer, Heidelberg (2010). https://doi.org/10.1007/978-3-642-12133-3_36

Best Practices

Survey of OpenMP Practice in General Open Source Software

Tim Jammer[✉][ID], Christian Iwainsky[ID], and Christian Bischof[ID]

Technical University Darmstadt, 64283 Darmstadt, Germany
{tim.jammer,christian.iwainsky,christian.bischof}@tu-darmstadt.de

Abstract. OpenMP, a widely adopted standard for shared memory parallel programming, is known for its simplicity and portability, making it accessible to programmers across various domains, not just HPC experts. This study aims at providing an overview of the current practice of OpenMP usage in open source projects. We focus our study on the considerations necessary for efficient OpenMP usage, as parallelizing an application with OpenMP comes with a certain overhead necessary for thread creation and management.

For this purpose, we developed a binary analysis tool that automatically estimates the complexity of a parallel region allowing a comparison with the complexity of thread creation and management overhead in bluk. We applied this tool on a large set of 537 open source applications. Specifically, we want to answer the question: "To what extent is the usage of OpenMP in general following known good practices from the HPC community?" In particular, we find that 45% of projects contain at least one example of a rather simple parallel region. In these cases, it is questionable whether parallelization is worth the overhead necessary for thread creation and management. We also observe from the codes analysed that the style of using OpenMP apparently did not change over the last decade.

Our analysis tool is available on GitHub: https://github.com/tudasc/openmp-analysis.

Keywords: OpenMP · Survey · Binary Analysis

1 Introduction

OpenMP is a widely adopted standard for shared-memory parallel programming, offering a portable and simple approach to exploit parallelism on multi-core systems. OpenMP simplifies the development of parallel applications by providing a set of compiler directives, library routines, and environment variables that enable programmers to parallelize their code with relative ease.

Parallelizing e.g. a for loop with OpenMP requires, in principle, minimal effort: in the best case only *one* simple pragma directive is needed. Hence,

---

T. Jammer and C. Iwainsky—Both authors contributed equally to this research.

OpenMP is suitable for programmers of all levels. Still, achieving an efficient parallelization requires effort and necessitates a deeper understanding of different aspects, such as involved overheads, impact of managing thread and task-pools as well as the impact of critical paths. The dependence of the overheads on the number of threads involved complicates this even more. These aspects are not directly visible to programmers, as these are either handled by the OpenMP runtime library or only become important at scale. With the increasing numbers of cores nowadays, managing these overhead aspects becomes increasingly important though, as they can limit scalability, especially for fine-grained parallelism or workloads with high synchronization requirements. Also the ratio of parallelized to serial program parts has a severe impact on the performance of OpenMP codes. Simply put, OpenMP programming is easy to learn, but difficult to master.

Anecdotal evidence and analysis of known HPC codes using OpenMP indicates, that programmers and researchers associated with HPC sites seem to be typically well trained in these aspects and, in addition, can call on the support of HPC experts. However, the question remains, how OpenMP is used in the wider community. To the best of our knowledge, a comprehensive study of how OpenMP is used in codes from "laymen", e.g. students, self-taught OpenMP users and industrial users, and to what extent good practices known in the HPC community are applied and their implications for performance is still lacking.

Therefore, this research aims to address the question: "To what extent is the usage of OpenMP in general following known good practices from the HPC community?" To achieve this goal, we developed an automated tool that analyzes the binaries of OpenMP applications. We mainly use control-flow information combined with the count of assembly instructions to get a *rough* estimation of the complexity of the parallel regions encountered, *without the need for programm execution*. Thus, we are able to statically analyze a diverse set of open-source projects that employ OpenMP to gain insights into the prevalent usage patterns.

The remainder of this paper is structured as follows: We first present a brief survey of related work, followed by our analysis approach and the resulting tool in Sect. 3. We present the results and discuss our findings in Sect. 4, before concluding in Sect. 5.

2 Related Work

Previous work that analyzed the usage of OpenMP in practice only reported the usage of different pragmas [10]. The most comprehensive study of OpenMP usage was conducted by Kadosh et al. [4]: They "compare the popularity of OpenMP as a function of total usage and usage over time relative to other parallel programming APIs. Next, [they] present specific statistics about OpenMP constructs and the extent to which users adopt them." Although Kadosh et al.'s study provides insights into the different pragmas used, it does not include a reflection of the overheads associated with the used OpenMP constructs. Kadosh et al. [4] mentions that: "The popularity of `parallel for` is a reminder to programming model designers; people often seek *good-enough* performance, not ultimate performance." In our work, we want to address the question what *good-enough* performance actually means in this context, considering the ever increasing core count of modern machines and the resulting need for more scalability. This is especially important as OpenMP is designed to be used by programmers of all fields and not limited to HPC performance experts. To the best of our knowledge, no further studies analyzing general OpenMP usage have been conducted yet. Kadosh et al. [4] also only references to "anecdotal data and feedback from user-support teams at supercomputing centers" [4].

3 Analysis

The idea of this study is to analyze the use of OpenMP in as many codes as possible. For example, we aim to assess for parallel regions if the decrease of runtime of the parallelized workload is likely higher than overhead of management of the OpenMP directives, such as the overhead of thread creation/activation and other management work. Ideally, one would use existing analysis tools to measure and analyse individual applications with real input-sets.

However, the manual analysis of a single code is a time consuming process prone with difficulties, such as measurement overhead, which makes this unpractiable for hundreds of codes. This mandates an automated analysis process. Executing the benchmarks unsupervised raised concerns regarding to a waste of compute ressources and security risks: The code could compute for a long time, idle while waiting for input, deadlock, access local data, or perform other malicious activities. While virtual machines and containers could mitigate some of the security concerns, the ressource requirements and potential wasted CPU time for such an endeavor would be considerable. While the security risks and compute-time requirements can be debated, the automated detection of input dataset and inference on how to use these dataset can not be automated. Therefore, we aim to avoid the execution of an applications entirely, and rely on estimates work derived from assembly-analysis as an proxy in our assessments.

Therefore, we analyze the compiler-generated assembly code of the OpenMP parallel region and contrast the count of instruction inside the parallel region with an estimation of how many assembly instructions are necessary for thread creation and management. We conduct this analysis at the binary level, as it is the compiler's responsibility to transform the OpenMP pragma directives into suitable parallel code. An analysis of some compiler-internal intermediate representation is much more difficult to implement on a large scale, as one needs to interject the different build processes of many different repositories. Different binaries, on the other hand, can be automatically analyzed in a standardized way. The binary level analysis has the additional advantage that it can also be performed on applications where the source code is not known or available. We do not include such applications in our study however, to avoid potential licensing conflicts when dis-assembling binaries.

In this section, we first discuss our approach in using the instruction count as a metric for thread creation and management overhead. Then, we explain the process of discovering open source repositories that utilize OpenMP in Sect. 3.2. Section 3.3 describes the process of how we build as many repositories as possible. Lastly, we describe our binary analysis approach in Sect. 3.4.

3.1 Thread Creation and Management Overhead

In order to compare the parallelized workload inside the OpenMP parallel region with the overhead, we need some measurement of the overhead. We estimate the complexity of the overhead in assembly instructions, regardless of how long an individual instruction takes to execute. Measuring the overhead of thread creation in terms of assembly instructions is not a direct representative, when one can measure the runtime on a particular system. In our case however, our analysis can not execute the applications on any particular CPU, as detailed earlier. We analyze the general trend by estimating the amount of work represented by the "body" of OpenMP constructs and contrast it with the amount of work the used OpenMP construct has to perform, such as synchronization or thread management.

To make comparisons easier, and to account for different potentially better CPUs or implementations, we set the number of assembly instructions required for the startup of a parallel region to 100 instructions. These 100 instruction are a low approximation and account for operations to (a) determine which threads are part of the current team (b) create or wake them up, (c) set up their stack, (d) set up and initialize the required private variables, (e) and other runtime library (RTL) activities for possibly hundreds of threads, even in a highly optimized implementation. Measurements of real OpenMP RTLs show counts higher than his. For example, in previous studies [2,3], we measured that during the time required for the startup of a parallel region, the CPU was able to execute more than 375 assembly instructions. Therefore, the 100 instructions provide a *conservative* estimate on the complexity of the overhead required. We consider this a lower estimate, as this number can be much higher, depending on the amount of threads created or when taking into account the time needed for other aspects of the overhead such as the necessary synchronization. We furthermore note, that thread creation results in a call to the operating system, implying, that the program has no direct control on how long the thread creation actually takes. We can compare this overhead metric against the complexity of a parallel region, as explained in Sect. 3.4.

3.2 Finding Repositories with OpenMP Codes

In order to identify suitable repositories for our study, we gathered any public OpenMP code on Github, as well as codes available in the HPC community, i.e. as well known mini-apps (MiniFE, Lulesh, etc.).

In our query to GitHub, we searched for all repositories that contained the keyword openmp and that were using C or C++ as their language. The query used is equivalent to entering "openmp language:c language:c++" in the github search bar. For our analysis pipeline, the codes from GitHub were identified using the query interface (GitHub REST API). For this work we omitted Fortran codes, as we are not yet familiar with the internals of how the Fortran compiler handles OpenMP, which is necessary for analysis of the binary. Adding Fortran would have only contributed 276 additional codes to the initial pool of 8.5k C/C++ codes. This approach ensured that we do not confine our analysis to the biased sets of HPC codes and extend our view to OpenMP usage in the generality of all public codes on GitHub.

This search still must be refined a bit, as some codes only contain the keywords, but do not actively use OpenMP in the code. Some projects have no parallel regions, e.g. only utilize the `omp simd` pragma or GPU offload constructs. We therefore only include projects, that contain at least one parallel region. Other than that, we included all repositories that we could build with reasonable effort in our study.

A brief survey revealed, that our dataset contains a great variety of applications, e.g. password cracker for security auditing, hydrodynamics simulations, unit root testing of algorithmic trading tools or Fourier transformations. This satisfies our goal of targeting the broader OpenMP community, and not only the expert crafted HPC codes. Additionally, the dataset also contains OpenMP tutorial exercises, both trainer crafted and trainee solutions, as well as several student projects. Not all those are probably not intended to be executed in any production setting, but might provide lots of insight into the adoption of OpenMP by a broader audience.

3.3 Building Repositories

In order to be able to analyze the binary of an application, we first need to build it. Although the building process itself is not standardized, many projects follow the best practices of the Linux system they use. These are, in particular, cmake, GNU autotools and GNU makefiles. For many repositories, a standard invocation of the respective build system is sufficient for building one or multiple binaries. For other repositories, some manual intervention was necessary, for example providing the path to a prerequisite library. We initially applied an automated build phase to build each repository using a standard invocation of the build system used. For projects that failed in the automated process, we referred to the projects readme, in order to find the options necessary for building. Repositories that we could not build, because we were not able to quickly infer the necessary steps from the readme are excluded from our analysis.

To ensure full reproducibility of our work, we include the exact steps to build all repositories as shell scripts alongside with the exact git commit hash used during checkout in our github repository: https://github.com/tudasc/openmp-analysis-data.

In order to have a comparable assembly code, we build all repositories with the same version of GCC (11.2). We also set the `CFLAGS` and `CXXFLAGS` environment variable to the same optimization level. We do note, that the build system may be configured to ignore the relevant environment variables and therefore can not guarantee that the compilation actually used the same compiler flags

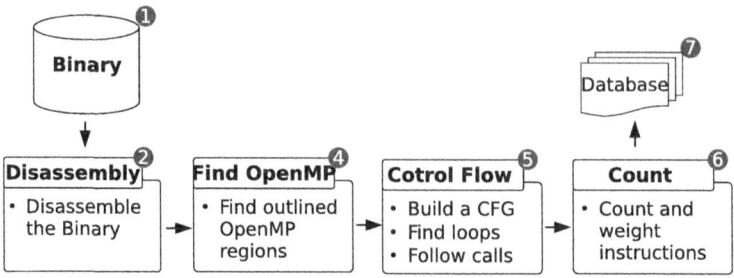

Fig. 1. Illustration of the analysis process. Starting from the Binary (1), in the disassembly (2), the OpenMP regions are located (3), by looking for the compiler generated symbols. Then a control flow graph is build (4) to analyze the loops, to be able to correctly count the assembly instructions, that are part of the parallel region (6). The results are collected in a database (6) for further investigation.

for all repositories. This does not change anything with our analysis and overhead assessment approach; it only prevents the direct comparison of the exact numbers from different projects. But as we analyze a large set of repositories, we consider the general trends identified are as valid.

3.4 Binary Analysis

We implemented the analysis of OpenMP regions in angr [9], which is an open-source binary analysis platform for Python. angr is often used for reverse engineering binaries, for example in the context of security vulnerability analysis [5,8] or detection of other defects [6,7]. Although we only tested our analysis with x86 binaries, the angr framework is capable of handling other architectures such as arm as well.

In order to estimate the complexity of the parallelized OpenMP regions, we analyze and count the assembly instructions in them, as illustrated in Fig. 1

The first step is to find the OpenMP parallel regions in the disassembled binary. This is achieved by looking for the `omp outlined` functions that are generated by the compiler to implement OpenMP parallel regions. Currently, we implemented this step specifically for the GCC version 11.2 that we used in this study, as the detailed naming conventions of the resulting `omp outlined` symbols might differ from other compilers like clang. This process, however, should still be applicable to different versions of GCC. As other compilers also implement OpenMP parallel regions by outlining functions, our tool is not directly bound to GCC or any specific compiler version, as long as it is provided with the correct symbol names of the internal OpenMP runtime library functions and the naming scheme of the automatically outlined ones.

When estimating the complexity of OpenMP regions via its assembly instruction count, we weigh each instruction by how often it is going to be executed. We use the control flow graph analysis built into angr for this purpose. Branches are weighted with an equal probability for each path taken. For loops, we try to infer the trip count to be used as the instructions weight, which in turn is used to scale the loob-bodys instruction, as they are executed multiple times. By analyzing the assembly instructions of the loop, we are in some, albeit rare, cases able to determine that a loop has a constant trip count. For all other loops we use a configurable default trip count to weight the instructions. As we are dealing with OpenMP parallel for loops, the loops trip count may depend on the number of threads, as the iterations are distributed between the different threads. In some cases, our analysis is able to determine that the loops execution depends on the number of threads present in the current team. We analyze this by utilizing the idea of a taint analysis. We taint all registers and memory locations whose value depends on the threadcount. This is possible, as we know the specific runtime library calls used in order to query the number of threads present, to be used as a starting point of our taint analysis. Loops with trip count depending on the number of threads are weighted as if the loop body is only executed once by each thread, as with higher amount of threads, less iterations are "available" per thread.

For instructions that can be executed multiple times by means of recursion instead of a loop, we do not change the instruction weighting. We only save the number of recursions detected in the parallel region for later analysis. It was not necessary to use the count of recursions in our dataset, as almost all parallel regions with recursions in our datasets also contain loops and are already complex enough to surpass our definition of overhead as described in Sect. 3.1.

We think that this metric, is able to give an initial overall assessment over all repositories. As it is designed to analyze general usage trends, it may not be accurate for any specific repository, as our approach does not take other aspects into account. For example, calls to dynamically loaded libraries are only counted as one assembly instruction, even though the called function is much more complex.

4 Assessment of OpenMP Usage Practice

In this section, we analyze the general usage practices of OpenMP in our dataset. We first give some general statistics about the analyzed repositories, before detailing the different pragma directives used and the resulting number of parallel regions in Sect. 4.2. We analyze the complexity of those regions in Sect. 4.3 and reflect how it compares with the necessary overhead in Sect. 4.4. Finally, in Sect. 4.5, we also take into account the parallelization coverage.

4.1 General Statistics of the Analyzed Repositories

We identified $\approx$ 4000 repositories with actual OpenMP usage, as described in Sect. 3.2. Of those, we could build 537 with the build process described in Sect. 3.3. The full set of queried projects, as well as the projects analyzed for this

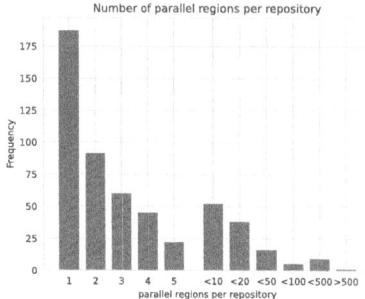
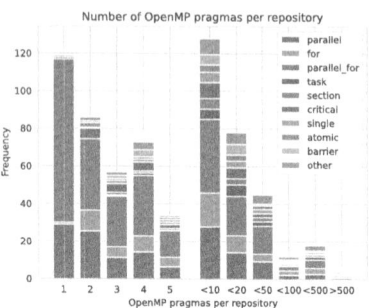

Fig. 2. Number of parallel regions per project

Fig. 3. Number of OpenMP pragma directives per project. The coloring of the bars shows the different pragmas used.

section is available at https://github.com/tudasc/openmp-analysis-data. The 537 analyzed repositories include both relatively old as well as projects with very recent commits. For all repositories, we analyzed the most recent commit on the repositories default branch. We did not perform any analysis on branches or tags. The analyzed commits range from October 2011 until the date when the analysis was carried out in May 2024. Half of the commits analyzed were from 2020 or later. As we do not observe any specific clustering of the commit dates (see Fig. 7), the analyzed repositories provides a statistically relevant base of overall wide spread OpenMP usage over the last decade.

For the top four projects we observed more than a thousand GitHub stars each. This indicates, that these projects are actively used. We will focus on these projects in the end of this section again.

4.2 Usage of Pragmas and Number of Parallel Regions

One of the aspects causing overhead on the OpenMP program is the repeated opening and closing of parallel regions, with threads having to be created or activated and other runtime library tasks to be completed. To limit the necessary overhead, a low number of parallel regions is preferable for a program using OpenMP, ideally with only one region for the entire program. Figure 2 depicts the number of parallel regions per analyzed code. We see that many codes ($\approx 30\%$) use only a single parallel region in their program. We also note that some codes have a high number of parallel regions, with $\approx 25\%$ of codes having more than five parallel regions, with two codes having more than 500 parallel regions.

While this is not a barrier to good performance per se, it is an indicator, that the work to collapse parallel regions into one is either too challenging, or the potential negative impact of multiple regions in unknown.

Figure 3 shows what OpenMP pragma directives are used in the codes. So, for example, in codes where only one pragma directive was used, it was a `parallel for` in ≈ 70% of cases. The coloring of the bars in Fig. 3 is determined by the usage frequency of the most relevant pragma directives.

The majority of codes relies on the one or multiple `pragma omp parallel for` directive(s). This widespread use indicates that most programmers stick to the "default" of `pragma omp parallel for`, shown in (online) tutorials and literature and follow the approach to parallelize the most important loop with `parallel for`. Most programmers stop at this stage and does not deem it necessary fo further dive into the possibilities of OpenMP.

We suspect users lack the training to use tools to actively investigate a programs hot-spots. This trend is also reflected by the complexity of the used pragma directives. ≈ 50% of pragma directives contain only a single clause, while only ≈ 25% specify more than two clauses, such as `reduction`, `schedule` or `private`. This leads us to the conclusion that fine-tuning the OpenMP usage is not widespread.

We note, that not all OpenMP pragma directives create a new parallel region and especially complex codes, such as the ones with many parallel regions, need addtional OpenMP directives for proper synchronization, such as barriers. This trend can be observed, when comparing the number of codes with high amount of directives (Fig. 3) against the number of codes with high amount of parallel regions (Fig. 2). We see that those pragma directives, such as `section`, `critical`, `task` are not heavily used. One explanation is that most programmers only apply parallelization to the part of the program that is trivially parallel, as parallelization of the other parts may be too difficult or seem not worthwhile. This could indicate a lack of knowledge on how to efficiently utilize synchronization to be able to parallelize a larger part of the application.

4.3 Complexity of Parallel Regions

Our main interest is in "how" the directives are used in relation to the workload they affect, in particular the work to be parallelized in the region. To this end, we analyzed the instruction count Fig. 4 and number of loops in parallel regions found by our analysis in depicted in Fig. 5.

For example, ≈ 25% of parallel regions contain only one loop. Of those, our analysis can identify ≈ 25% as loops, where the number of loop iteration certainly depends on the number of threads. However, we suspect that there are many more of such loops, considering that `pragma omp parallel for` is the most used pragma directive (see Fig. 3) and many parallel regions only contain one loop. More complex parallel regions with more than two loops also exist: < 40% of parallel regions contain more than two loops.

The work in a parallelized block of code plays a critical role for recuperating parallelization overheads. The more work, in our case assembly instructions, there is in such a region, the more favorable this region is in regards to a low overhead ratio. Figure 4 shows the number of weighted assembly instructions in a particular parallel region. We see that many parallel regions (≈ 40%) include less

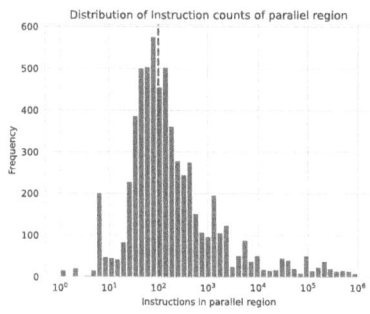
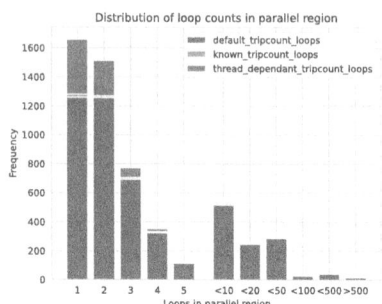

Fig. 4. Instructions per parallel region, the line denotes 100 instructions as our thread creation overhead estimation.

Fig. 5. Loops per parallel region. the green portion of the bar denotes the loops, where our binary analysis finds that the trip-count depends on the number of threads. (Color figure online)

than 100 assembly instructions, while 75% of parallel regions observed, contain less than 670 assembly instructions. Our estimate for overhead is 100 assembly instructions (Sect. 3.1), marked as the dotted line in Fig. 4.

If the weighted assembly instruction count is below this threshold, the OpenMP API overhead will dominate the execution by more than 50%. Considering that in HPC, an overhead-to-workload ratio of less than 10%, ideally less than 1%, is desirable. With our 100 instruction threshold, workloads above a 1000 (10.000 respectively) assembly instructions would be necessary to achieve such ratios. This leads us to the conclusion, that complex parallel regions are relatively rare. Of course this work-to-overhead assessment is strongly dependent on the weights applied for the weighted assembly instruction count algorithm. At the moment, we assume a default trip-count of 3, after parallelization. This may be a bit biased towards marking codes as unfavorable, but the reason why we used such a "low" trip-count *after parallelization* is, that the loop iterations are likely to be distributed among the different threads. Our raw data also includes the instruction counts with a trip-count of 1, but the difference in the figure was not detectable. This leads to the conclusion, that the trip count is not a strong factor and that a trip-count of 3 is already sufficient to distinguish complex from simple parallel regions.

4.4 Prevalence of "high Overhead" Parallel Regions

We define "high overhead" regions as regions that contain less than 100 weighted assembly instructions. Using the amount of "high overhead" regions as a metric, we investigate how many projects consist of only such regions or to what extent this changes over the years. Figure 6 shows the ratio of "high overhead" regions among all OpenMP regions in a particular repository. A ratio of 100% therefore

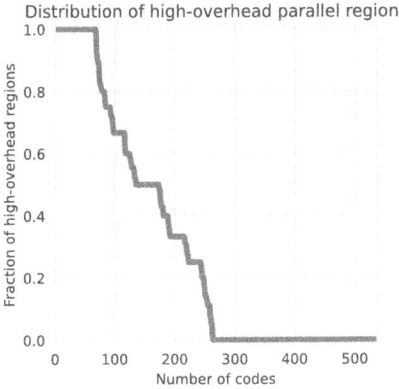
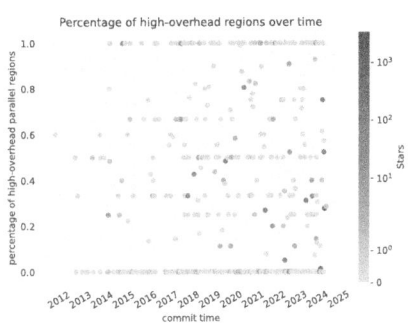

Fig. 6. Fraction of "high overhead" to all parallel regions. "high overhead" is defined as less than 100 assembly instructions in the parallel region (refer Sect. 3.1)

Fig. 7. Fraction of "high overhead" parallel regions over time correlated with the amount of GitHub stars.

reflects a code where all the parallel regions are considered "high overhead", whereas 0% indicates, that all regions have significant more work than approximated the parallelization overhead. We see, that about $\approx 20\%$ of all codes consist of "high overhead" regions, with additionally $\approx 40\%$ having a mix of "high overhead" and "normal overhead" regions. In sum, about $\approx 60\%$ of all analyzed codes have at least one region, that may not be suitable for thread parallelization with OpenMP, considering the overhead necessary for thread creation and management.

To analyze if there is an evolution in OpenMP of this pattern, e.g. due to trends in programming practice, we plotted the fraction of high "high overhead" regions over time. This is shown in Fig. 7. We see, that there is no discernible pattern on how the amount of "high overhead" regions are distributed over the years. Neither in the earlier years of OpenMP, nor in the more recent years is a clear trend visible. Codes with "high overhead" regions are equally as likely, as codes with normal overhead regions. We conclude, that OpenMP programming practices have not changed much in the last decade.

We also do not see any correlation between the amount of stars of a project and the presence of "high overhead" parallel regions. We note, however, that the top four repositories as measured by the amounts of stars do not contain examples of high overhead parallel regions.

For the identified "small" parallel regions, it may be worthwhile to execute them with low thread-counts, like only using two threads. But in those cases, we do think that our conclusion is still valid, as it is unlikely that execution of these regions with a high number of threads is worth the necessary overhead. As

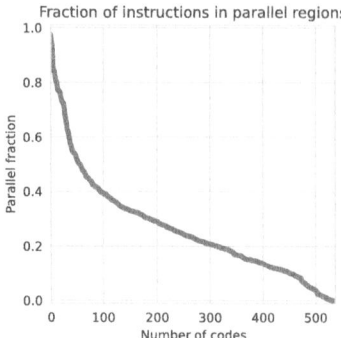

Fig. 8. Fraction of instructions in parallel region compared to all assembly instructions in the respective project.

core-counts of more than 100 are not unseen in modern machines, we wanted to analyze the potential scalability of those applications.

4.5 Parallelization Coverage

In order to evaluate the efficiency of parallelization, one also needs to take into account the part of the program that can be parallelized in relation to the total overall work (Amdahl's law [1]). As explained in Sect. 3, it is not feasible to collect runtime metrics for all codes, due to practical and security reasons. But we can still approximate the amount of work inside of the parallel part of a program by looking at the assembly instructions. Figure 8 shows the fraction of assembly instructions inside of the parallel part of a project. We see, that for $\approx 20\%$ of the codes, over 60% of the code-base is enclosed by an OpenMP parallel region, while for the majority of codes ($\approx 80\%$) only 40% or less of the code base is part of the OpenMP parallelization.

Having only 40% of a program running in parallel does not indicate that it would be reasonable to reserve many cores on a system, as most likely these cores will be idling most of the time. We note, that this metric was taken without the instruction weighting as described in Sect. 3.4 and may therefore be more miss-representative of highly complex parallel regions[1]. Regardless we consider this still a valid indicator, as most parallel regions are not particularly large and complex, so the general trend should still be valid.

5 Conclusion

In this work, we developed a workflow to automatically assess the complexity of OpenMP parallel regions by means of binary analysis without the need to execute the application. This allowed us to analyze the OpenMP usage patterns of 537 open source applications.

---

[1] We do not weigh all instructions due to the computational cost of the full control flow graph analysis necessary.

Many codes contain OpenMP, but the application of good OpenMP practices, particularly in managing overhead for thread creation and management, is questionable. Our study found numerous examples of "high overhead" parallel regions where the benefits of parallelization are likely outweighed by the associated overhead (in ≈ 40% of analyzed applications). This trend has persisted over the past decade, indicating that OpenMP programming practices have not significantly evolved. The prevalent use of high overhead regions and basic directives suggests that many developers may lack the training or knowledge to optimize OpenMP usage effectively. This highlights a need for improved education and resources on advanced OpenMP practices beyond specialized HPC training, especially since the current widespread usage predominantly showcases basic OpenMP applications, making it challenging to learn more advanced concepts from existing usage examples.

In the current study, we limited our analysis to C and C++ programs. In the future, we want to explore if the usage patterns of Fortran programs are different. Additionally, we want to further refine the overhead metric and binary analysis, for example by also taking into account the instruction mix of the parallel region, if vectorized instructions are used for example. We also want to extend the practical usability of the developed analysis tool, to be able to link the parallel regions back to the pragmas in the source code, so that the tool can also be used to guide programmers to the parallel regions, to be reviewed for thread creation and management overhead. It may be possible to achieve this by utilizing debug symbols of a binary.

The code for our analysis tool as well as the result data is available on GitHub: https://github.com/tudasc/openmp-analysis.

Acknowledgements. We thank René Sitt from the University of Marburg for invaluable assistance in building the Open source GitHub repositories, which greatly enhanced the scope and impact of this project.

This work was supported by the Hessian Ministry for Higher Education, Research and the Arts through the Hessian Competence Center for High-Performance Computing and by the Federal Ministry of Education and Research (BMBF) and the states of Hesse as part of the NHR program. Measurement for this work were conducted on the Lichtenberg high performance computer of TU Darmstadt.

References

1. Amdahl, G.M.: Validity of the single processor approach to achieving large scale computing capabilities. In: Proceedings of the April 18–20, 1967, Spring Joint Computer Conference, pp. 483–485, AFIPS 1967 (Spring), Association for Computing Machinery, New York, NY, USA (1967). ISBN 9781450378956, https://doi.org/10.1145/1465482.1465560
2. Iwainsky, C., et al.: How many threads will be too many? On the scalability of OpenMP implementations. In: Träff, J.L., Hunold, S., Versaci, F. (eds.) Euro-Par 2015. LNCS, vol. 9233, pp. 451–463. Springer, Heidelberg (2015). https://doi.org/10.1007/978-3-662-48096-0_35

3. Jammer, T., Iwainsky, C., Bischof, C.: A comparison of the scalability of OpenMP implementations. In: Malawski, M., Rzadca, K. (eds.) Euro-Par 2020. LNCS, vol. 12247, pp. 83–97. Springer, Cham (2020). https://doi.org/10.1007/978-3-030-57675-2_6
4. Kadosh, T., Hasabnis, N., Mattson, T., Pinter, Y., Oren, G.: Quantifying OpenMP: statistical insights into usage and adoption. In: 2023 IEEE High Performance Extreme Computing Conference (HPEC), pp. 1–7. IEEE (2023)
5. Machiry, A., et al.: BOOMERANG: exploiting the semantic gap in trusted execution environments. In: Proceedings of the 2017 Network and Distributed System Security Symposium (2017)
6. Parvez, M.R.: Combining static analysis and targeted symbolic execution for scalable bug-finding in application binaries (2016)
7. Pewny, J., Garmany, B., Gawlik, R., Rossow, C., Holz, T.: Cross-architecture bug search in binary executables. In: 2015 IEEE Symposium on Security and Privacy (SP), pp. 709–724. IEEE (2015)
8. Shoshitaishvili, Y., Wang, R., Hauser, C., Kruegel, C., Vigna, G.: Firmalice - automatic detection of authentication bypass vulnerabilities in binary firmware. In: Proceedings of the 2015 Network and Distributed System Security Symposium (2015)
9. Shoshitaishvili, Y., et al.: SoK: (State of) the art of war: offensive techniques in binary analysis. In: IEEE Symposium on Security and Privacy (2016)
10. Squar, J., Schroeter, N., Fuchs, A., Kuhn, M., Ludwig, T.: Content queries and in-depth analysis on version-controlled software. Proc. Comput. Sci. **207**, 1261–1270 (2022)

CI/CD Efforts for Validation, Verification and Benchmarking OpenMP Implementations

Aaron Jarmusch[1], Felipe Cabarcas[1,3], Swaroop Pophale[5], Andrew Kallai[1], Johannes Doerfert[2], Luke Peyralans[4], Seyong Lee[5], Joel Denny[5], and Sunita Chandrasekaran[1(✉)]

[1] University of Delaware, Newark, DE, USA
schandra@udel.edu
[2] Lawrence Livermore National Laboratory, Livermore, CA, USA
[3] Universidad de Antioquia, Medellin, Colombia
[4] University of Oregon, Eugene, OR, USA
[5] Oak Ridge National Laboratory, Bethel Valley Road Oak Ridge, Oak Ridge, TN, USA

Abstract. Software developers must adapt to keep up with the changing capabilities of platforms so that they can utilize the power of High-Performance Computers (HPC), including exascale systems. OpenMP, a directive-based parallel programming model, allows developers to include directives to existing C, C++, or Fortran code to allow node level parallelism without compromising performance. This paper describes our CI/CD efforts to provide easy evaluation of the support of OpenMP across different compilers using existing testsuites and benchmark suites on HPC platforms. Our main contributions include (1) the set of a Continuous Integration (CI) and Continuous Development (CD) workflow that captures bugs and provides faster feedback to compiler developers, (2) an evaluation of OpenMP (offloading) implementations supported by AMD, HPE, GNU, LLVM, and Intel, and (3) evaluation of the quality of compilers across different heterogeneous HPC platforms. With the comprehensive testing through the CI/CD workflow, we aim to provide a comprehensive understanding of the current state of OpenMP (offloading) support in different compilers and heterogeneous platforms consisting of CPUs and GPUs from NVIDIA, AMD, and Intel.

Keywords: OpenMP · Validation · CI · Compiler · Benchmarking

1 Introduction

Heterogeneous computing has reached a new milestone with the Frontier [21] and Aurora [3] supercomputers achieving exaflops, representing one quintillion floating point operations per second. This significant increase in processing speed has the potential to revolutionize application performance, provided that software developers can keep up with the growing demand for tools and platforms that can harness the power of these devices. To achieve this, current languages and models include OpenMP [24], OpenACC [22], CUDA [20], HIP [5], and OpenCL [31]. However, each of them has its own unique features and their usage depend on what developers are comfortable with.

While some languages like NVIDIA's CUDA, and AMD's HIP, can be challenging for beginners to learn and require significant rewriting of programs to achieve optimal performance, portable programming models such as OpenMP and OpenACC offer a simpler approach. They use a directive-based approach for parallel programming, allowing users to include these directives on top of existing C, C++, or Fortran code, without compromising on performance. These models play a major role with heterogeneous systems equipped with accelerators such as GPUs, FPGAs, APUs, and more, and can be parallelized on ARM-based systems with ease.

Since more real-world applications have adopted OpenMP, it has been used in various domains. For instance, miniQMC [9], primarily used in the study of electronic molecular structures and 2D/3D solid states, is a simplified version of QMCPACK [14]. Other applications include miniMD [26], LULESH [13], GAMESS [4], HPGMG [7]. With the adoption of OpenMP in modern computing, it is crucial to validate and verify the compilers' implementations of this standard. To simplify the evaluation process for developers, we have established a Continuous Integration (CI) and Continuous Development (CD) workflow, which provides faster feedback for developers. This approach allows us to evaluate the support of OpenMP across different compilers more frequently, reducing the waiting time for developers between evaluations. By implementing this workflow, our goal is to improve the development process and ultimately make OpenMP easier for developers to use in their applications.

This work's focus is on the CI/CD efforts to evaluate the support of OpenMP across different compilers using established validation suites and benchmarks such as OpenMP Validation and Verification (V&V) suite [25], SPEChpc [30], HeCBench [11], and Smoke [1] tests. The main contributions of this paper are:

– Building a Continuous Integration and Continuous Development pipeline for automating testing of OpenMP implementations
– Analysis of output from the CI/CD pipeline that includes verification of OpenMP implementations from AMD, HPE, GNU, LLVM, NVIDIA, and Intel
– Discussion and evaluation of the performance and quality of OpenMP offloading compiler implementations on supercomputers such as Frontier, Perlmutter, Sunspot, and Summit using SPEChpc benchmarking suite.

2 Background and Motivation

OpenMP is a widely used application programming interface (API) that enables programmers to develop parallel applications in C, C++, and Fortran with access to multi-platform shared memory and multi-processing capabilities. With its straightforward adaptable interface, OpenMP enables developers to create efficient parallel programs on multi-core processors. Key features of OpenMP include directives for parallel programming, runtime library routines, thread management, and environment variables.

Over the years OpenMP has refined support for computations on CPU and, starting with OpenMP 4.0 [23], added support for devices such as accelerators. Although GPGPUs are most widely used accelerator devices used in HPC, OpenMP directives are designed to work with any devices that have memory and are capable of performing computations. That makes OpenMP an attractive choice for future-proofing codes and minimizing developer effort for adapting to different architectural trends.

With multiple vendor implementations of OpenMP and more and more real-world applications porting/developing codes using OpenMP programming model, it is crucial to validate and verify the compilers' implementations of the OpenMP standard. It is often unclear to the application developers if adequate OpenMP features are supported by an implementation and if they are performant. This effort takes that stress away from developers by providing nightly runs of established and curated set of benchmarks and testsuites.

3 Related Work

The current work's focus is to enhance the testing of OpenMP offloading implementations using a CI/CD workflow, which has become increasingly popular in recent years due to its ability to automate various stages of the development process [32,33]. Clacc [8], an open source project that offers support of OpenACC in Clang and LLVM, employs a CI/CD workflow to detect errors quickly. However, the main focus of the current work is to bring a workflow to OpenMP implementation. Even though both OpenACC and OpenMP are directive-based models, their compiler implementations differ, resulting in distinct use cases. LLVM Buildbots[1], another well-known project in the LLVM community, has been used for commit checking of LLVM, but not exclusively for testing OpenMP. However, there are only a few buildbots dedicated to testing OpenMP Offloading, highlighting an area of opportunity for further development. Additionally, CI/CD workflows have also been applied to Machine Learning (ML) through MLOps. Toward MLOps [12], is a case study demonstrating the use of CI/CD workflows to train ML models with different configurations, analyzing the results to identify potential performance bottlenecks and improve the process. Finally, CI/CD workflows have been utilized on the RMACC Summit supercomputer [2] for deploying user-facing software environments and automating benchmark testing [28]. Overall, the current work builds upon these existing efforts to create a more comprehensive and efficient CI/CD workflow for OpenMP Offloading implementations.

---

[1] https://lab.llvm.org/buildbot/.

4 Continuous Integration and Continuous Development Workflow

Manual software testing methods are insufficient for hardware evolution and new software releases. To address this challenge, we use an automation tool to test compilers when they are updated. Leveraging a CI/CD workflow allows us to continuously identify failed tests at all times, not just before an official software release, and to automate the manual testing process. As a result, we reduce the time and effort required for compiler testing, leading to faster development cycles and higher quality software.

4.1 CI/CD Pipeline

We have established an OpenMP CI/CD workflow that involves setup of source code, building and installing the compiler, and suite execution, to reduce the developers time required for testing.

Within our CI/CD workflow a **pipeline** refers to a single run of our workflow, which can be triggered by a scheduled time or by new commits. A pipeline contains **stages** which defines when to run a job. A **job** is a set of steps that defines what you want to accomplish. A pipeline's success depends on the completion of each job, which are labeled as "Pass" or "Fail." If any job within a stage fails, the entire pipeline fails. In other words, each job serves as a building block for the overall pipeline, and its outcome determines whether the pipeline is successful or not. The separation of jobs within a pipeline allows isolation of issues from different parts of an implementation during the collection of source code (setup), build/install of the compiler, or suite execution.

With this idea of separation, as indicated in Fig. 1, our workflow (for LLVM Clang/Flang) is divided into three stages: setup, build, testing followed by cleanup.

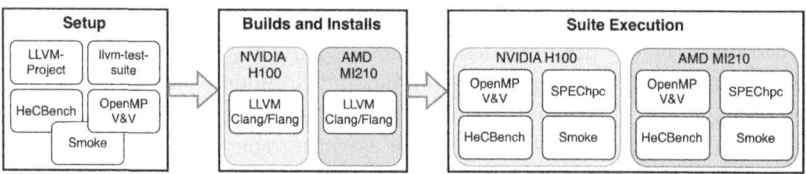

Fig. 1. CI/CD Workflow for LLVM Clang and Flang

In the first stage (i.e., setup), the CI/CD clones any necessary source codes such as the LLVM source, LLVM testsuite infrastructure, and other suites (OpenMP V&V, Smoke, and HeCBench). However, we do not clone SPEChpc suite because the benchmark is not released via GitHub or any other public software storage platform. https://www.spec.org/hpgdownload.html. We download the source codes at a specific commit (for OpenMP V&V, Smoke and HeCBench) to forgo any new changes coming into the suite after the specific commit we have chosen. For the LLVM compiler source, we download the commit (GitHub commit hash) from the latest trunk.

In the build/install stage, that comes next, we build only the LLVM compiler from the identified commit. We then, proceed to testing with OpenMP V&V, Smoke, HeCBench as well as SPEChpc suite.

In the suite execution stage, the CI/CD is using the LLVM Integrated Tester (LIT) [16] in conjunction with the LLVM-test-suite [17] to compile and execute the OpenMP V&V, HeCBench, and Smoke suites. We designed CMake files for each testsuite, located in the LLVM-test-suite GitHub repository[2]. These CMake files allow us to specify which languages we want to run and which tests or applications to execute. For instance, the OpenMP V&V testsuite consists of a large number of tests, and to make a job pass or fail, we need to provide specific criteria for the CI/CD to determine this. Therefore, we manually ran each suite to create a green and red list of tests for capturing pass and fail results respectively, with each compiler. Additionally, we created green and red lists per accelerator that we target.

In our CI/CD pipelines, we only run the green lists of tests, which ensures reliable and accurate testing results. By integrating both correctness checking and real-world application testing into a single workflow, we can ensure that our compilers are not only correct but also reliable in real-world scenarios.

Experimental Setup: Since hardware evolves at a rapid pace, The University of Oregon (UO) has setup the Frank Cluster which is comprised of a multitude of servers hosted by UO Oregon Advanced Computing Institute for Science and Society (OACISS) with different hardware setups. At the time of writing, across different servers they have an NVIDIA H100, AMD MI210, and an Intel Data Center Max 1100 (Ponte Vecchio). Utilizing the Frank Cluster to implement our first CI/CD to test software means we can easily change to new hardware configurations. For our CI/CD, we are using GitLab and focusing on the AMD MI210 and the NVIDIA H100 within the Frank Cluster. This means we build compilers and execute each suite for both AMD and NVIDIA GPUs for target-specific errors. For instance, we are building LLVM Clang and Flang for AMD and NVIDIA GPUs, which makes two jobs. We also run each suite on both AMD and NVIDIA GPUs. In total, this makes eight jobs. Two and six for the build and testing stages respectively.

On the Frank Cluster we test LLVM Clang and Flang hourly with the OpenMP V&V, HeCBench, and Smoke suites. We run the SPEChpc suite weekly, due to long execution times. The hourly testing is done to provide commit-level feedback to developers because LLVM is open-source and most compiler developers upstream LLVM into their own compiler [15]. All other compilers are tested on a weekly basis with the SPEChpc suite, since the frequency of compiler releases or changes to those compilers are more on a monthly basis. Table 1 is our configuration with the compilers being tested on what hardware. Since we wanted to include testing for Cray we reproduced our CI/CD workflow onto

---

[2] https://github.com/llvm/llvm-test-suite/tree/main/External.

Table 1. CI/CD pipeline hardware and software configuration.

System		Compilers			
UO Frank Cluster	H100	LLVM Clang & Flang	GNU	NVIDIA	–
UO Frank Cluster	MI210	LLVM Clang & Flang	GNU	AMD	–
ORNL Frontier	MI250X	LLVM Clang & Flang	GNU	AMD	Cray

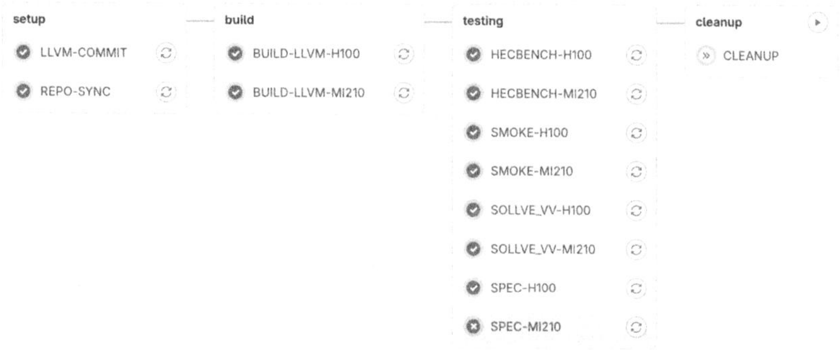

Fig. 2. The CI/CD output for a LLVM Clang and Flang pipeline. The green checkmark marks the job as "Pass" while the red 'x' marked the job as "Fail". (Color figure online)

Frontier at ORNL. This also gave us another system to validate our results against. An example of the CI/CD pipeline is shown in Fig. 2.

Discussion: The development and testing of compilers require rigorous testing to ensure quality. While automating these tasks can accelerate the process, it's crucial to maintain effective communication with developers to provide timely feedback on testsuites' failures. To address this challenge, we have implemented two forms of automatic communication. First, for LLVM, we have integrated a messaging service to notify a team of compiler developers interested in LLVM's implementation of OpenMP offloading when a pipeline has failed. This provides the developers with immediate feedback in case a recent commit has broken the compiler. However, due to LLVM's open-source nature and large project aspect, it may not be possible to identify the root cause of a build failure solely through automated means, it may or may not be the fault of LLVM Clang or Flang OpenMP offloading implementation. The cause may have risen from other parts of the LLVM toolchain. Therefore, we still require some form of human interference to differentiate between failed jobs and identify the specific issue.

Similarly, build-bots have been used in LLVM to test every commit. These build-bots notify the commit creator if a failure occurs; however they primarily focus on CPU code testing and building. Consequently, our primary concern is not build failures but failures within the testsuites themselves. Therefore, it might not be advantageous to notify commit creators of these failures. Instead, we should track them specifically for developers working on OpenMP Offloading.

For the second form of communication, we are utilizing the LLVM Nightly Testing (LNT) [18] infrastructure to create a server that stores testsuite information about the kernel. This information is visualized in a graph to track performance over time[3]. Overall, these methods of communication with developers about the results of the pipelines have been effective so far. However, we continue to evaluate and improve our approaches to ensure optimal effectiveness in the development and testing of compilers.

5 OpenMP Validation and Verification Suite and SPEChpc Benchmarking Suite

In this section, we will elaborate further on the OpenMP V&V testsuite and SPEChpc benchmarking suite exercised by our CI/CD workflow. The OpenMP V&V testsuite is primarily concerned with verifying compiler correctness, whereas the SPEChpc benchmarking suite evaluates the quality of compiler implementations. By integrating both correctness verification and application-based benchmarking into a CI/CD workflow, we can ensure more robust and reliable compiler testing.

5.1 OpenMP Validation and Verification Suite

The OpenMP Validation and Verification (OpenMP V&V) suite [10,25] started as a sub-project of the SOLLVE (Scaling OpenMP With LLVM for Exascale) Exascale Computing Project (ECP) [29]. The sub-project was born out of the lack of open, unbiased testsuite to evaluate aspects of OpenMP that were most critical for exascale applications. Yet, there is still more work to be done. ECP marked a significant achievement with the push towards exascale computing resources. ECP ended in December 2023. As a path forward, the Next Generation Science Software (S4PST) project [27] aims to push the boundaries even further. This focuses on creating a more predictive ecosystem for sustainability in HPC software, with a particular emphasis on node-level programming systems and tools. The tests in the OpenMP V&V are organized based on the specification version. They contain feature and kernel tests in C, C++ and Fortran.

Coverage: Table 2 shows there are 742 total tests in the testsuite covering new features starting with the OpenMP 4.5 specification up to the 5.2. The OpenMP testsuite is under active development and the numbers here represent a snapshot at the time of this writing. The number of test per specification is mainly related to the number of new features introduced in the specification (Table 3).

Results: Figure 3 shows the number of tests that pass for each compiler in each system, for C/C++ and Fortran separately[4]. The left axis represents C/C++, while the right is Fortran. AMD C/C++ compiler on Frontier and GNU on

---
[3] https://crpl.cis.udel.edu/lnt-sollve/.
[4] zenodo.org/doi/10.5281/zenodo.12571032: allCompilerSystemsResults.json.

Table 2. Number of tests in C, C++, and Fortran for each OpenMP Specification currently in the OpenMP Validation and Verification Suite.

Version	C	C++	Fortran	Total
4.5	134	14	104	252
5.0	191	13	128	332
5.1	99	2	28	129
5.2	16	8	5	29
Total	440	37	265	742

Table 3. Systems and compiler versions used for validation

System	Vendor	Accelerator	Compiler and Versions
Perlmutter	HPE	NVIDIA A100	NVIDIA 24.5, Cray 17.0.0, LLVM 19.0.0 commit (18ec885a), and GNU 14.1
Frontier	HPE	AMD MI250X	AMD's ROCm 6.0.0, Cray 17.0.0, LLVM 19.0.0 commit (18ec885a), and GNU 14.1
Sunspot	Intel	Intel GPU Max Series	OneAPI 18.0.0

Perlmutter pass the most, with GNU is the compiler that passes most tests over all. In the case of Fortran, in both systems GNU passes the most tests. LLVM Flang for offloading is under development. Table 4 shows the results for each OpenMP Version.

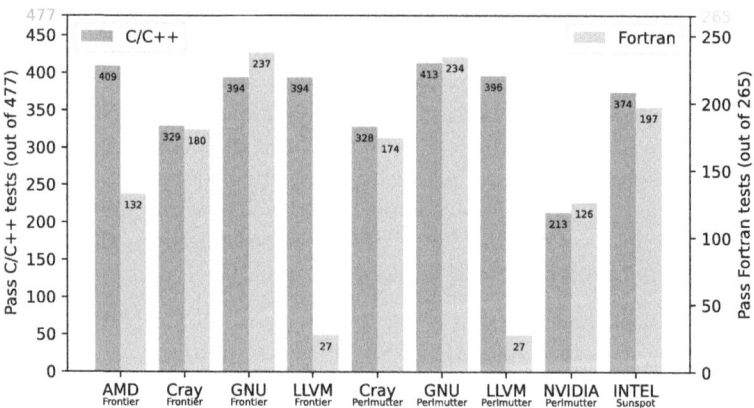

Fig. 3. No. of tests passing per system out of total 477 C/C++ & 265 Fortran tests

Figure 4 shows the compiler evolution over a period of two years for Perlmutter and Frontier[5]. The chosen compilers are the recommended compilers in the

---

[5] zenodo.org/doi/10.5281/zenodo.12571032: compilerVersionsPerlmutterFrontier-Results.json.

Table 4. OpenMP Validation and Verification Suite pass results per OpenMP Version.

Ver.	Lang.	Frontier				Perlmutter				Sunspot
		AMD	Cray	GNU	LLVM	Cray	GNU	LLVM	NVIDIA	INTEL
4.5	C & C++	146	142	137	147	142	145	148	131	142
5.0		179	147	170	171	146	175	172	67	162
5.1		68	39	75	66	39	75	66	13	67
5.2		16	1	12	10	1	18	10	2	3
Total		**409**	**329**	**394**	**394**	**328**	**413**	**396**	**213**	**374**
4.5	Fortran	86	89	104	15	88	104	15	97	97
5.0		40	86	110	9	81	107	9	24	85
5.1		2	3	19	0	3	19	0	2	12
5.2		4	2	4	3	2	4	3	3	3
Total		**132**	**180**	**237**	**27**	**174**	**234**	**27**	**126**	**197**

given system for OpenMP offloading application development. It can be seen in the graph that the compiler development for Fortran has been slow during this period. In the case of C/C++ there has been greater improvement over time, specially for LLVM. NVIDIA supports till OpenMP 4.5.

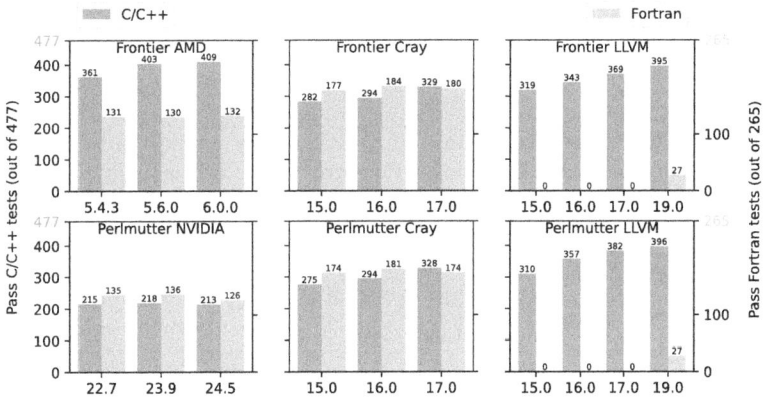

Fig. 4. Evolution of compilers on Frontier and Perlmutter

5.2 SPEChpc HPG Benchmarking Suite

We present SPEChpc V1.1.8 HPG [30] benchmark for evaluating the performance and quality of OpenMP offloading features [6]. The benchmark contains 9 MPI applications written in different programming models, including OpenMP-offloading (TGT) and OpenACC (ACC), where 6 of them are C/C++ and 3 are Fortran. While we focus on the OpenMP offloading versions of the applications, we also present the OpenACC results as a performance reference of another directive programming model. Table 5 summarizes the SPEChpc applications.

We use the smallest size (tiny) versions of the benchmarks, which can run on a single node of each of the tested systems. In addition to these tests, we include a modified *532.sph_exa*, which we will reference as *532.sph_exaM*. The modified version was a result of code analysis as we noticed a bigger performance difference with the OpenACC version compared to OpenACC (we discuss this in more detail at the latter half of this section).

Table 5. SPEChpc 2021 version 1.1.8 applications taken from SPEC website [30].

Benchmark Name	Size: Tiny	Language	Application Area
LBM D2Q37	505.lbm	C	Computational Fluid Dynamics
SOMA	513.soma	C	Polymeric Systems
Tealeaf	518.tealeaf	C	High Energy Physics
Cloverleaf	519.clvleaf	Fortran	High Energy Physics
Minisweep	521.miniswp	C	Nuclear Engineering
POT3D	528.pot3d	Fortran	Solar Physics
SPH-EXA	532.sph_exa	C++14	Astrophysics and Cosmology
HPGMG-FV	534.hpgmgfv	C	Cosmology, Astrophysics
miniWeather	535.weather	Fortran	Weather

SPEChpc Results: Table 6 presents estimated base time results of SPEChpc 2021 Version 1.1.8 on Frontier[6] and Perlmutter[7] using available compilers.

Table 6. Estimated **Base Run Time** of SPEChpc tiny applications on Perlmutter and Frontier using one node. **EE** is execution error, while **BE** is build error.

	Estimate Base Time (seconds)							
	Perlmutter				Frontier			
Compiler	GNU	LLVM	Cray	NVIDIA	GNU	LLVM	Cray	ROCm
Version	14.1	19.0.0	17.0.0	24.5	14.1	19.0.0	17.0.0	6.0.0
505.lbm	484.89	38.29	*28.34*	35.9	2813.46	43.44	40.82	54.64
513.soma	855.05	69.61	*56.75*	65.64	**BE**	87.98	**BE**	70.05
518.tealeaf	2200.95	90.84	49.09	40.49	337.12	43.58	*40.41*	48.51
519.clvleaf	**BE**	**BE**	**EE**	*45.54*	**BE**	**BE**	58.73	72.73
521.miniswp	**EE**	209.55	96.76	573.09	**EE**	160.44	*93.59*	142.61
528.pot3d	926.24	**BE**	55.34	61.54	**BE**	**BE**	*45.64*	92.61
532.sph_exa	1454.46	849.6	**EE**	491.41	**BE**	*203.34*	226.33	207.4
532.sph_exaM	5973.46	179.41	*128.36*	**EE**	**BE**	145.61	164.87	144.83
534.hpgmgfv	**EE**	156.75	*71.2*	163.33	**BE**	102.32	87.5	95.59
535.weather	1391.84	**BE**	38.51	42.72	2569.96	**BE**	*32.51*	53.19

---

[6] zenodo.org/doi/10.5281/zenodo.12571032: Frontier_SPEC_PaperResults.zip.
[7] zenodo.org/doi/10.5281/zenodo.12571032: Perlmutter_SPEC_PaperResults.zip.

Looking at the results from the perspective of the applications, only **505.lbm** and **518.tealeaf** can be built and executed with all compilers (both are C/C++ applications). Fortran's **519.clvleaf** can only be built and executed by NVIDIA's compiler in Perlmutter and by AMD's ROCm and Cray compilers in Frontier. From the point of view of the compilers, only AMD's ROCm compiler could build and execute all applications. The performance of LLVM C/C++ applications is similar to that from vendor compilers. LLVM Flang is under development so it could not build Fortran applications. Even though the GNU compiler can build Fortran and C/C++ applications, its performance is very low compared to all others, specially on Frontier, where many of the applications don't even build. This is an interesting observation, as we found GNU compilers doing a better job with correctness (Fig. 3).

As mentioned before, AMD's compiler was the only one that built and executed all applications with good performance. For this to happen, AMD required special flags suggested by the developers, like (*-fopenmp-target-xteam-reduction-blocksize=128, -Mx,201,2, -fno-openmp-assume-no-nested-parallelism, –mca topo basic*). Finally, as a performance reference for the Perlmutter system, we present SPEChpc results for the OpenACC programming model(See footnote 7) as shown in Table 7. We noticed significant performance differences between OpenMP and OpenACC outputs for some applications, especially **532.sph_exa** and **521.miniswp**. As mentioned before, a direct comparison of results from both the models should not and cannot be made without understanding the intricate details of feature implementations and understanding the reasoning behind performance gaps.

Listing 1.1 contains the OpenMP annotation added to **532.sph_exa**. We found that this memory allocation on the device was missing for the OpenMP offloading version, while it was present for the OpenACC version. The modified version is referenced in this document as **532.sph_exaM**[8]. In the original OpenMP version, because these pragmas were missing, every time these arrays were accessed in a target region they have to be allocated in the device. By adding these lines, the arrays are allocated in the device before multiple iterations of device kernel calls. In Perlmutter, while the original version does not execute correctly with Cray compiler (it is a memory allocation error), the modified version doesn't run correctly with NVIDIA and GNU Compilers (it is also a memory allocation error). In the case of Frontier, neither versions compile with GNU, but the error doesn't have anything to do with the modification, it is a compiler bug.

---

[8] zenodo.org/doi/10.5281/zenodo.12571032: SqPatch.hpp.diff.

Listing 1.1. These are the pragmas added to the benchmark **532.sph_exa**. The new benchmark is **532.sph_exaM**. These lines were added to the original file **SqPatch.hpp** on the function **resizeN(size_t size)**.

```
// OpenACC annotation present in the original code
#pragma acc exit data delete(hNptr, hNCptr)
// First OpenMP Directive added
#pragma omp target exit data map(delete: hNptr[:Nsze],
                                        hNCptr[:NCsze])

// OpenACC annotation present in the original code
#pragma acc enter data create(hNptr[:size*ngmax],
                              hNCptr[:size])
// Second OpenMP Directive added
#pragma omp target enter data map(alloc: hNptr[:size*ngmax],
                                         hNCptr[:size])
```

Table 7. OpenACC estimated **base run time** of SPEChpc tiny applications on Perlmutter with NVIDIA compiler.

Version	Estimate Base Time (seconds)								
	505 lbm	513 soma	518 tealeaf	519 clvleaf	521 miniswp	528 pot3d	532 sph_exa	534 hpgmgfv	weather
24.5	28.48	45.82	48.23	35.69	52.38	53.58	129.08	64.27	37.23

Discussion: We observed that it should not be concluded that one compiler is better over the other as the results largely depends on the applications and optimizations. Having said that, Cray demonstrated some of the best results. Furthermore, Cray's results on Perlmutter are very similar to the OpenACC results for **505.lbm**, **528.pot3d** and **535.weather**. Moreover, the results of **532.sph_exaM** for Cray compiler is similar to the OpenACC version of **532.sph_exa**. These also suggest that the large performance gaps for codes such as **521.miniswp** between OpenMP and OpenACC could be an implementation difference, not necessarily a compiler optimization difference. SPEChpc uses only 4.5 specification features, but as seen, the compilers are still having trouble, after almost 10 years of the release of the specification, to produce efficient code for all applications. Moreover, the performance is not as good as the OpenACC versions. As seen with **532.sph_exa**, the lack of performance of the applications may not be caused only by compiler optimization issues, but it could also be application implementation differences as a result of not using OpenMP features that compilers don't support or that their performance is low. The performance of larger versions of SPEChpc would correlate to the results shown here, but they would also depend on the network, and the performance of the MPI implementation. We expect that the performance per node would be similar, but we can not extrapolate to the performance of larger versions of the benchmark.

6 Conclusion

This paper sheds light on the pass/fail of OpenMP features from version 4.5 and above. We do so by building a CI/CD workflow comprising of OpenMP V&V, Smoke, HeCBench, and SPEChpc suites to automate the testing of OpenMP implementations with a goal to fail fast and provide feedback to LLVM compiler developers especially since several vendor compilers are LLVM-based. This paper further provides details of the current status of correctness of OpenMP compilers via the V&V testing infrastructure and tests running on Frontier, Perlmutter, and Sunspot. As we know, manual test creation is a time consuming process for developers; this challenge is currently being explored by using Large Language Models (LLM) for test generation [19]. The work also discusses the quality of OpenMP compiler implementations on different GPUs when using SPEChpc benchmarking suite. The discussion also offers suggestions and room for further implementation improvement.

Building on the workflow developed in this work, future works could include the implementation of "expected fail" testing, the continous development of tests as the specification evolves, and enabling developers to reproduce and debug problems effectively.

In conclusion, the OpenMP offloading features represent a crucial environment for the HPC community as the systems continue to evolve. The model has been bringing legacy and new applications to run on novel systems, which makes it time critical to closely track correctness and quality of implementations guiding the developers accordingly.

Acknowledgments. This research used resources of the OLCF at ORNL supported by the Office of Science of the U.S. DOE under Contract No. DE-AC05-00OR22725; used resources of the ALCF, a U.S. DOE Office of Science user facility at Argonne National Laboratory and is based on research supported by the U.S. DOE Office of Science-ASCR program, under Contract No. DE-AC02-06CH11357; used resources of NERSC, a U.S. DOE Office of Science User Facility located at LBNL, operated under Contract No. DE-AC02-05CH11231 using NERSC ERCAP0029463. This material is also based upon work supported by the U.S. DOE under Contract DE-FOA-0003177, S4PST: Next Generation Science Software Technologies Project.

References

1. AMD: AMD ROCm Smoke Tests. https://github.com/ROCm/aomp/tree/aomp-dev/test/smoke
2. Anderson, J., Burns, P., Milroy, D., Ruprecht, P., Hauser, T., Siegel, H.: Deploying RMACC summit: an HPC resource for the rocky mountain region, pp. 1–7, July 2017. https://doi.org/10.1145/3093338.3093379
3. Argonne National Laboratory: Argonne's aurora supercomputer breaks exascale barrier, May 2024. https://www.anl.gov/article/argonnes-aurora-supercomputer-breaks-exascale-barrier
4. Bak, S., et al.: Openmp application experiences: porting to accelerated nodes. Parallel Comput. **109**, 102856 (2022)

5. Bauman, P., et al.: Introduction to AMD GPU programming with hip. Presentation at Oak Ridge National Laboratory (2019). https://www.olcf.ornl.gov/calendar/intro-to-amd-gpu-programming-with-hip
6. Brunst, H., et al.: First experiences in performance benchmarking with the new SPEChpc 2021 suites. In: 2022 22nd International Symposium on Cluster, Cloud and Internet Computing (CCGrid), pp. 675–684. IEEE Computer Society, Los Alamitos, CA, USA, May 2022. https://doi.org/10.1109/CCGrid54584.2022.00077, https://doi.ieeecomputersociety.org/10.1109/CCGrid54584.2022.00077
7. Daley, C., Ahmed, H., Williams, S., Wright, N.: A case study of porting HPGMG from CUDA to OpenMP target offload. In: Milfeld, K., de Supinski, B.R., Koesterke, L., Klinkenberg, J. (eds.) IWOMP 2020. LNCS, vol. 12295, pp. 37–51. Springer, Cham (2020). https://doi.org/10.1007/978-3-030-58144-2_3
8. Denny, J.E., Lee, S., Vetter, J.S.: CLACC: translating OpenACC to OpenMP in clang. In: 2018 IEEE/ACM 5th Workshop on the LLVM Compiler Infrastructure in HPC (LLVM-HPC), pp. 18–29. IEEE (2018)
9. Huber, J., et al.: Efficient execution of OpenMP on GPUs. In: 2022 IEEE/ACM International Symposium on Code Generation and Optimization (CGO), pp. 41–52. IEEE (2022)
10. Huber, T., et al.: ECP SOLLVE: validation and verification testsuite status update and compiler insight for openMP. In: 2022 IEEE/ACM International Workshop on Performance, Portability and Productivity in HPC (P3HPC), pp. 123–135 (2022). https://doi.org/10.1109/P3HPC56579.2022.00017
11. Jin, Z., Vetter, J.S.: A benchmark suite for improving performance portability of the SYCL programming model. In: 2023 IEEE International Symposium on Performance Analysis of Systems and Software (ISPASS), pp. 325–327 (2023). https://doi.org/10.1109/ISPASS57527.2023.00041
12. John, M.M., Olsson, H.H., Bosch, J.: Towards MLOps: a framework and maturity model. In: 2021 47th Euromicro Conference on Software Engineering and Advanced Applications (SEAA), pp. 1–8 (2021). https://doi.org/10.1109/SEAA53835.2021.00050
13. Karlin, I., et al.: Early experiences porting three applications to OpenMP 4.5. In: Maruyama, N., de Supinski, B.R., Wahib, M. (eds.) IWOMP 2016. LNCS, vol. 9903, pp. 281–292. Springer, Cham (2016). https://doi.org/10.1007/978-3-319-45550-1_20
14. Kim, J., et al.: QMCPACK: an open source ab initio quantum Monte Carlo package for the electronic structure of atoms, molecules and solids. J. Phys.: Condens. Matter **30**(19), 195901 (2018)
15. Lambert, J., Monil, M.A.H., Lee, S., Malony, A.D., Vetter, J.S.: Leveraging compiler-based translation to evaluate a diversity of exascale platforms. In: 2022 IEEE/ACM International Workshop on Performance, Portability and Productivity in HPC (P3HPC), pp. 14–25 (2022). https://doi.org/10.1109/P3HPC56579.2022.00007
16. LLVM Compiler Infrastructure: lit - LLVM Integrated Tester. https://llvm.org/docs/CommandGuide/lit.html
17. LLVM Compiler Infrastructure: LLVM Test Suite. https://github.com/llvm/llvm-test-suite
18. LLVM Compiler Infrastructure: LNT infrastructure for performance testing. https://llvm.org/docs/lnt/tests.html
19. Munley, C., Jarmusch, A., Chandrasekaran, S.: LLM4VV: developing LLM-Driven testsuite for compiler validation. Futur. Gener. Comput. Syst. **160**, 1–13 (2024)

20. NVIDIA: CUDA. https://developer.nvidia.com/cuda-toolkit
21. Oak Ridge National Laboratory: Frontier supercomputer debuts as world's fastest, breaking exascale barrier, May 2022. https://www.ornl.gov/news/frontier-supercomputer-debuts-worlds-fastest-breaking-exascale-barrier
22. OpenACC Organization: OpenACC. https://www.openacc.org/
23. OpenMP Architecture Review Board: OpenMP application program interface version 4.0 (2013). https://www.openmp.org/wp-content/uploads/OpenMP4.0.0.pdf
24. OpenMP Architecture Review Board: OpenMP application program interface version 5.2 (2021). https://www.openmp.org/wp-content/uploads/OpenMP-API-Specification-5-2.pdf
25. ORNL and University of Delaware: OpenMP validation and verification suite. https://github.com/OpenMP-Validation-and-Verification/OpenMP_VV
26. Pennycook, S.J., Sewall, J.D., Hammond, J.R.: Evaluating the impact of proposed OpenMP 5.0 features on performance, portability and productivity. In: 2018 IEEE/ACM International Workshop on Performance, Portability and Productivity in HPC (P3HPC), pp. 37–46. IEEE (2018)
27. S4PST: Sustainability for Programming Systems and Tools: S4PST. https://ornl.github.io/events/s4pst2023/
28. Sampedro, Z., Holt, A., Hauser, T.: Continuous integration and delivery for HPC: using singularity and Jenkins. In: Proceedings of the Practice and Experience on Advanced Research Computing. PEARC '18, Association for Computing Machinery, New York, NY, USA (2018). https://doi.org/10.1145/3219104.3219147
29. SOLLVE: Scaling OpenMP With LLVm for Exascale Performance and Portability : SOLLVE. https://www.exascaleproject.org/research-project/sollve/
30. Standard Performance Evaluation Corporation: SPEChpc^{TM} 2021 benchmark suites. https://www.spec.org/hpc2021/
31. The Khronos Group: OpenCL. https://www.khronos.org/opencl/
32. Varrette, S., Bouvry, P., Cartiaux, H., Georgatos, F.: Management of an academic HPC cluster: the UL experience, July 2014. https://doi.org/10.1109/HPCSim.2014.6903792
33. Yu, L., Alégroth, E., Chatzipetrou, P., Gorschek, T.: A roadmap for using continuous integration environments. Commun. ACM **67**(6), 82–90 (2024). https://doi.org/10.1145/3631519

Evaluation of Directive-Based Programming Models for Stencil Computation on Current GPGPU Architectures

Baodi Shan[1](✉), Mauricio Araya-Polo[2], and Barbara Chapman[1]

[1] Stony Brook University, Stony Brook, NY 11794, USA
{baodi.shan,barbara.chapman}@stonybrook.edu
[2] TotalEnergies EP Research & Technology US, LLC, Houston, TX 77002, USA

Abstract. Stencil calculations are a widely-used computing pattern, and tracking the performance of such computing pattern on modern GPGPUs is of interest to the computational community. In this document we focus on how directive-based programming models profit from the GPGPUs computing power and how they compare with the native programming model. One major takeaway is that OpenMP and OpenACC are still behind native code but closing the gap with newer generations of accelerators and SW stack. In particular, to address programmability we do compare the development effort of implementing optimized kernels with all the above mentioned programming models. Finally, we further extend the analysis to cover power consumption aspects, which complements the programming and performance perspectives.

Keywords: Stencil Computation · OpenACC · OpenMP · Performance · Programmability · Power consumption

1 Introduction

HPC-based on General Purpose Graphic Processing Units (GPGPUs) has mostly replaced Central Processing Units (CPUs)-based computing, becoming the primary source of computational power for supercomputing systems. In the latest TOP500 supercomputer rankings released in June 2024 (top500.org), seventeen out of the twenty fastest systems use GPGPUs as accelerators, mostly made by NVIDIA and AMD. Therefore it is relevant to continue updating and optimizing workloads that rely on this kind of accelerators.

The evolution of GPGPUs architectures is driven by different markets/applications needs, it is unknown which and to what extent the new features might be useful for specific numerical workflows, this is another reason to evaluate how well-established workflows map to new hardware [16]. In this work's case, the target application is subsurface characterization [20], through wave equation solving, which at the core sports high-order stencil computations. Research on stencil computing continuously produces technical advances [2,7,18,19] given its importance for many scientific and industrial applications [3], from weather prediction [4] to earthquake modeling [11].

In this work, through performance evaluation of different programming models and data sizes, profiling analysis, and comparison of hardware parameters between GPGPUs, we provide suggestions for developers. Thus, this work has the following main contributions:

- On the comparison between OpenACC's async and OpenMP's nowait, we proposed an effective optimization strategy for asynchronously executing parallel regions, enabling the code to fully utilize the ability of the GPGPUs' multiple streams to execute concurrently. Compared with the original implementation, the performance of the enhanced code has been improved by up to **30%**.
- We compared the performance and portability of three different GPGPU-based programming models, and evaluated and analyzed the performance and changes of the three models on different generations of NVIDIA GPGPUs. Based on our evaluation results and analysis, we provide recommendations to developers of scientific programs using stencil computations.
- We compare the power consumption of Ampere and Hopper architectures under three different programming models. This reflected the relationship between energy consumption and performance.

The paper is organized as follows: Sect. 2 introduces stencil computation and relevant related work. Section 3 elaborates on the implementation of the stencil computation program using OpenACC and OpenMP, presents our newest optimization scheme and its performance on the A100 and H100. Section 4 compares the portability of three different programming models, by evaluating them on three generations of GPGPU's architectures. In Sect. 5 power consumption aspects are analyzed. Finally, in Sect. 6 conclusions and takeaways are summarized.

2 Stencil Computation and Related Work

Stencil computations are at the core of many scientific applications. The one under analysis in this computes the differential operators required by Finite Difference scheme to solve the wave equation, in this case an acoustic isotropic approximation of it. The implementation in this work build upon what was introduced in [10] and optimized versions tailored for GPGPUs presented in [15]. In this case, the spatial part of the wave equation is discretized using a 25-point stencil in 3D (8th order in space), with eight points in each direction plus the centre point, therefore the pattern has a characteristic 3D cross-shaped form.

Multiple works in the literature introduced implementations and optimization strategies for stencil computations. A selected few references relevant to our work are described as follows. The time skewing approach, as discussed in [21,22], enhances the performance of stencil computations by augmenting data reuse and

Table 1. System Specifications

GPU	H100	A100	T4
CPU	NVIDIA Grace	AMD EPYC 7F52	Intel(R) Xeon(R) 5217
Cores	16896	6912	2560
GRAM	96 GB	40 GB	16 GB
Memory Bandwidth	4TB/s	1555 GB/s	320 GB/s
CUDA Compiler	12.2	12.0	
OpenACC Compiler	NVHPC (nvc)		
OpenMP Compiler	NVHPC (nvc)		
GPU Driver	535.129.03	525.105.17	
Compiler Arch	sm_90	sm_80	sm_75

cache locality. Tiling is a popular technique where exchanging redundant computation along the boundaries of overlapped tiles decreases the required memory bandwidth [6,8]. An alternative strategy for accelerating computation is split tiling, as described in [5]. Instead of using overlapped tiles, which can induce significant amounts of redundant computation, split tiling computes points in two distinct phases. Nguyen et al. [12] propose a 3.5D blocking algorithm that blends 2.5D spatial blocking with 1D temporal blocking. 2.5D spatial blocking involves blocking in a 2D plane and streaming along a third dimension to increase data reuse, storing active 2D planes in GPGPU shared memory.

3 Exploration and Optimization of OpenACC and OpenMP Target Offloading

In this section, we will present and analyze the evaluation results of our stencil implementations with two directive-based parallel computing programming model. First, we introduce the evaluation setup along with two directive-based programming models. Second, we discuss their corresponding implementations and the new optimization strategies that we propose. Finally, we present the analysis of profiling on the Ampere and Hopper architectures.

3.1 Evaluation Setup and Programming Model

The primary testing platform is a NVIDIA Grace Hopper Superchip with NVIDIA GH200. In the comparative evaluations, we also utilized computing nodes equipped with A100 and T4. Refer to Table 1 for the hardware and software specifications of the systems.

OpenACC is a programming standard designed to simplify parallel computing, particularly for programming with accelerators like GPUs. It offers a directive-based programming model that lets developers indicate which parts of the code should run in parallel by inserting directives, without needing to specify how to parallelize in detail. The primary goal of OpenACC ([13]) is to provide a simple way to optimize and parallelize applications with minimal effort from the developer.

OpenMP is an application programming interface (API) that supports multi-platform shared memory multiprocessing programming in C, C++, and Fortran. OpenMP ([14]) provides a simple and flexible interface for developing parallel applications for platforms ranging from desktop computers to supercomputers. OpenMP's `target` directive is part of its support for offloading computation to accelerators, such as GPUs [1,9]. Currently, in the implementation of OpenMP in LLVM, the OpenMP target offloading support NVIDIA GPU, AMD GPU, Intel Phi and remote devices [17].

3.2 Implementations and Optimization on OpenACC and OpenMP Target Offloading

The original inner region implementations of the program in OpenACC and OpenMP are similar, both implementing parallelism at the outermost loop of the 3D data as shown in Fig. 1 and Fig. 2. The OpenACC implementation uses the directive #pragma acc loop gang vector collapse(3), while the OpenMP target offloading implementation uses #pragma omp target teams distribute parallel for simd collapse(3).

```
#pragma acc parallel
#pragma acc loop gang vector collapse(3)
for (llint i = x3; i < x4; ++i) {
    for (llint j = y3; j < y4; ++j) {
        for (llint k = z3; k < z4; ++k) {
            # Computation
        }}}
```

Fig. 1. OpenACC code for inner region

```
#pragma omp target teams distribute parallel for simd collapse(3)
for (llint i = x3; i < x4; ++i) {
    for (llint j = y3; j < y4; ++j) {
        for (llint k = z3; k < z4; ++k) {
            # Computation
        }}}
```

Fig. 2. OpenMP target offloading code for inner region

Both of these implementations face memory bandwidth bottlenecks and difficulties to hide latency, problems that asynchronous computation can effectively address. In CUDA, streams are used to implement asynchronous instructions provided by the host. In OpenACC and OpenMP, stream management is not possible with the same fine granularity as in CUDA. Alternatively, both OpenACC and OpenMP provide methods for implementing stream asynchronicity. For OpenACC, the async clause can be used to specify the CUDA stream ID. In the case of OpenMP, the nowait clause can be used to dispatch target tasks to the GPGPU, allowing the GPGPU to manage its own scheduling. In this process, each target task will be executed asynchronously.

Runtime Optimization 1: Fine-Grained Concurrent Kernels. In OpenACC, the parallel region is moved from the outermost loop to the second nested loop, and then uses the third nested loop to iterate over the stream IDs, thereby distributing by streams. This approach allows for different parallel regions to be executed asynchronously, particularly enabling memory read/write tasks and compute tasks from different parallel regions to effectively hide latency caused by insufficient bandwidth. However, adjusting the original parallel region from the third nested loop to the second nested loop means that the number of times the parallel region is executed, i.e., the number of CUDA kernels, has increased by several orders of magnitude (the specific increase depends on the size of the data). This implies an increase in kernels launch with corresponding streaming overhead, thus potentially producing performance degradation.

Fig. 3. Tracing results for OpenACC (Grid Size: 1024^3, 1000 iterations)

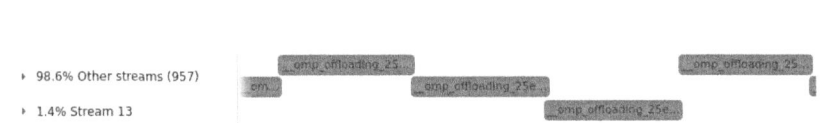

Fig. 4. Tracing results for OpenMP target offloading (Grid Size: 1024^3, 1000 iterations)

Due to the limited number of CUDA kernels that GPGPU can execute simultaneously, excessive CUDA streaming does not lead to greater overlap, meaning it does not bring effective concurrency. Therefore, we limited the number of CUDA streams available in OpenACC to **2** and ensured that the CUDA Stream IDs between two adjacent kernels are different. In this way, we can reduce the overhead of launching streams while ensuring concurrency. The tracing result provided by the NVIDIA Nsight System is shown in Fig. 3. It can be seen that

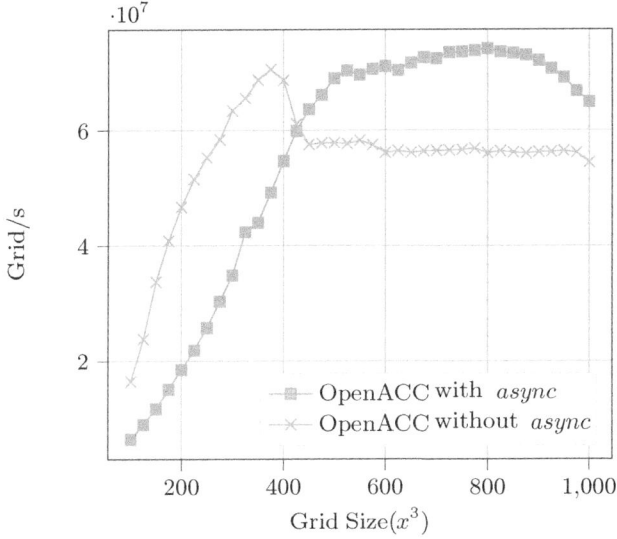

Fig. 5. Performance of OpenACC with and without *async* on A100

the program mainly uses two CUDA streams to perform the inner part of the computation, while other streams handle boundary computation.

Figure 5 shows performance of the async version of OpenACC and the original version of OpenACC under different grid sizes. In order to better reflect the computing power of the stencil computation program under different grid sizes, we did not use the number of floating-point operations per second (FLOPS) as the evaluation standard, but chose the number of grids processed per second (grid/s) as the performance reference indicator. It can be seen that when the grid size is large, the original version reach a performance bottleneck and the throughput does not increase with the grid size. But the asynchronous execution of parallel regions can effectively hide the latency caused by memory read/write and kernel launch, thereby improving performance.

In OpenMP target offloading, there is no directive equivalent to that in OpenACC that can specify CUDA streams. The asynchronous execution can only be indirectly achieved through the nowait clause.

Table 2. The kernel performance of asynchronous execution on the second layer loop in OpenMP and OpenACC.

	Kernel Time(us)	Cycles	Performance(GFLOPs)	Arithmetic Intensity
OpenMP	101.18	109660	381.254	0.88
OpenACC	35.74	38805	1079.255	0.88

Initially, the same code optimization as in the OpenACC version was used on the OpenMP implementation, i.e. reducing the target task to the second layer loop and making it execute asynchronously. However, compared with OpenACC, the reduced OpenMP kernel does not yield any performance improvement. On the contrary, we found that the same "small kernel" can be executed in 35us with OpenACC, while OpenMP requires more than 101us to complete. In terms of the aggregated kernel time, the OpenMP code using this optimization strategy has no improvement at all, but rather a significant decrease. The Table 2 shows the performance comparison between OpenMP kernel and OpenACC kernel when using the same approach. It can be seen that OpenMP target offloading shows significantly weaker performance when facing this relatively small kernel.

On the one hand, this behavior mainly comes from the differences in how OpenACC and OpenMP handle the working mechanisms of CUDA kernels. In OpenACC, the kernel code region is compiled into machine code by the compiler and then directly run on the GPGPU. However, the OpenMP target offloading region includes some necessary device runtime when running on the GPGPU. In OpenMP, this runtime code includes but is not limited to kernel launching, fine-grained memory management, and potential multi-device support. Particularly, with regards to fine-grained memory management, OpenMP target offloading supports loading necessary data into the shared memory of the GPGPU, which OpenACC does not support. This runtime support provided by OpenMP can effectively improve the program's running efficiency in some cases, but it backfires for the small kernels in this optimization scheme. This is because the additional runtime overhead on the GPGPU is hard to be hidden by the kernel code, and thus the runtime overhead becomes an unavoidable part of the execution time.

On the other hand, OpenMP target offloading has a non-negligible overhead for the creation and deletion of CUDA streams. Since the `nowait` clause cannot specify the CUDA stream ID, OpenMP target offloading can create at most as many CUDA streams as there are kernels. Figure 4 shows the tracing result of the OpenMP target offloading program in the Nsight System. It can be seen that the program has launched nearly 1000 CUDA streams, which brought significant overhead.

Runtime Optimization 2: Coarse-Grained Concurrent Kernels. The second performance optimization approach is to keep the original size of the target task unchanged, and make the inner loop and the boundary task execute asynchronously. Since the boundary task is significantly smaller than the inner task, the performance improvement yielded by this optimization method is relatively small.

The Fig. 6 shows the changes in execution time of the original version and the asynchronous version under different grid sizes. Unlike the optimization approach of reducing the kernel to make it execute asynchronously in OpenACC, this optimization method does not change the kernel itself. Therefore, in subsequent

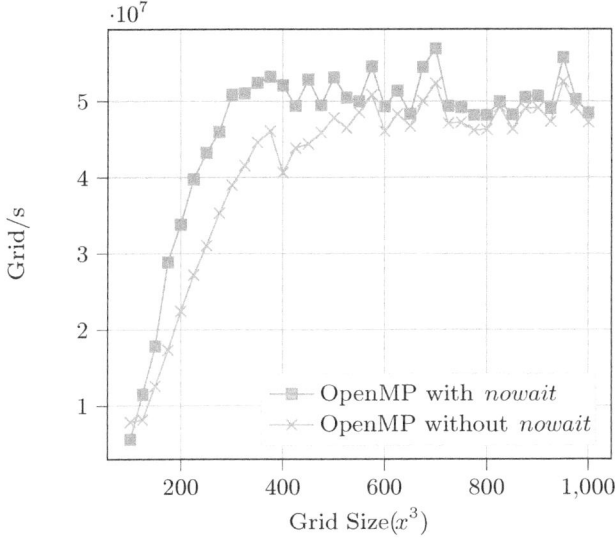

Fig. 6. Performance of OpenMP Target Offloading with and without *nowait* on A100

discussions, we will only address the optimized kernel and no longer distinguish between the two versions of the kernel.

Compilation Optimization. In addition, we further improved the performance of OpenACC programs by optimizing the number of registers. The number of registers affects the performance of GPGPU programs. On one hand, excessive use of registers may limit the number of parallel threads, thereby affecting performance; on the other hand, when there are not enough registers to store all variables, some variables need to be stored in local memory (which is part of global memory), which we refer to as spillover storage and loading. Excessive spillover storage and loading will also lead to a decrease in performance.

3.3 Performance and Profiling Results on OpenACC and OpenMP

Table 3 shows execution time for OpenACC, OpenACC-*async*, OpenMP on A100 and H100. The grid size used in the experiments is 1024^3, and the kernel allocates in total about 22.1 GB GPGPU memory. The number of time steps per experiments is 1000.

In Fig. 7, the implemented kernels are placed in the roofline plot close to optimal utilization of main memory for their respective arithmetic intensity, which aligns with previous publications ([7]) about similar kernels. Table 4 and Table 5 show memory profiling and computing profiling information respectively. These two profiling results are based on grid size of 1024^3 and 1000 time steps.

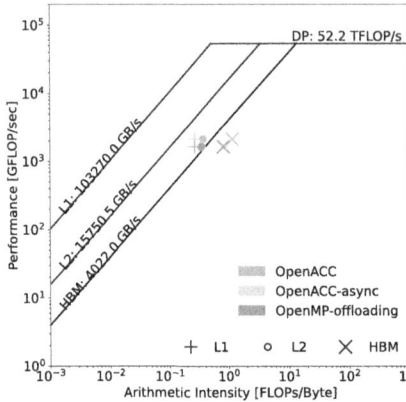

Fig. 7. Roofline Model of Minimod on H100. OpenACC-async and OpenMP are overlapping

Table 3. Execution time of OpenACC and OpenMP programs on A100 and H100 (Grid Size: 1024^3, 1000 iterations)

Programming Model	Device	Execution Time(s)
OpenACC	A100	53.188
	H100	23.196
OpenACC-async	A100	44.222
	H100	19.229
OpenMP	A100	58.568
	H100	29.527

Table 4. Profiling results of memory information of OpenACC and OpenMP code on A100 and H100 GPUs.

Kernel	Device	Memory Throughput Rate	Memory Throughput(GB/s)	L1 Hit Rate	L2 Hit Rate	Device Memory Read-/Write(Bytes)
OpenACC	A100	60.95%	947	42.97%	55.16%	47,612,893,312
	H100	60.22%	2,422	43.44%	45.31%	45,280,361,216
OpenACC-async	A100	56.18%	872	48.93%	48.41%	46,209,280
	H100	52.26%	2,097	46.13%	43.74%	44,710,400
OpenMP	A100	54.39%	845	47.04%	54.51%	46,086,569,472
	H100	30.03%	1,208	46.01%	56.66%	32,045,994,240

3.4 Comparative Analysis of OpenACC/MP on A100 and H100

The performance gap between OpenMP and OpenACC originates both from memory management and from differences in computational efficiency. As shown in Table 4, the memory throughput of OpenMP is significantly less than that of the OpenACC version, and yet the volume of memory read/write operations is not less than that of the OpenACC version, thus, memory read/write operations will introduce significant latency. As shown in Table 5, the elapsed cycles of OpenMP kernel are also significantly higher than the OpenACC version.

In addition, in OpenACC, the program can relatively automatically configure GPGPU-related settings, such as automatically adjusting the GPGPU's grid size according to the size of the data. OpenMP developers can manually select the grid size through num_teams. However, compared to OpenACC's automatic setting of grid Size, choosing ideal grid Size is difficult, and the optimal value often changes with problem size. In Fig. 5, the curve of OpenACC is smoother than the curve of OpenMP in Fig. 6, which indicates that OpenACC can make fuller and more reasonable use of GPGPU resources.

Table 5. Profiling results of compute information of OpenACC and OpenMP code on A100 and H100 GPUs.

Kernel	Device	Compute Throughput	SM Frequency	Elapsed Cycles	Theoretical Occupancy		Achieved	
					Occupancy	Active Warps Per SM	Occupancy	Active Warps Per SM
OpenACC	A100	40.87%	764,999,157.62	38,427,322	37	24	37	24
	H100	45.15%	1,529,167,787.04	28,593,676	37	24	37	24
OpenACC-async	A100	47.21%	765,073,370.74	40,523	31	20	27	17
	H100	48.40%	1,508,094,031.53	32,408	37	24	32	20
OpenMP	A100	42.83%	764,998,995.17	41,677,024	25	16	24	15
	H100	58.30%	1,529,855,754.88	40,585,290	25	16	23	14

4 Programming Models Comparison

4.1 Programmability and Portability of Different Programming Models

In terms of performance alone, within the NVIDIA GPU-based programming models, CUDA thanks to its fine-grained control over instructions and memory, as well as the vendor-specific implementation of certain instructions (such as __fmaf_rn), is far ahead when effectively exploited. However, when developing software other aspects needs to be considered, portability and implementation complexity should not be overlooked. Table 6 shows the LoC counts of different kernel implementations, OpenACC and OpenMP Target Offloading are less demanding than CUDA in terms of code length and implementation complexity. Further, portability-wise, OpenMP Target Offloading supports a variety of accelerators, making this programming model an excellent choice for HPC developers that are planning to deploy single code-base among multiple platforms.

Table 6. Lines of code (LoC) for the a single kernel implementation with different programming models for GPGPUs

Programming Model	Lines of Code
CUDA-opt1	142
CUDA-opt2	172
OpenACC	71
OpenMP Target Offloading	69

4.2 Performance Comparison of Different Generations of NVIDIA GPGPUs on Multiple Programming Models

We evaluate the performance on Turing (T4), Ampere (A100) and Hopper (H100) architectures. We compare the execution time for 1000 time steps on a 3D grid of size 700^3, the results can be seen in Table 7. We also calculated the performance differences of different models on different generations of GPGPUs and made some interesting findings. As can be seen from the last three rows of Table 7, as new generations of GPGPUs are introduced, the gap between the three programming models is gradually narrowing. Compared to the Turing, the performance of the OpenACC version on the Hopper has increased by 13.0×, while the performance of the OpenMP version has achieved an 14.4× increase; the optimized CUDA version, however, only saw a 9.4× improvement with respect Turing baseline.

Table 7. Execution time of same kernel implemented on different programming models on three generations of NVIDIA GPGPUs

	Turing	Ampere	Hopper
CUDA	31.775 s	5.706 s	3.364 s
OpenACC	81.718 s	11.260 s	6.276 s
OpenMP	139.358 s	18.012 s	9.651 s
(OpenACC - CUDA)/OpenACC	0.611	0.493	0.464
(OpenMP - CUDA)/OpenMP	0.772	0.683	0.651
(OpenACC - OpenMP)/OpenMP	0.414	0.375	0.349

Although the performance of OpenMP target offloading and OpenACC is off by 3× and 2× the optimized CUDA version, this is a result obtained at the expense of portability. The optimized CUDA version in the chart is selected from a massive number of CUDA implementations, and selecting the optimal CUDA version requires a costly grid-like search, further in terms of code length and debugging difficulty. Therefore, we believe that OpenMP and OpenACC, whose performance continues to improve along with newer GPGPUs generations and compiler progress, are becoming development options worth considering when portability is a must.

In terms of architectural comparison, we use the rate of improvement (ri) as metric, it is defined as

$$ri(Arch_{i+1}|Arch_i, prog\_model) = \frac{time\ Arch_i}{time\ Arch_{i+1}} \quad (1)$$

It remarkable that ri(Ampere|Turing, CUDA) is 5.6, which is ahead of ri(Hopper|Ampere, CUDA) = 1.7. The highest ri computed from Table 7 is ri(Ampere|Turing, OpenMP) = 7.7, and both OpenACC and OpenMP achieve higher ri on Ampere versus Hopper when comparing with CUDA. This last finding support our claim that these programming models are catching up with CUDA.

5 Power Consumption Analysis

In this section, we evaluated the power consumption of Ampere and Hopper architectures when running the presented kernels. Figure 8 shows the energy consumption curves of two different GPGPUs across three distinct programming models. The grid size of this evaluation is 1024^3, and the number of timesteps for CUDA is 10000, and for OpenACC/OpenMP is 5000.

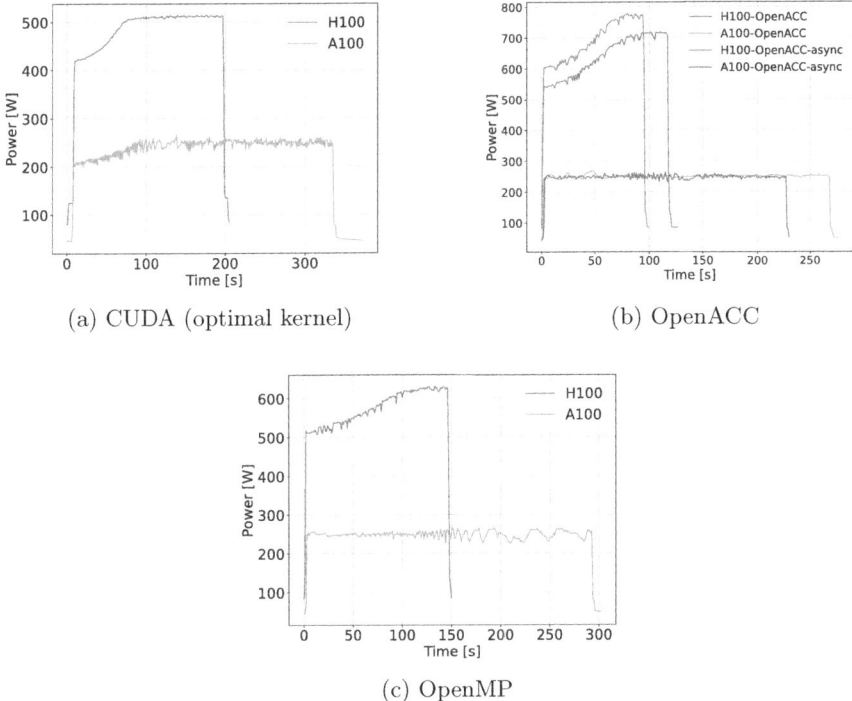

Fig. 8. Power consumption on Ampere and Hopper across different programming models

The measurements revealed that the H100 GPU tends to consume more energy for equivalent computational tasks compared to the A100. This increased energy consumption is particularly evident for OpenMP Target Offloading and OpenACC (up to 3× the power consumption, see Fig. 8.b) implementations. However, a notable advantage of the H100 is its time to solution efficiency, where it significantly reduces computing time for similar tasks. On the CUDA programming model side, both GPGPUs showed a significant increase in power consumption during the peak computational phases of the stencil computations. However, the A100 GPU maintained a more stable energy profile. During the OpenACC power consumption evaluation (Fig. 8.b), unlike the behavior with CUDA implementations, the H100 exhibited greater fluctuations in energy consumption compared to the A100. This observation suggests that NVIDIA's newer Hopper architecture may not be as refined in energy management for OpenACC as it is for Ampere. Notice that OpenACC-async version consumes more energy but in return it finished the task quicker.

The outcomes observed with OpenMP (Fig. 8.c) are akin to those witnessed with CUDA (Fig. 8.a), wherein the energy consumption fluctuations of the H100 are relatively stable. Overall, plenty of room for the application and SW stack to improve and take better advantage of the Hopper architecture. For instance, for the CUDA implementation, time to solution reduced from 340 s to 200 s (1.7×) but the power consumption raised from 250W to 510W (2×), so at least 0.3× (power to time solution ratio) to catch-up.

6 Conclusion

Performance evaluation of optimized 3D stencil kernels was conducted on two directive-based programming models for the latest generation GPGPUs. Our findings indicate that the H100 demonstrates performance improvements of up to 58% compared to the previous GPU generation. Simultaneously, we proposed CUDA stream-based asynchronous execution strategies for the OpenACC and OpenMP of stencil computation programs, resulting in performance enhancements of up to 30% over the original versions.

We also compared the performance and portability of the three programming models on multiple GPGPU generations. Our observations reveal that as architectures and performance progress, the performance gap between OpenMP, OpenACC, and optimized CUDA versions narrows. Particularly, in scenarios demanding portability, OpenMP and OpenACC are gradually becoming more viable alternatives.

Finally, in terms of power consumption, computing performance is not quite catching up with the increase in energy spent during computation, ecosystem (compilers and runtime) development effort is required to address this issue.

Acknowledgements. We would like to thank TotalEnergies E&P Research and Technologies US for their support of this work.

References

1. Bak, S., et al.: OpenMP application experiences: porting to accelerated nodes. Parallel Comput. **109**, 102856 (2022). https://doi.org/10.1016/j.parco.2021.102856
2. Denzler, A., et al.: Casper: accelerating stencil computations using near-cache processing. IEEE Access **11**, 22136–22154 (2023)
3. Dubey, A.: Stencils in scientific computations. In: Proceedings of the Second Workshop on Optimizing Stencil Computations, p. 57. WOSC '14, Association for Computing Machinery, New York, NY, USA (2014). https://doi.org/10.1145/2686745.2686756
4. Fuhrer, O., et al.: Towards a performance portable, architecture agnostic implementation strategy for weather and climate models. Supercomput. Front. Innov. Int. J. **1**(1), 45–62 (2014). https://doi.org/10.14529/jsfi140103

5. Grosser, T., Cohen, A., Kelly, P.H.J., Ramanujam, J., Sadayappan, P., Verdoolaege, S.: Split tiling for GPUs: automatic parallelization using trapezoidal tiles. In: Proceedings of the 6th Workshop on General Purpose Processor Using Graphics Processing Units, pp. 24–31. GPGPU-6, Association for Computing Machinery, New York, NY, USA (2013). https://doi.org/10.1145/2458523.2458526
6. Holewinski, J., Pouchet, L.N., Sadayappan, P.: High-performance code generation for stencil computations on GPU architectures. In: Proceedings of the 26th ACM International Conference on Supercomputing, pp. 311–320. ICS '12, Association for Computing Machinery, New York, NY, USA (2012).https://doi.org/10.1145/2304576.2304619
7. Jacquelin, M., Araya-Polo, M., Meng, J.: Scalable distributed high-order stencil computations. In: SC22: International Conference for High Performance Computing, Networking, Storage and Analysis, pp. 1–13. IEEE (2022). https://doi.org/10.1109/SC41404.2022.00035
8. Krishnamoorthy, S., Baskaran, M., Bondhugula, U., Ramanujam, J., Rountev, A., Sadayappan, P.: Effective automatic parallelization of stencil computations. In: Proceedings of the 28th ACM SIGPLAN Conference on Programming Language Design and Implementation, pp. 235–244. PLDI '07, Association for Computing Machinery, New York, NY, USA (2007). https://doi.org/10.1145/1250734.1250761
9. Lu, W., et al.: Towards efficient remote OpenMP offloading. In: Klemm, M., de Supinski, B.R., Klinkenberg, J., Neth, B. (eds.) OpenMP in a Modern World: From Multi-device Support to Meta Programming. IWOMP 2022. LNCS, vol. 13527, pp. 17–31. Springer, Cham (2022). https://doi.org/10.1007/978-3-031-15922-0_2
10. Meng, J., Atle, A., Calandra, H., Araya-Polo, M.: Minimod: a finite difference solver for seismic modeling (2020)
11. Moczo, P., Kristek, J., Gális, M.: The Finite-Difference Modelling of Earthquake Motions: Waves and Ruptures. Cambridge University Press, Cambridge (2014). https://doi.org/10.1017/CBO9781139236911
12. Nguyen, A., Satish, N., Chhugani, J., Kim, C., Dubey, P.: 3.5-D blocking optimization for stencil computations on modern CPUs and GPUs. In: SC'10: Proceedings of the 2010 ACM/IEEE International Conference for High Performance Computing, Networking, Storage and Analysis, pp. 1–13. IEEE (2010)
13. OpenACC-Standard.org: Openacc (2023). https://www.openacc.org/. Accessed 14 Aug 2023
14. OpenMP.org: Openmp (2023). https://www.openmp.org/. Accessed 14 Aug 2023
15. Sai, R., Mellor-Crummey, J., Meng, X., Araya-Polo, M., Meng, J.: Accelerating high-order stencils on GPUs. In: 2020 IEEE/ACM Performance Modeling, Benchmarking and Simulation of High Performance Computer Systems (PMBS), pp. 86–108 (2020). https://doi.org/10.1109/PMBS51919.2020.00014
16. Shan, B., Araya-Polo, M.: Evaluation of programming models and performance for stencil computation on current GPU architectures (2024). https://arxiv.org/abs/2404.04441
17. Shan, B., Araya-Polo, M., Malik, A.M., Chapman, B.: MPI-based remote OpenMP offloading: a more efficient and easy-to-use implementation. In: Proceedings of the 14th International Workshop on Programming Models and Applications for Multicores and Manycores, pp. 50–59. PMAM'23 (2023). https://doi.org/10.1145/3582514.3582519
18. Sun, B., Li, M., Yang, H., Xu, J., Luan, Z., Qian, D.: Adapting combined tiling to stencil optimizations on sunway processor. CCF Trans. High Perform. Comput. 1–12 (2023)

19. Sun, Q., Liu, Y., Yang, H., Jiang, Z., Luan, Z., Qian, D.: StencilMART: predicting optimization selection for stencil computations across GPUs. In: 2022 IEEE International Parallel and Distributed Processing Symposium (IPDPS), pp. 875–885. IEEE (2022)
20. Tylor-Jones, T., Azevedo, L.: A Practical Guide to Seismic Reservoir Characterization. Springer, Cham (2023). https://doi.org/10.1007/978-3-030-99854-7
21. Wonnacott, D.: Using time skewing to eliminate idle time due to memory bandwidth and network limitations. In: Proceedings 14th International Parallel and Distributed Processing Symposium. IPDPS 2000, pp. 171–180 (2000). https://doi.org/10.1109/IPDPS.2000.845979
22. Wonnacott, D.: Achieving scalable locality with time skewing. Int. J. Parallel Program. **30** (1999). https://doi.org/10.1023/A:1015460304860

Tools

Finding Equivalent OpenMP Fortran and C/C++ Code Snippets Using Large Language Models

Naveed Sekender[1], Pei-Hung Lin[2(✉)], and Chunhua Liao[2]

[1] University of California, Davis, CA 95616, USA
nsekender@ucdavis.edu
[2] Lawrence Livermore National Laboratory, Livermore, CA 94550, USA
{lin32,liao6}@llnl.gov

Abstract. This paper investigates the feasibility of using Large Language Models (LLMs) to identify semantically equivalent code snippets across different programming languages. Motivated by the need for cross-language translation datasets between OpenMP Fortran and C/C++, this study aims to determine the optimal LLMs and methodology for finding equivalent OpenMP Fortran vs. C/C++ code pairs. We propose a novel approach involving: (1) the construction of a ground truth dataset using DataRaceBench, (2) experimentation with multiple commercial and open-weight LLMs, (3) comparison of two distinct methods (code embedding-based cosine similarity analysis vs. question-answering prompting), and (4) impact analysis of code preprocessing techniques (comment removal vs. inclusion). Our preliminary evaluation encompasses performance metrics and overhead analysis. The findings provide a systematic understanding of LLMs' capabilities in cross-language code snippet identification, ultimately offering actionable recommendations for practitioners seeking to leverage these models for automated dataset generation.

Keywords: OpenMP · Large Language Models · Code Similarity · DataRaceBench · Cross-Language Code Equivalence

1 Introduction

OpenMP, a crucial standard for parallel programming on shared memory systems, is widely used in high-performance computing (HPC) communities to develop scalable parallel applications in languages like C, C++, and Fortran. Recently, there has been a growing interest in the HPC community in leveraging large language models (LLMs) [15] for code translation between OpenMP Fortran and C/C++ to facilitate the migration of legacy codes. However, creating training and evaluation datasets with equivalent OpenMP Fortran and C/C++ code pairs is challenging [8].

Recent advancements in Large Language Models, including GPT-4 [2], Gemini [13], and StarCoder [9], have shown significant potential in understanding and generating code. These models can create dense vector representations (embeddings) that encapsulate the semantic meanings of code snippets, facilitating the identification of semantically similar code fragments across different languages. Furthermore, LLMs like OpenAI GPT-4 Turbo, GPT-4o, and open source models such as GPT-Neo [3] and Llama3-8b [1] can answer questions about code equivalence using natural language prompting. Therefore, one may exploit LLMs to automatically extract equivalent OpenMP Fortran and C/C++ code snippets from existing large source code corpus such as the Stack v2 [12].

This research explores the capabilities of LLMs in identifying equivalent code snippets across Fortran and C/C++ within the OpenMP domain. The study addresses key research questions: 1) To what extent can various LLMs effectively identify semantic similarities between OpenMP code snippets written in Fortran and C/C++? 2) How does preprocessing, specifically comment removal, impact the accuracy of code similarity detection using LLMs? 3) What are the comparative advantages of utilizing LLMs through embedding-based methods versus direct prompting for detecting code snippet equivalence? 4) What is the associated overhead of using LLMs processing code snippets to generate code equivalence analysis results?

Our approach starts with the creation of a reference dataset based on DataRaceBench [10] as the ground truth of equivalent code snippet detection. We then select a set of language models to experiment with two different ways of exploiting LLMs: using embeddings or direct prompting. We also study the impact of source code comments for code equivalence checking across different programming languages. Finally, we assess the models' performance and overhead.

This paper has the following contributions:

- We create a novel dataset with both positive and negative equivalent code pairs across OpenMP Fortran and C/C++ languages.
- We benchmark a set of LLMs using two different methods to extract equivalent analysis results. The first method involves cosine similarity computing based on embeddings generated by LLMs while the second method uses question answering based on direct prompting.
- We conduct an impact analysis of source code comments in the context of equivalence code pair analysis.
- We evaluate the models with performance and overhead metrics and provide actionable suggestions.

The findings from this study offer valuable insights for enhancing code similarity detection, which is essential for applications such as code translation, plagiarism detection, and code search within the OpenMP and broader HPC domain. By evaluating both open-source and proprietary models, we highlight the strengths and limitations of different approaches, emphasizing the importance of scalable and open-source solutions in HPC.

2 Background and Motivation

In this section, we briefly discuss the background and motivation of this paper.

2.1 HPC Code Migration from Fortran to C++

HPC has evolved significantly, with OpenMP emerging as a key standard for parallel programming on shared memory systems. OpenMP directives, used in languages like C, C++, and Fortran, facilitate the development of scalable parallel applications. For some code teams, migrating from OpenMP Fortran codes to equivalent OpenMP C++ codes might be desired due to various technical and organizational reasons.

Technically, C++ often has more advanced compilers and performance tools that might offer better code optimization opportunities. Modern C++ language features such as lambda expressions, smart pointers, and advanced template meta-programming can enable more portable, efficient, and expressive parallel codes, including those using RAJA or Kokkos. C++ applications also have access to the C++ Standard Library (STL) and many other modern HPC C++ libraries. C++ often offers better access to low-level hardware features, including those available on GPUs, for better performance optimizations.

Organizationally, there are more C++ developers available compared to Fortran, making it easier to hire new talent and maintain the code base. There is also a larger C++ community to better support C++ code development.

2.2 Large Language Models and HPC Code Analysis and Refactoring

Modern large language models, such as GPT-4 by OpenAI, have revolutionized the field of natural language processing (NLP) and beyond by demonstrating unprecedented capabilities in understanding and generating human language. These models are built using deep learning architectures, particularly transformer models, that enable them to process vast amounts of text data. By leveraging billions of parameters and training on diverse datasets, these models are capable of performing a wide range of tasks with remarkable fluency and coherence. The ability to understand context, generate human-like text, and even engage in complex reasoning makes large language models versatile tools applicable across various domains.

One of the most promising applications of large language models is in the domain of HPC software development [4,5], particularly in understanding and refactoring source code. These models can analyze and comprehend code in multiple programming languages, making them invaluable for tasks such as code review, bug detection, and automated documentation. By understanding the semantics and structure of source code, large language models can provide meaningful insights and suggestions to developers, thereby enhancing productivity and code quality. They can also assist developers in transforming and optimizing HPC code. A recent study [8] has demonstrated that it is feasible to fine-tune open-weight LLMs to enable translation between OpenMP Fortran and C/++ code snippets. However, generating large-scale datasets for training and evaluating such cross-language translation models remains a challenge.

2.3 Code Equivalence Analysis and LLMs

Identifying equivalent code snippets across different programming languages in HPC has many valuable applications [14]. First of all, cross-language code equivalence checking enhances the effectiveness of code search tools, enabling the reuse of existing solutions across different projects and languages. This is especially beneficial in large code repositories where similar functionality may be implemented in multiple languages. By identifying equivalent snippets, developers can avoid redundant implementations and leverage existing, tested code. One might also build large-scale datasets enabling OpenMP Fortran vs. C/++ code translation using LLMs.

Secondly, in multi-language projects, ensuring that code changes and updates are consistently applied across different languages is crucial. Cross-language equivalence checking ensures that an update in a C++ codebase, for example, is reflected accurately in the corresponding Fortran code, maintaining consistency and reducing the risk of bugs.

Lastly, by comparing code snippets against databases of known issues, LLMs can detect potential security vulnerabilities and suggest best practices. This proactive approach to code quality ensures that security and performance standards are maintained across different languages.

Internally, LLMs process input (text or code) and generate corresponding dense vector representations, called embeddings. These vectors capture semantic meanings in a high-dimensional space. One can check the semantic similarity between code pairs using cosine similarity, Euclidean distance, dot product, or other similar metrics. This method can even be agnostic to the programming language used, as different programming languages may express similar algorithmic semantics. Alternatively, LLMs support question-answering interactions with users via natural language prompting. One might directly frame the problem of code equivalence analysis as a question, asking if two code snippets are semantically equivalent.

However, with the many choices of different LLMs and various ways to obtain equivalence analysis, we are curious about which model and method might be most effective in identifying equivalent OpenMP Fortran vs. C/C++ code snippets.

3 Methodology

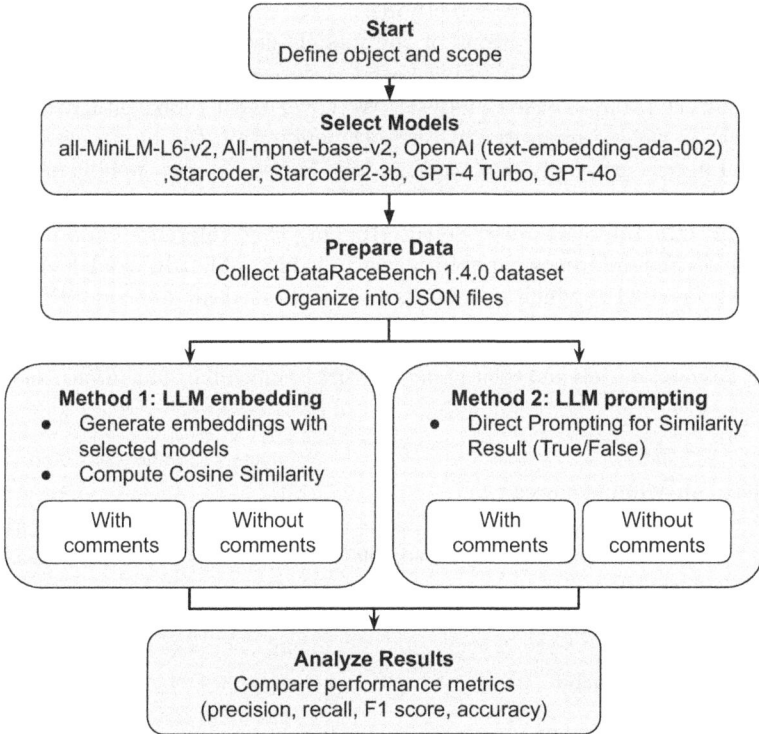

Fig. 1. Flowchart of the experiment steps

The paper designs a set of experiments to answer key research questions (mentioned in Sect. 1) about using LLMs to find equivalent OpenMP Fortran and C/C++ code snippets.

As shown in Fig. 1, our experiments start with the selection of a set of representative models, followed by the dataset preparation based on DataRaceBench 1.4.0 [10,11]. After that, this study aims to benchmark various LLMs to identify similar code snippets derived from the DataRaceBench dataset. It evaluates the effectiveness of two methods of using LLMs for detecting equivalent code snippets. For each method, two versions of the code snippets are used: one with source comments and one without them. Finally, we analyze the results, including accuracies, F-1 scores, overhead, and so on. We elaborate on these steps in the following subsections.

3.1 Models Used

In our study, we employ multiple language models to assess the similarity between code snippets. These models differ widely in parameter sizes, architectures, dimensions, and access methods.

Table 1 lists the specifications of the models used. Two categories of models are selected: one for embedding-based code equivalence analysis, and the other for direct prompt-based analysis. We cover both representative commercial models as well as open-weight ones. Depending on the model used, we use either API access or locally deployed models. For some open-weight models, we may also access them through Hugging Face due to the difficulties of deploying them locally. HF Inference refers to the Hugging Face Inference endpoint, which provides real-time inference capabilities with dedicated hardware. HF API refers to Hugging Face API, which provides access to hosted models via API calls.

Table 1. Selected models and their parameter sizes, embedding dimensions, and access methods.

Category	Model	Parameters	Dimensions	Access
Embeddings	all-MiniLM-L6-v2	22M	384	HF API
	all-mpnet-base-v2	109M	768	HF API
	OpenAI (text-embedding-ada-002)	350M	1536	OpenAI API
	Starcoder	15.5B	6144	Local
	Starcoder2-3b	3B	3072	Local
Prompting	GPT-4o	175B	N/A	OpenAI API
	GPT-4 Turbo	Not specified	N/A	OpenAI API
	GPT-Neo	2.7B	2560	HF API
	Llama-3-8b	8B	4096	HF API

Each model has unique characteristics tailored to specific tasks. For example, all-MiniLM-L6-v2 and all-mpnet-base-v2 are versatile tools for a range of text-based applications, while Starcoder and Starcoder2-3b are specifically optimized for coding-related tasks. GPT-4o, GPT-4 Turbo, GPT-Neo, and Llama3-8b are utilized for their strong capabilities in language generation and understanding, making them suitable for evaluating code snippet equivalence using LLM prompts.

3.2 Dataset Preparation

One of the main challenges in assessing a model's capability for equivalence analysis is how to prepare datasets that include ground truth. We leverage an existing OpenMP benchmark, DataRaceBench, to create a new dataset for equivalence analysis. The new dataset is named DRB-EQ. The goal of DRB-EQ is to contain two subsets of code snippet pairs between OpenMP Fortran and C/C++: one subset with equivalent pairs while the other with different pairs.

DataRaceBench [10,11], developed by Lawrence Livermore National Laboratory (LLNL), is a comprehensive benchmark suite designed to evaluate the performance of tools and techniques for detecting data races in OpenMP programs. This dataset includes a variety of compilable microbenchmarks written in languages such as C/C++ and Fortran, specifically annotated to indicate the presence or absence of data races. The dataset includes a range of complexities, from simple loops to advanced algorithms, covering functionalities such as sorting algorithms, matrix operations, and stencil computations. By providing a standardized set of examples, DataRaceBench facilitates the development and comparison of different approaches to identifying and analyzing data race conditions in parallel computing environments.

DataRaceBench 1.4.0 comprises 172 Fortran (.f95) and 209 C (.c) code snippets. These programs follow a specific naming convention (e.g., DRB001-antidep1-orig-yes.f95), indicating identifier, dependency type, status, and data race presence, which aids in systematic organization and referencing.

For our study, we utilized the first 168 snippets from each language (DRB001 to DRB168) due to their functional equivalence across Fortran and C/C++. They are designed to represent similar OpenMP coding patterns using Fortran or C/C++. There are a few exceptions such as DRB041-3mm-parallel-no.c, DRB042-3mm-tile-no.c, DRB055-jacobi2d-parallel-no.c, and DRB056-jacobi2d-tile-no.c. These snippets are excluded because there are no equivalent Fortran versions. Snippets beyond DRB168 were excluded as they differ between the two languages.

To generate pairs of different OpenMP Fortran vs. C/C++ snippets, we leverage the existing labels of DataRaceBench. These labels indicate high-level categories of OpenMP programs, such as unresolvable dependencies, missing data sharing clauses, missing synchronization, SIMD data races, accelerator data races, and so on. While we cannot conclude that two programs from the same high-level category are equivalent, if two programs are from different categories, they must be different since they represent distinct OpenMP code patterns.

For instance, consider a C snippet named DRB001-antidep1-orig-yes.c categorized under the Unresolvable dependencies category. This snippet would be compared against a Fortran snippet from a different category, such as DRB011-minusminus-orig-yes.f95, which belongs to the Missing synchronization category. This approach ensures that the comparisons are conducted between code snippets that are fundamentally different in terms of their category, thereby eliminating any potential bias that could arise from comparing snippets within the same category.

In the end, DRB-EQ has 165 equivalent pairs and 165 different pairs. They serve as the ground truth for evaluating LLMs in code equivalence analysis. To efficiently manage the snippets in DRB-EQ, we employed a specific naming convention: For equivalent pairs of programs, such as DRB001-antidep1-orig-yes.f95 and DRB001-antidep1-orig-yes.c, we assigned names ranging from 1a to 164a. The suffix 'a' indicates that the snippets in these pairs are expected to be equivalent. For the different pairs, they are named from 1b to 164b, with 'b' indicating that they are fundamentally different.

3.3 Code Variants With or Without Comments

Source code comments may either positively or negatively impact code equivalence analysis, depending on their consistency with the code and the ratio of comments to code. Good and consistent comments can improve LLMs' understanding of the code, while outdated or distracting comments may mislead LLMs. Some models may be trained with source code comments preserved, while others may have comments stripped off.

To study the impact of source code comments on equivalence analysis, we prepared two versions of the DRB-EQ dataset: one with original comments kept intact and the other with comments removed. For C/C++ DRB-EQ programs, we implemented a Python program to remove single-line (//) and multi-line (/* */) comments in C code. For Fortran programs, we removed comments marked by !, C, c, or *, while preserving OpenMP directives.

The ultimate goal of this research is to identify semantic similarities between Fortran and C/C++ code snippets, not similarities in the comments. To ensure the analysis focuses on actual code structure and semantics, removing comments by default may be a reasonable choice. This ensures LLMs evaluate the true code logic, leading to more accurate identification of equivalent code snippets.

3.4 Using Two Methods to Determine Code Snippet Equivalence

We use two different methods to obtain equivalence results of two code snippets. The first method uses the LLM embeddings, generating a floating point cosine similarity number (of a value between 0.0 to 1.0) first and then using a threshold (such as 0.8) to determine if the code snippets are equivalent. We split this into two different experiments: one with code comments and one with comments removed, as described earlier.

The Python code that extracts embedding looks like the following:

```
import openai
openai.api_key = 'your-api-key-here'
embedding = openai.Embedding.create
    (input="code here", model="text-embedding-ada-002")
```

We calculate cosine similarity once embeddings (in the form of vectors) are obtained, as follows:

$$\text{Cosine Similarity} = \frac{\mathbf{A} \cdot \mathbf{B}}{\|\mathbf{A}\|\|\mathbf{B}\|}$$

where $\mathbf{A}$ and $\mathbf{B}$ represent the embedding of each code snippet. A threshold is needed to decide if a pair is considered equivalent based on the similarity score between 0.0 and 1.0.

The second method prompts several LLMs to assess whether pairs of code snippets are equivalent. Specifically, we provided each LLM with 165 pairs of code snippets (1a to 165a labeled TRUE and 1b to 165b labeled FALSE). The task was to output 1 if the LLM believed the code snippets were equivalent and 0 otherwise.

The prompt used for this method is given below:

```
Determine if the two code snippets are equivalent.
OpenMP C: {code_snippet_1}
OpenMP Fortran: {code_snippet_2}
Are the two code snippets equivalent? Answer 'yes' or 'no'.
```

4 Preliminary Results

We present preliminary results of our experiments in this section.

4.1 Hardware Configuration

The experiments were conducted using two distinct computing systems, each selected based on the specific demands of the computational tasks and models involved. For computationally intensive tasks and large-scale models like Star-Coder, we utilized the Lassen supercomputer at Lawrence Livermore National Laboratory. Lassen is equipped with high-performance IBM Power9 processors and NVIDIA Volta V100 GPUs, delivering a peak performance of 23 petaflops, making it ideal for handling large models requiring significant memory and processing power. For less intensive tasks and convenience, a personal laptop, featuring 24 GB DDR5 RAM, an Intel i5-13420H processor, and an NVIDIA RTX 3050 6 GB GPU, is employed for running smaller models via the Hugging Face and OpenAI APIs. This setup provided ease of use and sufficient computational capabilities for models with lower resource demands. This dual-setup approach allowed us to efficiently manage computational resources while achieving the desired outcomes for various experiments.

4.2 Classification Metrics

We briefly explain the metrics used to evaluate the performance of similarity analysis. For each code pair, there are four possible outcomes based on whether the analysis result matches the ground truth (whether the codes are equivalent or not): True Positive (TP), False Positive (FP), True Negative (TN), and False Negative (FN). A TP occurs when the analysis correctly identifies a code pair labeled as equivalent. An FP occurs when the analysis incorrectly labels a code pair as equivalent when it is actually labeled as not equivalent. Similarly, we can define true negative and false negative cases. Based on the counts of these categories, four metrics can be computed: precision, recall, accuracy, and F1 score.

Precision measures how many of the pairs labeled as equivalent by the analysis are actually equivalent.

$$\text{Precision} = \frac{\text{TP}}{\text{TP} + \text{FP}}$$

Recall measures how many of the actual equivalent pairs were correctly identified by the analysis.

$$\text{Recall} = \frac{\text{TP}}{\text{TP} + \text{FN}}$$

Accuracy measures the overall correctness of the analysis, considering both equivalent and non-equivalent pairs.

$$\text{Accuracy} = \frac{\text{TP} + \text{TN}}{\text{TP} + \text{FP} + \text{TN} + \text{FN}}$$

F1 Score is the harmonic mean of precision and recall, providing a single score that balances both.

$$\text{F1 Score} = 2 \times \frac{\text{Precision} \times \text{Recall}}{\text{Precision} + \text{Recall}}$$

These metrics help us understand the effectiveness of the similarity analysis in correctly identifying equivalent and non-equivalent code pairs.

4.3 Results Using Embedding and Cosine Similarity Scores

For the DRB-EQ ground truth pairs labeled 1a to 165a (TRUE) and 1b to 165b (FALSE), we calculated the cosine similarity for each pair. Based on the cosine similarity threshold being tested, we evaluated the precision, recall, F1 score, and accuracy by determining TP (True Positive), FP (False Positive), FN (False Negative), and TN (True Negative).

We experimented with three different thresholds to determine the most effective ones in identifying equivalent or different code snippets. The LLMs utilized in this embedding study include all-mpnet-base-v2, all-MiniLM-L6-v2, OpenAI (text-embedding-ada-002), Starcoder, and Starcoder 2-3b. We used the cosine similarity thresholds of 0.6, 0.7, 0.8, and 0.9.

The experiment results, as depicted in Fig. 2, provide actionable insights for selecting models and cosine similarity thresholds for determining code snippet equivalence using LLM embeddings with cosine similarity. OpenAI and Starcoder 2 are good choices if source files have comments preserved. The configuration with the highest F1 score with comments is OpenAI at threshold 0.8 (F1 score: 0.849). Startcoder 2 has an F1 score of 0.674 at a threshold of 0.7.

If the comments are removed, mpnet Base v2 and mini LM 16 are recommended. For example, mpnet Base v2 using a threshold of 0.7 has an F1 score of 0.929.

Some models are sensitive to the presence of comments. For example, mpnet Base v2 only achieves an F1 score of 0.442 at the threshold of 0.7 with comments

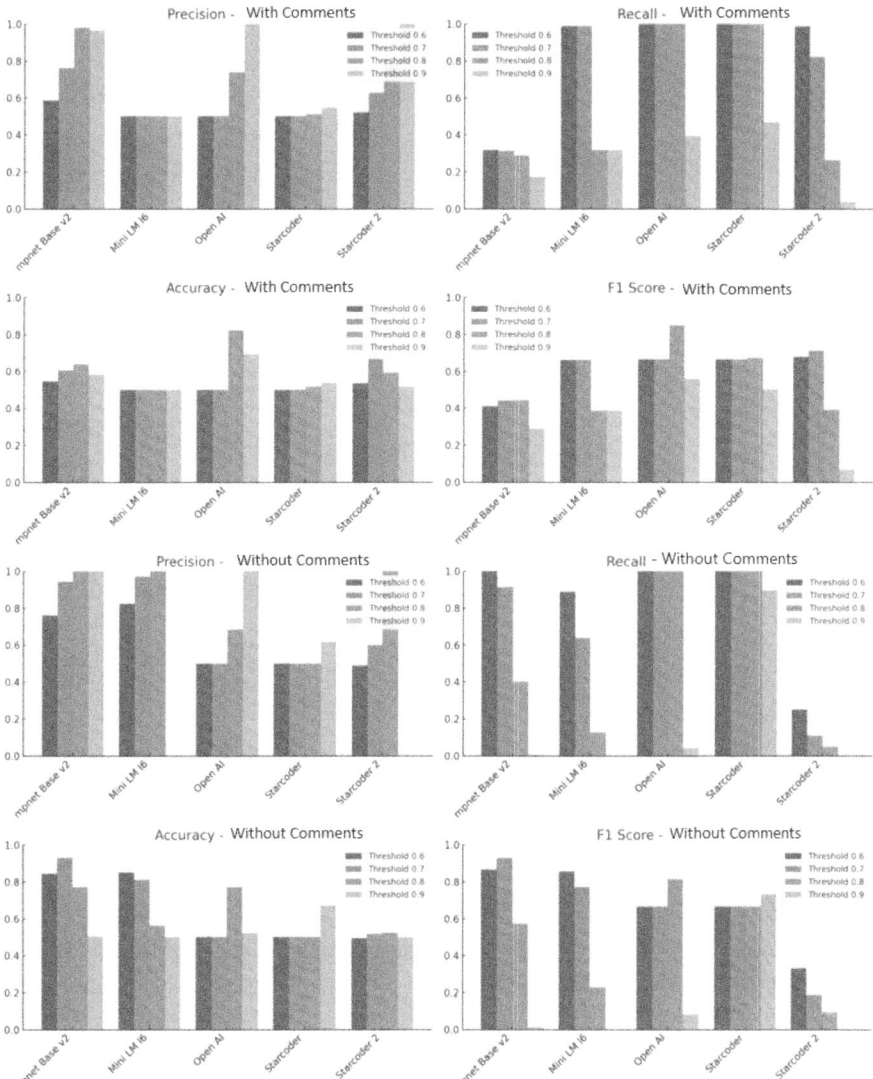

Fig. 2. Results of the Embedding Method using DRB-EQ With (top four plots) and Without Comments (bottom four)

preserved in source codes. However, its F1 score jumps to 0.929 when comments are removed. Startcoder2 behaves exactly the opposite. Its F1 scores significantly drop (0.712 to 0.185 at a threshold of 0.7) if comments are removed.

Picking the right threshold numbers can have a big impact on most models. For example, OpenAI's embedding model performs best if the threshold is set to 0.8, regardless of whether comments are present (F1 = 0.849) or not

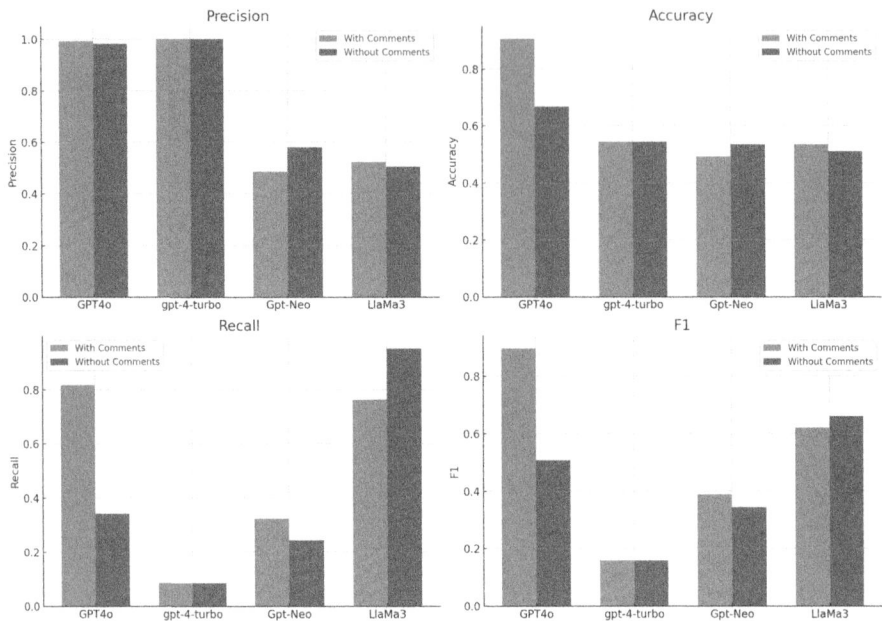

Fig. 3. Results using the LLM prompting method

(F1 = 0.814). However, using 0.9 as a threshold may hurt its performance when comments are removed. Startcoder is an exception here since its F1 scores are relatively stable across different thresholds.

4.4 Results Using LLM Prompts

Figure 3 compares the selected models' performance using the prompting method to extract equivalence analysis information. The models evaluated include OpenAI GPT-4 turbo, OpenAI GPT-4o, GPT-Neo 2.7B, and Llama3-8b models. The metrics considered are Accuracy, Precision, Recall, and F1 Score.

For the DRB-EQ dataset with comments, OpenAI GPT-4o performs very well. It achieved the highest scores for Accuracy (0.906), Recall (0.817), and F1 Score (0.896). This indicates that GPT-4o is highly reliable in predicting the correct class when comments are present. GPT-4 turbo, while achieving perfect Precision (1.000), had a very low Recall (0.085) and F1 Score (0.157). This suggests that GPT-4-turbo is highly conservative, predicting the positive class only when it is very confident, leading to many false negatives.

For input codes without comments, OpenAI GPT-4o demonstrated good performance in Precision (0.982) and Accuracy (0.669). However, its F1 Score (0.507) is lower than LlaMa3's F1 Score of 0.660. GPT-4 turbo, similar to its performance with comments, achieved perfect Precision (1.000) but very low Recall (0.085) and F1 Score (0.157), indicating a high number of false negatives.

Based on the evaluation metrics, OpenAI GPT-4o stands out as the best performer, achieving the highest overall metrics with comments per (Accuracy: 0.906, F1 Score: 0.896) and strong performance without comments (Accuracy: 0.669, F1 Score: 0.507). The best open-weight model is Llama3-8b and it does the best when there are no comments present(Accuracy: 0.511, F1 Score: 0.660).

4.5 Impact of Comments on Model Performance

In this section, we analyze the impact of source code comments on the performance of various language models in identifying equivalent OpenMP Fortran and C/C++ code snippets. For the two sets of code snippets (one with comments included and one with comments removed), we compare the F1 score ratios between them across different models.

For the embedding methods, we used a threshold of 0.8 to compute the F1 score ratios. This threshold was chosen because it provides a good balance between precision and recall, making it a reliable choice for evaluating model performance.

Figure 4 shows the F1 score ratios for different models using embedding methods (left) and LLM prompts (right). The F1 score ratio is calculated by dividing the F1 score obtained with comments removed by the F1 score obtained with comments included. A horizontal line at the ratio of 1.0 is drawn to indicate the same performance with and without comments. This ratio indicates the relative performance improvement or degradation when comments are removed from the code snippets.

For embedding models, we observe that *mpnet_base_v2*, *MiniLM_L6* and *Starcoder_2* are sensitive to the comment removal. The former two have 2.00 and 1.25 performance improvement respectively and the *Starcoder_2* shows performance degradation instead. Whereas the comment removal degrades the LLM prompts for *GPT4o* and is not as sensitive to the other prompting models. Overall, these results suggest that the impact of comments on model performance varies depending on the model and the method used. While some models benefit from the additional context provided by comments, others perform better when comments are removed, possibly due to reduced noise and distractions.

4.6 Overhead Analysis

We measured each model's time and memory overhead. For embedding modes, we measure the overhead by generating embeddings for 10 input code snippets. For models used via prompting, we measure their overhead by asking for analysis for 10 pairs of input code snippets. Table 2 provides a comparison of the overhead metrics for various language models, focusing on both embedding and prompting operations.

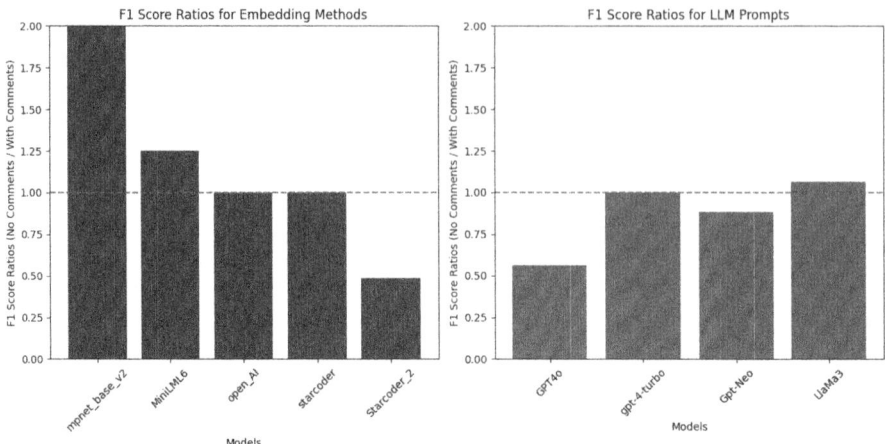

Fig. 4. F1 Score Ratios (No Comments/With Comments) for Embedding vs. Prompting

Table 2. Overhead when embedding 10 snippets or prompting using 10 pairs.

Model	Usage Type	Execution Time (sec)	Memory Usage (MB)
all-MiniLM-L6-v2	Embedding	0.42	23.69
all-mpnet-base-v2	Embedding	2.54	29.28
text-embedding-ada-002	Embedding	1.78	136.00
Starcoder	Embedding	521.90	713.04
Starcoder2-3b	Embedding	221.80	112.37
GPT-4-turbo	Prompting	207.32	0.19
GPT4o	Prompting	56.76	0.19
Llama3	Prompting	5.56	0.05
GPT Neo	Prompting	4.66	0.05

For embedding tasks, *all-MiniLM-L6-v2* is the most efficient model, with the fastest embedding time of 0.417 s and low memory usage of 23.694 MB. OpenAI's *text-embedding-ada-002* offers a balanced performance with a reasonable embedding time and moderate memory usage. In contrast, *starcoder* and *starcoder2-3b* show significantly higher embedding times and memory usage, indicating they are less efficient for embedding tasks.

For prompting operations, *Code Llama3* and *GPT Neo* demonstrate exceptional efficiency with the lowest query times and minimal memory usage. *GPT-4-turbo* has the longest query time, although its peak memory usage is low. The choice of model depends on the specific use case, whether the priority is embedding efficiency or query performance.

4.7 Cost Comparison: Open-Weight vs. Commercial Models

Evaluating large language models involves considering their costs, especially since our future goal is to scale up the analysis to large datasets. The cost of GPT-4 can be calculated by the formula:

$$\text{Total Cost} = \left(\frac{\text{Total Tokens}}{1000}\right) \times \text{Token Cost}$$

The total tokens can be defined as: Total Tokens = Total Snippets × Average Tokens per Snippet. The cost for GPT-4 is 3 cents per 1k input tokens. For our estimations, we only considered input tokens, since the output is very short - just a "1" or "0".

We estimate that "The Stack v2" dataset has 42,079,717 total snippets and 500 average tokens per code snippet. Therefore, the total token number is estimated to be 21,039,858,500 $(42,079,717 \times 500)$. The total cost can be calculated in the following:

$$\text{Total Cost} = \left(\frac{21,039,858,500}{1000}\right) \times 0.03 = 631,195.755$$

Many research projects might not have sufficient budget to afford the GPT-4 cost ($631k USD) to deploy an experiment for extracting equivalent pairs from a large-scale dataset. On the other hand, open-weight models can be deployed locally or accessed via Hugging Face APIs. The costs are primarily associated with API usage, typically more cost-effective than commercial models.

5 Related Work

LLMs have been introduced into software development and HPC communities to assist in various tasks. For language translation and code generation tasks, Lachaux et al. [7], have explored unsupervised translation of programming languages using machine learning models, demonstrating the potential of these methods in overcoming language barriers. Godoy et al. [6] evaluated the capability of OpenAI Codex in generating HPC parallel programming kernels, highlighting the role of advanced language models in enhancing code generation and optimization. LLMs are also applied for analytical tasks, Chen et al. [4] introduced LM4HPC, a framework designed to support HPC tasks through the application of large language models, focusing on parallelism detection and code similarity analysis. Question-answering systems for HPC leveraging LLMs are proposed by Ding et al. [5]. HPC-GPT, a specialized LLaMA-based model fine-tuned with domain-specific question-answer instances, was developed to address the unique challenges in HPC tasks. To address the inadequate quality of existing dataset to address HPC-specific translation tasks, Lei et al. [8] create a unique dataset tailored for translating between OpenMP Fortran and C++ in the HPC domain. This dataset has shown significant improvement in the translation capacities of language models through fine-tuning.

Despite these advancements, existing datasets often lack the comprehensive coverage needed for efficient translation between HPC-specific languages like OpenMP Fortran and C++. Our work aims to determine the optimal LLMs and methodology for finding equivalent code pairs across OpenMP Fortran and C/C++ languages, paving the way for using LLMs to automatically generate high-quality paired translation datasets in the context of HPC code migration.

6 Conclusion

This study explored the feasibility of using LLMs to identify semantically equivalent code snippets across OpenMP Fortran and C/C++ programming languages. By creating a novel ground truth dataset derived from DataRaceBench, we conducted experiments with various commercial and open-weight LLMs, comparing embedding-based similarity analysis with direct prompting for code equivalence detection.

Our findings indicate that different LLMs excel in various aspects of identifying code snippet equivalence, depending on the method and context used. Overall, the embedding method results in better performance compared to the prompting method. While OpenAI's commercial models often demonstrate superior performance, their associated costs may prevent research groups from applying them for large-scale datasets.

For free open-weight embedding models, **all-mpnet-base-v2** is the best choice with a cosine similarity threshold set to 0.7, achieving an F1 score of 0.9288 without comments. This model is efficient and memory-sensitive, making it suitable for scenarios where low cost is a priority. When high true positive rates are required, **all-mpnet-base-v2** remains the best choice for embedding methods, providing high precision at a threshold of 0.8. Although the F1 score is not the highest for prompting methods, **Llama3-8b** still provides a reasonable balance with its efficient performance without comments.

Removing comments generally improves precision and F1 scores for embedding methods, as comments can mislead LLMs to focus on comment similarity rather than code similarity. Therefore, we recommend removing comments by default to ensure that the analysis focuses purely on code structure and semantics.

The recommendations in this study are based on comprehensive experiments and highlight which models perform best under specific conditions. For practitioners, understanding the context-such as the trade-off between cost and accuracy, or the need for high precision vs. high recall-is crucial. These recommendations aim to guide users in selecting the most appropriate model and configuration for their specific needs.

Future work will include extracting equivalent code snippets across OpenMP Fortran and C/C++ snippets from the Stack v2 dataset, using parallel computing resources at LLNL. This will help further validate the findings and explore the scalability of the approach. We can also have future work in analyzing the energy usage and cost analysis of running these LLMS.

Acknowledgement. Prepared by LLNL under Contract DE-AC52-07NA27344. LLNL-CONF-866090. This research was performed under an appointment to the Minority Serving Institutions Internship Program (MSIIP) administered by the Oak Ridge Institute for Science and Education (ORISE) for the National Nuclear Security Administration (NNSA) and U.S. Department of Energy (DOE). ORISE is managed by Oak Ridge Associated Universities (ORAU). All opinions expressed in this publication are the author's and do not necessarily reflect the policies and views of NNSA, DOE, ORISE or ORAU. This material is also based upon work supported by the U.S. Department of Energy, Office of Science, Office of Advanced Scientific Computing Research, Scientific Discovery through Advanced Computing (SciDAC) program.

References

1. Introducing Meta Llama 3: The most capable openly available LLM to date — ai.meta.com. https://ai.meta.com/blog/meta-llama-3/. Accessed 26 July 2024
2. Achiam, J., et al.: GPT-4 technical report (2023). arXiv preprint arXiv:2303.08774
3. Black, S., Gao, L., Wang, P., Leahy, C., Biderman, S.: GPT-Neo: large scale autoregressive language modeling with Mesh-Tensorflow, March 2021. https://doi.org/10.5281/zenodo.5297715
4. Chen, L., Lin, P.H., Vanderbruggen, T., Liao, C., Emani, M., de Supinski, B.: LM4HPC: towards effective language model application in high-performance computing. In: McIntosh-Smith, S., Klemm, M., de Supinski, B.R., Deakin, T., Klinkenberg, J. (eds.) OpenMP: Advanced Task-Based, Device and Compiler Programming. IWOMP 2023. LNCS, vol. 14114, pp. 18–33. Springer, Cham (2023). https://doi.org/10.1007/978-3-031-40744-4_2
5. Ding, X., et al.: HPC-GPT: integrating large language model for high-performance computing. In: Proceedings of the SC'23 Workshops of The International Conference on High Performance Computing, Network, Storage, and Analysis, pp. 951–960 (2023)
6. Godoy, W., Valero-Lara, P., Teranishi, K., Balaprakash, P., Vetter, J.: Evaluation of OpenAI codex for HPC parallel programming models kernel generation. In: Proceedings of the 52nd International Conference on Parallel Processing Workshops, pp. 136–144 (2023)
7. Lachaux, M.A., Roziere, B., Chanussot, L., Lample, G.: Unsupervised translation of programming languages. arXiv preprint arXiv:2006.03511 (2020)
8. Lei, B., Ding, C., Chen, L., Lin, P.H., Liao, C.: Creating a dataset for high-performance computing code translation using LLMS: a bridge between OpenMP Fortran and C++. In: 2023 IEEE High Performance Extreme Computing Conference (HPEC), pp. 1–7. IEEE (2023)
9. Li, R., et al.: Starcoder: may the source be with you! arXiv preprint arXiv:2305.06161 (2023)
10. Liao, C., Lin, P.H., Asplund, J., Schordan, M., Karlin, I.: Dataracebench: a benchmark suite for systematic evaluation of data race detection tools. In: Proceedings of the International Conference for High Performance Computing, Networking, Storage and Analysis, pp. 1–14 (2017)
11. Lin, P.H., Liao, C.: High-precision evaluation of both static and dynamic tools using dataracebench. In: 2021 IEEE/ACM 5th International Workshop on Software Correctness for HPC Applications (Correctness), pp. 1–8. IEEE (2021)
12. Lozhkov, A., et al.: Starcoder 2 and the stack v2: the next generation (2024)

13. Team, G., et al.: Gemini: a family of highly capable multimodal models. arXiv preprint arXiv:2312.11805 (2023)
14. Zakeri-Nasrabadi, M., Parsa, S., Ramezani, M., Roy, C., Ekhtiarzadeh, M.: A systematic literature review on source code similarity measurement and clone detection: techniques, applications, and challenges. J. Syst. Softw. 111796 (2023)
15. Zhao, W.X., et al.: A survey of large language models. arXiv preprint arXiv:2303.18223 (2023)

Visualizing Correctness Issues in OpenMP Programs

Feiyang Jin[✉], Alan Tao[✉], Lechen Yu, and Vivek Sarkar

Georgia Institute of Technology, Atlanta, GA 30332, USA
{fjin35,atao31,lechen.yu,vsarkar}@gatech.edu

Abstract. Past work on OpenMP program visualization has mainly centered on performance analysis. This paper explores how the visualization of *computation graphs* assists programmers in debugging issues related to program correctness. The motivation is twofold. First, researchers widely use computation graphs to analyze dynamic program behavior. Second, most past work focused on visualizing performance bottlenecks rather than correctness issues. This paper's contributions are as follows. First, we introduce techniques for building computation graphs using the OpenMP Tools Interface (OMPT). Second, we present a computation graph visualizer for OpenMP programs built upon these techniques. The visualizer specifically highlights data races as the correctness issue under study. Finally, the paper includes an empirical study of the performance and effectiveness of our prototype. The evaluation demonstrates that our graph builder introduces minimal overhead when integrated with state-of-the-art race detectors. We also conducted a user study involving a control group and an experimental group. The results show that our visualization greatly aids programmers in understanding and debugging data races. Beyond our main contribution, which focuses on data races, we also integrate host-device data movement in the visualization. This serves as a first step toward visualizing data mapping issues. To the best of our knowledge, our work is the first to explore understanding of correctness issues in OpenMP programs through interactive visualization of computation graphs.

Keywords: OpenMP Programs · Computation Graphs · Data Races · Host-Device Data Movement · Dynamic Program Analysis · Visualization

1 Introduction

A *computation graph* is a dynamically constructed directed graph that captures the execution of parallel programs in a partial order. In the research community, computation graphs are extensively used to model the dynamic behavior of parallel programs. Debugging and analysis of parallel programs leverage computation graphs in various ways:

1. Data race detection: a data race happens if two nodes in the computation graph access the same memory locations, at least one performs a write, and

there is no directed path in the computation graph connecting the two. This property is utilized by many dynamic race detectors [9,14,17,18,22,23].
2. Deadlock detection: a deadlock arises when a cycle is formed in the computation graph [19]. If the program is deadlock-free, the generated computation graph will be a *directed acyclic graph* (DAG).
3. Determinacy validation: researchers have proven that programs with certain kinds of parallel constructs (e.g., spawn-sync task parallelism and async-finish task parallelism) have the property that data race freedom also guarantees determinacy [6,9]. One key feature of determinate programs is that given the same input, different executions of the same program will always generate the same computation graph [8,9].

While computation graphs have gained widespread conceptual usage, there remains a distinct lack of tools designed for OpenMP programmers to visualize them, together with any correctness issues detected. Most existing debugging tools use computation graphs internally. When detecting a correctness issue (e.g., data race, buffer overflow), these tools simply dump the collected trace with an error message. Given the complexity of OpenMP programs, manually analyzing the trace and figuring out the root cause can be challenging, even for experienced programmers (as illustrated by our user study results in Sect. 6.2). On the contrary, there have been a large amount of prior work dedicated to visualizing the results of performance analysis [1,3,4,12,15,21], many of which are for OpenMP programs. These tools usually apply sampling/instrumentation techniques to obtain performance data and embed these data into a customized graph; later a visualization tool will display the performance data in a group of interactive view (e.g., thread view, trace view) to highlight detected performance issues.

Despite the limited efforts in visualizing correctness issues, the need for such a feature remains evident. First, as mentioned above, computation graphs are widely used to identify correctness issues in parallel programs. Introducing visualization offers an effective means to comprehend program behavior and identify the root causes of bugs. Secondly, perhaps less obvious but equally essential, visualization aids developers in recognizing certain tools' limitations. For instance, dynamic race detectors often encounter false positives (reporting non-existing races) due to design choices or implementation errors. Integrating the debug information of detected races with visualization can give a clearer view of a tool's limitations (user study results in Sect. 6.2 proved this).

In this paper, we take the lead in exploring how visualization of data races can help OpenMP programmers better understand the problems. We have designed and implemented a computation graph visualizer for OpenMP programs. The tool consists of two parts: an on-the-fly graph builder written in C++ and an interactive visualization interface written in Javascript. The graph builder uses *OpenMP Tools Interface* (OMPT) to build computation graphs based on runtime events. The tool provides interfaces for existing race detectors to report race information. We have integrated one race detector [23] into our tool, as an example of how the interface can be used. A second major contribution is a research user study that evaluates the efficacy of our tool. As with any software, the ultimate goal of our tool is to help programmers. Since no similar user study has been conducted to study how visualization helps programmers understand data races, we performed such one. The user study demonstrates that developers significantly benefit from using our tool to analyze data races.

In the remaining section of this paper, we first describe the high-level design of our visualization tool. Subsequently, we propose three *language-centric* approaches to build the computation graph. These approaches ensure that the graph is tightly connected to the OpenMP programming and execution model. A previous work on OpenMP performance analysis shares the same approach [3]. After introducing the graph builder, we present our visualization interface. The visualization is interactive and connected to the source code so users can follow the program's execution trace through graph navigation. In short, the key contributions of this work are:

1. A set of techniques for utilizing OMPT callbacks to build computation graphs and an implementation of the graph builder using our techniques (Sect. 4). The graph builder integrates an existing race detector to get race information.
2. A web-hosted visualization interface for the computation graph. The visualizer combines the graph, source code, trace, and race information. When interacting with developers, it uses carefully designed animation and interaction to highlight data races (Sect. 5).
3. An evaluation of the graph builder's performance is included and shows that the overhead compared to stand-alone race detection is bound by a 1.32x slowdown (Sect. 6.1). A research user study indicates that participants found visualization significantly helped them comprehend data races (Sect. 6.2).
4. An initial step towards visualizing data mapping issues. We explored how to model and present host-device data movements in the computation graph. This includes a new OMPT callback to handle data movement precisely (Sect. 7), an unprecedented feature among existing callbacks.

2 Background

Computation Graph: A *node* in the computation graph represents a sequence of code without any parallel constructs; the only exception is that the last statement of the node may generate parallelism by task creation or synchronization. There are three kinds of edges [17]: *continuation*, *fork* and *join*. Continuation edges mark the execution order for nodes within the same task. Fork edges represent new task creation. Join edges represent synchronization.

We say node u *happens before* node v if and only if there is a directed path from u to v in the computation graph. We denote it as $u \rightsquigarrow v$. If $u \not\rightsquigarrow v$ and $v \not\rightsquigarrow u$, we say u, v *may happen in parallel* and denote it as $u \parallel v$.

Data Races: A *data race* occurs if and only if nodes u and v access the same memory location, at least one of them conducts a write, and $u \parallel v$.

A dynamic race detector usually consists of two parts [6,9,11,14,17,18,23]: *shadow memory* and *reachability structure*. Shadow memory records previous reads and writes for each memory location; the reachability structure answers happens-before queries for pairs of nodes. In practice, reachability structures are often designed to save only the necessary parts of a computation graph.

OpenMP: In this work, we focus on the *task parallelism* constructs in OpenMP. In task parallelism, work is divided into tasks, and each available worker thread will be assigned a task to execute. An OpenMP program starts as an *initial task*, and the program executes sequentially until it encounters a *parallel* construct, which will initiate a *parallel region* consisting of parallel tasks. By default, a *barrier* occurs at the end of a parallel region to synchronize all tasks. All tasks created before the barrier must be completed before any task created after the barrier can start execution. The pattern is shown in Fig. 2.

3 Design

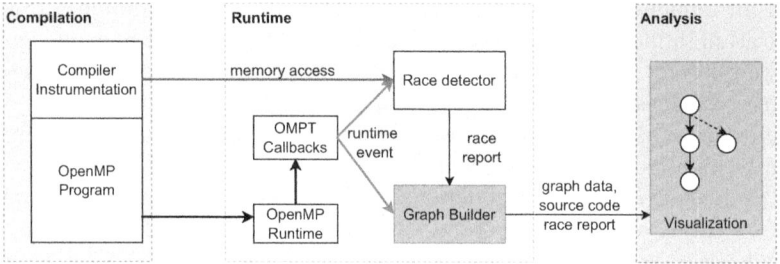

Fig. 1. Application workflow

As shown in Fig. 1, our tool consists of two fundamental components: 1) on-the-fly computation graph construction written in C++, and 2) graph visualization written in JavaScript. Upon receiving an OpenMP program to analyze, the tool executes the program with race detection enabled. During runtime, the computation graph is dynamically built using OMPT. OMPT provides callbacks to capture runtime events with marginal time overhead, and we update the graph correspondingly in each callback. The race detector we integrated is TSAN-SPD3 [23]. It relies on computation graphs to detect data races, though it does not explicitly keep the graph. At runtime, if TSAN-SPD3 detects a data race, it will report the race information to our graph builder; the graph builder will save the information in the graph. After the program is completed, the tool outputs all the information into a JSON file. The visualization component reads this JSON file to present the computation graph integrated with the source code and race report. Visualization is implemented in *D3*, a JavaScript library renowned for creating interactive visualization.

Regarding conceptual exploration, our tool is the first to spotlight correctness issues by visualizing computation graphs. Consequently, our approach lacks precedence for reference. The best experience we can learn from is visualization work for OpenMP program performance analysis [1,3,12,21]. On one hand, we share similarities. We both build a graph during execution and visualize it offline. As they integrate performance information into the graph, we integrate correctness issues detected. On the other hand, our contributions are quite different from theirs. The graphs built have different granularity, and we carefully designed the graph structure to enhance comprehension. Our graph builder also has an interface for existing tools to report information. Instead of asking programmers to find issues themselves, we allow them to utilize existing tools.

Regarding implementation, we have tested several tools mentioned in Sect. 8 related work and explored existing graphing software such as yEd[1], Cytoscape [16] and Intel Advisor's FGA [1]. Nevertheless, we opted to construct our own graph builder and visualization for several reasons. First, the installation process of other tools posed challenges. For example, many tools in Sect. 8 require administrative permissions to trace programs, potentially limiting accessibility. In contrast, our graph builder is an OMPT tool compatible with any OpenMP version that supports OMPT. The visualization part is browser-based, ensuring ease of use without installation. Additionally, the dynamic nature of our visualization, facilitated by JavaScript, enables powerful animations that play a pivotal role in highlighting data races - a feature that could be more robustly supported by the alternatives we explored.

4 Graph Construction Techniques

4.1 Language-Centric Approaches

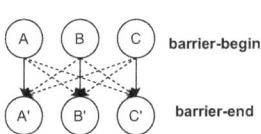

Fig. 2. OpenMP barrier pattern

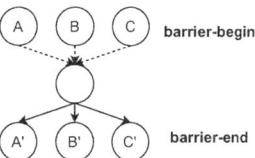

Fig. 3. Barrier visualization in our tool

These approaches aim to enhance programmers' comprehension by connecting computation graphs to OpenMP's programming model.

Approach 1: Designing for Programmers (rather than the specification). While adhering closely to the OpenMP specification is always essential, we have made adjustments in several instances to optimize the graph's presentation for improved comprehension. Here, we will use barriers as an example. In OpenMP, when a barrier occurs, all tasks must hit the barrier before any can proceed – a synchronization pattern depicted in Fig. 2. Previous work has used this presentation to illustrate barrier [13,23].

However, such visualization would contaminate the computation graphs with overlapping, crowded edges. The situation worsens when the number of threads

---

[1] www.yworks.com/products/yed

becomes large (we usually test benchmarks with eight threads). To avoid the problems, we opted to redesign the barrier presentation, as shown in Fig. 3. Theoretically, this representation means "all tasks will join a single task's synchronization node before continuation." While a slight deviation from the formal specification, this redesign significantly enhances the graph's clarity and simplifies navigation.

Approach 2: Leveraging Implicit Coherence in the Context. By using the implicit coherent context, we do not need to handle all OpenMP constructs explicitly. Our existing code already handles many "quietly". We will use the `single` construct as an example. In OpenMP, a single construct specifies that only one task will execute the associated code block. An implicit barrier occurs at the end of a single construct unless a `nowait` clause is specified. When a single construct begins and ends, the OMPT `callback_work` event is invoked; the callback tells programmers which task will execute the code block.

We could utilize `callback_work` and correspondingly update the computation graph: add a continuation node for the selected task while leaving others untouched. However, such handling is unnecessary: as only one task will execute the code region, other OMPT events in the region will automatically extend the graph. Similarly, the `nowait` clause is implicitly handled by another OMPT callback, which will only be invoked if a barrier occurs. If a `nowait` clause is present, the callback will not be invoked because no barrier exists. Consequently, we do not need to save additional information when a single construct occurs. Existing OMPT callbacks will correctly record the execution.

Approach 3: Applying Sufficient and Minimized Serialization. The dynamic nature of OpenMP programs requires the analysis tool itself to be aware of the parallelism. Concurrent tasks can invoke the same OMPT callbacks simultaneously during runtime, potentially creating data races within the analysis tool. On the other hand, excessive serialization can impede the tool's performance.

Here, we will explain how we handle parallel regions as an example. Recall that a parallel region creates a group of new tasks. Ideally, the solution to updating the graph is to add a start node for each new task and connect the current node to each new node by a fork edge. In this case, the callback provided by OMPT is `implicit_task`; unfortunately, it will only be invoked after each new task is created. As a result, if we add a fork edge for each new task inside this callback, we introduce data races because many tasks can invoke the callback simultaneously. The resulting graph could miss several fork edges.

To safely update the graph when a group of tasks is created, we use a concurrent vector to save all the newly generated fork edges. Each call to `implicit_task` will add a fork edge to the vector. The edges will be added to the graph just before we output it. On the other hand, additional serialization is not required at the end of a parallel region. When a parallel region starts, we already know the number of new tasks being created (assume the number is n). Thus, we can create a vector v of size n and assign an index i for each new task. When each task finishes, it only needs to put its last node into $v[i]$. When the parallel region ends, one task will iterate through the vector and add join edges to the graph. Notice that this iteration is sequential, so we do not need extra synchronization.

4.2 Implementation

Our graph builder's source code can be accessed here[2]. The graph builder is implemented as a stand-alone OMPT tool. During execution, the computation graph is stored in memory and exported to a JSON file if the program completes without crashing. Many OMPT callbacks provide the program counter as a parameter. When available, we leverage this to extract trace information, such as line numbers and file names. For existing race detectors to report races, we provide functions they can call to pass the information. The functions are implemented in OMPT, so existing tools need to define them as weak functions in their code.

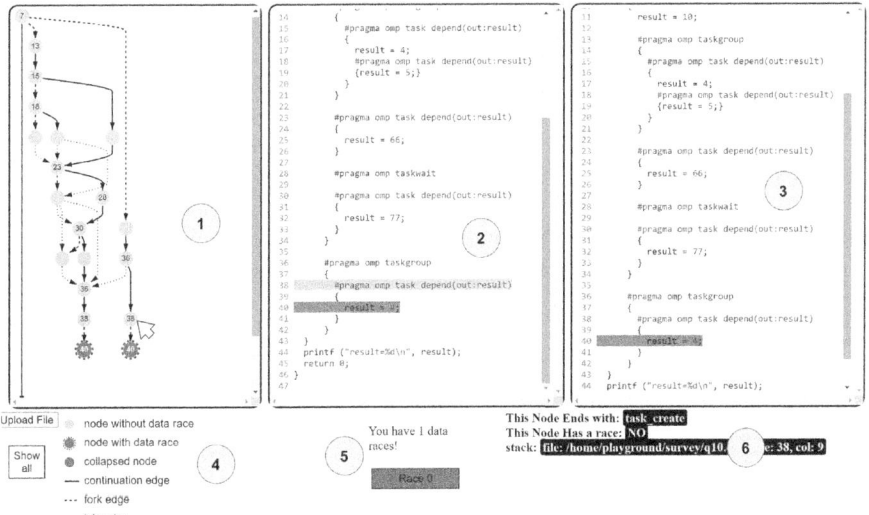

Fig. 4. User interface for the visualization tool. We have hosted the tool on Amazon's Amplify web service (https://www.drvis.ninja). Users can access the website, view preset examples, or upload their graphs to visualize.

5 Visualization

Figure 4 presents the UI for the visualization. It consists of 6 divisions (Div). Div 1 is the computation graph. Each node in the graph contains:

1. Stack trace information (if available). If the stack is captured, hovering the mouse cursor over the node will highlight the line in the source code. As

---

[2] https://github.com/lechenyu/llvm-project/tree/ompt52_dpst.

shown in Fig. 4, line 38 is highlighted in this manner. At the same time, Div 6 will display the trace information, including the OMPT event this node ends with, if it has a race or not, and the text information of the stack. Users can move the mouse along the graph to follow the program's execution trace while examining the highlighted source code.
2. The feature to be collapsed. If an open node is clicked, it will be collapsed by hiding its outgoing edges. A node will be hidden if it is unreachable from the root node, and the process will propagate to its children recursively. This feature allows programmers to center the scope on racy nodes or regions of interest.

Div 2 and 3 contain the source code. The footer section consists of three parts: Div 4 contains the legend and file upload, Div 5 has buttons to select races, and Div 6 displays node information. Clicking on a race button in Div 5 highlights the two racy lines in Div 2 and 3. The computation graph in Div 1 will also be updated to display only up to those two racy nodes; any subsequent nodes are hidden. In Fig. 4, the racy accesses lie on the same line because two tasks concurrently execute the line. In real life, a race can be caused by two different lines or even two lines in different files.

6 Empirical Study

In this section, we study the implementation of our graph builder and visualization interface to answer the following research questions:

1. Performance (Sect. 6.1): How much slowdown does the graph builder introduce to the original program execution?
2. Efficacy (Sect. 6.2): To what extent does the visualization help programmers better understand data races compared with traditional log reports?

6.1 Performance Evaluation

The evaluation aims to examine the amount of slowdown the graph builder introduced. To measure this slowdown, we record the execution time from the program's start to completion. The graph dumping and visualization parts are not considered because they are not integral to assessing the graph builder's performance. We also plan to support a more advanced graph aggregation strategy in the future and treat it as an independent research topic.

For a better performance comparison, the benchmarks and inputs we select are the same used in the original TSAN-SPD3 (the integrated race detector in our tool) paper [23]. A total of nine programs from BOTS [5] are included. The experiment was conducted on a single-node AMD server machine, which consists of a 12-core Ryzen9 3900X operating at 3.8 GHZ with 128 GB memory (RAM). All benchmarks were compiled by Clang/LLVM 15.0.1 running on Ubuntu 18.04.6. The reported execution times are presented for four configurations: Base, Race, Graph, and Full. For each configuration, we report each benchmark's mean execution time of five runs. The coefficient of variation for each configuration, benchmark, and five runs is within 4.5%.

The "Base" configuration measures the execution time of the original programs. The "Graph" configuration enables only the graph builder but not the race detection. The "Race" configuration enables race detection using TSAN-SPD3 but not the graph builder. Finally, the "Full" configuration encompasses race detection and the graph builder.

Table 1. Graph builder performance and graph metrics

Benchmark	Base	Graph	Race	Full	Full/Race	#node	#edges	#fork	#join
align	1.45	1.59	10.01	10.08	1.01x	9927	14891	4958	4965
fft	1.74	17.21	30.13	39.74	1.32x	77221537	134838680	28808574	57617144
fib	1.56	23.05	58.02	71.11	1.23x	74651782	134373200	29860710	59721419
health	1.67	9.40	18.89	23.16	1.23x	52547254	87578509	17515629	35031256
nqueens	3.80	49.11	77.92	98.12	1.26x	124231833	243862475	59815322	119630643
sort	2.62	3.06	21.13	26.77	1.27x	6138550	11119286	2490373	4980737
sparselu	2.39	2.62	119.28	120.17	1.01x	588669	884345	292533	295677
strassen	1.22	1.24	25.17	27.30	1.08x	294149	568676	137265	274528
uts	0.29	2.48	19.19	20.47	1.07x	12338710	20564510	4112905	8225801

The performance and graph information are shown in Table 1. The first four columns report the average execution time in seconds for the four configurations. The column "Full/Race" is the slowdown of full configuration over race configuration. The last four columns show the number of nodes, edges, fork edges, and join edges for the computation graph generated from each benchmark. Figure 5 shows the time overheads.

Concerning only the graph builder, the data in Table 1 indicates that its slowdown correlates to the generated graph's size. The three benchmarks exhibiting the highest overhead (fft, fib, and nqueens) correspond precisely to the top three largest computation graphs generated (nodes+edges). Moreover, they also have the largest number of join edges.

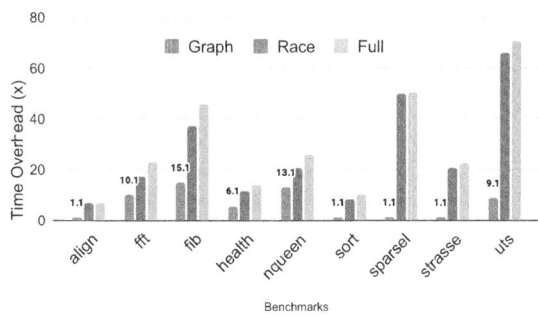

Fig. 5. Time overhead over base configuration

The increasing size of the graph and join edges bring more serialized operations within our tool, as discussed in Sect. 4.1. Similarly, the three benchmarks with the lowest overhead (align, strassen, and sparselu) generate the smallest computation graphs and the fewest join edges.

A second crucial finding is that integrating our graph builder with the race detector introduces no more than 1.32x overhead (Full over Race configuration).

The logic is coherent because, unlike a race detector, the graph builder does not need to record the access history for each memory location or check for races when memory access occurs. As a result, the overhead imposed by the graph builder is mostly subsumed by the overhead introduced by the race detector.

6.2 Efficacy Study

To evaluate the efficacy of our visualization, we conducted an anonymous user study among graduate-level students, faculty members, and software engineers from different institutions. Participants were randomly divided into a control group and an experimental group. The control group received traditional log race reports from TSAN-SPD3, while the experimental group used race reports presented by our visualization tool. We received a total of 25 responses. After removing poor-quality and irregular data (responses with extreme response times), the experimental group had 8 valid responses, while the control group had 10.

The study consisted of three parts. **Part 1**: Both groups received an introduction to data races along with examples of race reports. In addition, participants of both groups were asked to rate their familiarity, on a scale from 1 to 10, with the following concepts: Parallel Computing or Multithreading, OpenMP, Data Races or Race Conditions and Computation Graphs. The response results are shown in Table 2. The self-reported proficiency ratings indicate that differences in individual skill in parallel computing had little impact on the user efficacy study.

Table 2. Average Self-Declared Proficiency

Group	Part	Average Proficiency by Topic			
		Parallel Computing	OpenMP	Data Races	Computation Graphs
Control	1	6.4	4.8	6.1	4.4
Experimental	1	6.125	5	6.75	4.75

Part 2: For 5 programs (Q1–Q5), participants were asked to identify whether the reported races were true reports or false alarms. **Part 3 (optional)**: For 3 programs (B1–B3), we showed the first line involved in the race; participants needed to identify the second line. We analyzed the responses using two metrics. 1) The percentage of correct responses and 2) The average response time.

Table 3. Accuracy, average time elapsed (seconds), and participation rate

Group	Part	Accuracy and Average Response time					Participation		
		Q1	Q2	Q3	Q4	Q5	Q1 ~ Q5		
Control	2	50% (119s)	38% (115s)	50% (118s)	75% (82s)	50% (64s)	100%		
Experimental	2	50% ( )	(145s)	( )	( )	( )	100%		
		B1	B2	B3			B1	B2	B3
Control	3	17% (60s)	0% (106s)	0% (81s)	N/A	N/A	60%	50%	50%
Experimental	3	(117s)	( )	( )	N/A	N/A	100%	100%	100%

Table 3 reveals interesting trends. For part 2, a required section, the experimental group demonstrated equivalent or superior accuracy to the control group across all five questions while spending significantly less time overall (except for Q2). For part 3, an optional section, all participants in the experimental group finished all questions, in contrast to the control group's 50% completion rate. Control group members may encounter challenges using traditional log reports, even if the reports contain stack traces and line numbers. These challenges could contribute to the observed lower completion rates and accuracy.

After part 3, both groups rated the difficulty of understanding data races on a scale from 1 to 10. Results indicate that participants in the control group (avg. 8.4) found data races challenging to comprehend. Upon viewing a screenshot of our tool, they strongly agreed (avg. 8) that visualization would facilitate their understanding of data races. Conversely, the experimental group rated the difficulty of understanding data races as fair (avg. 4.6) and strongly agreed (avg. 7.3) that visualization aids comprehension.

These results suggest that our visualization tool offers the advantage of enhanced productivity. It enables programmers to gain a deeper understanding of data races and expedites the process of identifying root causes, thereby reducing time spent. Moreover, the tool helps programmers recognize a race detector's limitations by visualizing false negatives. By utilizing the graph, developers can more confidently identify false results reported. Any tool's ultimate goal is to assist programmers, and the user study indicates that our tool, although not perfect, is clearly on the right track.

7 Extending Beyond Data Races: Visualizing Data Mapping Issues

OpenMP programs suffer from various correctness issues. For example, previous work [24] has shown that many bugs can arise from misunderstandings of data movement behavior. These bugs include data races, uninitialized memory, stale data, and more. We currently support host-device data movement in our visualization. In an ongoing project, we are integrating Arbalest [24] to report bugs caused by incorrect use of data movement. Figure 6 shows our current visualization. OpenMP programmers can use the *target offloading* feature to migrate code onto heterogeneous devices for execution. Data is moved between the host (CPU) and the target/device (GPU) at the begin/end of an offloading. Users can specify options to control this movement. For example, the *to* option copies data from host to device at the beginning but not the other way around at the end.

```
#pragma omp target map(to:a[0:N]) map(from:c[0:N]) map(alloc:b[0:N*N]) device(0)
```

However, no current OMPT callbacks accurately model host-device data movements. Two possible but inferior solutions using existing callbacks exist. The first callback handles *data mapping*, a high-level abstraction of data movement. Unfortunately, data mapping does not necessarily lead to data movement. This may happen when the same data mapping is declared multiple times in a

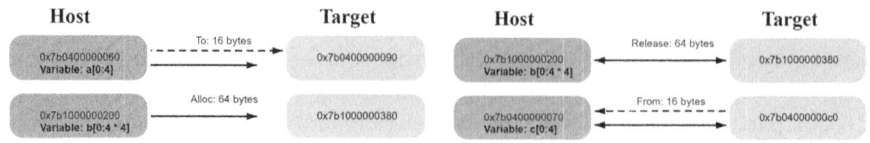

Fig. 6. Data movement code and visualization. The left-hand side shows transferring data from host to target when the offloading begins. The right-hand side shows transferring data back to host when the offloading ends. Variable address, name, and size are included for each transfer.

GPU kernel. Tool developers could handle data movement in this callback, but they must track if a movement is incurred every time, leading to significant time overhead. The second callback handles *data operations*, which are low-level GPU memory operations such as allocation. These operations are used to implement data mapping. The challenge is that it is up to the runtime to determine how to utilize operations to accomplish a mapping, which means this callback may not have enough information about the movement.

We introduced a new OMPT callback `device_mem` to model host-device data movement precisely. This callback is associated with each data mapping and combines all data operations conducted. Therefore, it avoids problems faced by existing callbacks and provides debugging information for the mapped variable, including name, size, file name, and line number. These details are unavailable with existing callbacks for data mappings and data operations.

8 Related Work

Using visualization to explore performance bottlenecks is an active research field. Muddukrishna et al. proposed grain graphs [12], which considers grain (a task or a parallel for-loop) as the unit for performance measuring. Langdal et al. implemented three OMPT callbacks to build grain graphs [10]. Reissmann and Muddukrishna proposed a strategy to aggregate grain graphs to ease navigation [15]. Agrawal et al. visualized OpenMP task dependencies using OMPT to analyze performance [1]. Aftermath is a performance analysis tool for detecting performance bottlenecks in task parallel programs [4]. A subsequent work extends Aftermath by providing an instrumented version of OpenMP [3]; similar to our work, the authors applied a language-centric approach. AfterOMPT [21] further extends Aftermath by incorporating OMPT events to trace programs.

The work mentioned above was designed to provide insights into performance issues. A handful of projects have also contributed to debugging visualization. DAGViz is a tool that captures and visualizes computation graphs [7]. However, users must write programs using a generic model, which only supports three parallel constructs. Temanejo [2] acts at the task level and gives users the dependency graph while debugging the program in its GUI. ThreadScope visualizes multithreaded applications [20]. The graph generated shows memory operations, and the authors propose that users can identify graph-based problems from it.

However, all previous works have merely stopped at "presenting the graph" without displaying any correctness problems, leaving users to debug on their own. In contrast, our work allows existing tools to report issues and incorporates dynamic animation and interaction. Additionally, we adopt a language-centric approach to relate the graph to the OpenMP context. These innovations are crucial in helping programmers understand the problems without getting lost in the debugging process.

9 Conclusion

In this paper, we studied how visualization can help programmers understand data races in OpenMP programs. Our contribution lies in formulating techniques to correctly and efficiently construct computation graphs. A new OMPT callback is introduced by us to model host-device data movements accurately. The ensuing implementation of our graph builder, tailored for OpenMP programs, provides a robust foundation for visualizing correctness-related aspects. The interactive visualization interface allows programmers to review data races and data movements. To our knowledge, our tool is the first to explore and highlight correctness issues in OpenMP programs through a customized visualization interface. It is also a trailblazer for future successors because the graph builder and visualization are independent of any debugging tool; developers can integrate their tool with our work. A key opportunity for future work is to develop an improved aggregation approach to facilitate easier graph navigation. Loop parallelism can also be supported by utilizing OMPT events to collect information and visualizing in the graph.

References

1. Agrawal, V., Voss, M.J., Reble, P., Tovinkere, V., Hammond, J., Klemm, M.: Visualization of OpenMP* task dependencies using Intel® advisor – flow graph analyzer. In: de Supinski, B., Valero-Lara, P., Martorell, X., Mateo Bellido, S., Labarta, J. (eds.) Evolving OpenMP for Evolving Architectures. IWOMP 2018. LNCS, vol. 11128, pp. 175–188. Springer, Cham (2018). https://doi.org/10.1007/978-3-319-98521-3_12
2. Brinkmann, S., Gracia, J., Niethammer, C.: Task debugging with TEMANEJO. In: Cheptsov, A., Brinkmann, S., Gracia, J., Resch, M., Nagel, W. (eds.) Tools for High Performance Computing 2012. Springer, Berlin, Heidelberg (2013). https://doi.org/10.1007/978-3-642-37349-7_2
3. Drebes, A., Bréjon, J.-B., Pop, A., Heydemann, K., Cohen, A.: Language-centric performance analysis of OpenMP programs with aftermath. In: Maruyama, N., de Supinski, B.R., Wahib, M. (eds.) IWOMP 2016. LNCS, vol. 9903, pp. 237–250. Springer, Cham (2016). https://doi.org/10.1007/978-3-319-45550-1_17
4. Drebes, A., Pop, A., et al.: Interactive visualization of cross-layer performance anomalies in dynamic task-parallel applications and systems. In: 2016 IEEE International Symposium on Performance Analysis of Systems and Software (ISPASS), pp. 274–283. IEEE (2016)

5. Duran, A., Teruel, X., et al.: Barcelona OpenMP tasks suite: a set of benchmarks targeting the exploitation of task parallelism in OpenMP. In: 2009 International Conference on Parallel Processing, pp. 124–131. IEEE (2009)
6. Feng, M., Leiserson, C.E.: Efficient detection of determinacy races in Cilk programs. In: Proceedings of the Ninth Annual ACM Symposium on Parallel Algorithms and Architectures, pp. 1–11 (1997)
7. Huynh, A., Thain, D., et al.: Dagviz: A dag visualization tool for analyzing task-parallel program traces. In: Proceedings of the 2nd Workshop on Visual Performance Analysis. pp. 1–8 (2015)
8. Jin, F., Jacobson, J., et al.: Minikokkos: a calculus of portable parallelism. In: 2022 IEEE/ACM Sixth International Workshop on Software Correctness for HPC Applications (Correctness), pp. 37–44. IEEE (2022)
9. Jin, F., Yu, L., Cogumbreiro, T., et al.: Dynamic determinacy race detection for task-parallel programs with promises. In: 37th European Conference on Object-Oriented Programming (ECOOP 2023). Schloss-Dagstuhl-Leibniz Zentrum für Informatik (2023)
10. Langdal, P.V., Jahre, M., Muddukrishna, A.: Extending OMPT to support grain graphs. In: de Supinski, B.R., Olivier, S.L., Terboven, C., Chapman, B.M., Müller, M.S. (eds.) IWOMP 2017. LNCS, vol. 10468, pp. 141–155. Springer, Cham (2017). https://doi.org/10.1007/978-3-319-65578-9_10
11. Mellor-Crummey, J.: On-the-fly detection of data races for programs with nested fork-join parallelism. In: Proceedings of the 1991 ACM/IEEE Conference on Supercomputing, pp. 24–33 (1991)
12. Muddukrishna, A., Jonsson, P.A., et al.: Grain graphs: openmp performance analysis made easy. In: Proceedings of the 21st ACM SIGPLAN Symposium on Principles and Practice of Parallel Programming, pp. 1–13 (2016)
13. Protze, J., Hahnfeld, J., Ahn, D.H., Schulz, M., Müller, M.S.: OpenMP tools interface: synchronization information for data race detection. In: de Supinski, B.R., Olivier, S.L., Terboven, C., Chapman, B.M., Müller, M.S. (eds.) IWOMP 2017. LNCS, vol. 10468, pp. 249–265. Springer, Cham (2017). https://doi.org/10.1007/978-3-319-65578-9_17
14. Raman, R., Zhao, J.: et al.: Scalable and precise dynamic datarace detection for structured parallelism. Acm Sigplan Notices **47**(6), 531–542 (2012)
15. Reissmann, N., Muddukrishna, A.: Diagnosing highly-parallel OpenMP programs with aggregated grain graphs. In: Aldinucci, M., Padovani, L., Torquati, M. (eds.) Euro-Par 2018. LNCS, vol. 11014, pp. 106–119. Springer, Cham (2018). https://doi.org/10.1007/978-3-319-96983-1_8
16. Shannon, P., Markiel, A.: et al.: Cytoscape: a software environment for integrated models of biomolecular interaction networks. Genome Res. **13**(11), 2498–2504 (2003)
17. Surendran, R., Sarkar, V.: Dynamic determinacy race detection for task parallelism with futures. In: Falcone, Y., Sánchez, C. (eds.) RV 2016. LNCS, vol. 10012, pp. 368–385. Springer, Cham (2016). https://doi.org/10.1007/978-3-319-46982-9_23
18. Utterback, R., Agrawal, K., et al.: Efficient race detection with futures. In: Proceedings of the 24th Symposium on Principles and Practice of Parallel Programming, pp. 340–354 (2019)
19. Voss, C., Cogumbreiro, T., Sarkar, V.: Transitive joins: a sound and efficient online deadlock-avoidance policy. In: Proceedings of the 24th Symposium on Principles and Practice of Parallel Programming, pp. 378–390 (2019)
20. Wheeler, K.B., Thain, D.: Visualizing massively multithreaded applications with threadscope. Concurr. Comput. Pract. Exp. **22**(1), 45–67 (2010)

21. Wodiany, I., Drebes, A., Neill, R., Pop, A.: AfterOMPT: an OMPT-based tool for fine-grained tracing of tasks and loops. In: Milfeld, K., de Supinski, B.R., Koesterke, L., Klinkenberg, J. (eds.) IWOMP 2020. LNCS, vol. 12295, pp. 165–180. Springer, Cham (2020). https://doi.org/10.1007/978-3-030-58144-2_11
22. Xu, Y., Singer, K., Lee, I.T.A.: Parallel determinacy race detection for futures. In: Proceedings of the 25th ACM SIGPLAN Symposium on Principles and Practice of Parallel Programming, pp. 217–231 (2020)
23. Yu, L., Jin, F., et al.: Leveraging the dynamic program structure tree to detect data races in openmp programs. In: 2022 IEEE/ACM Sixth International Workshop on Software Correctness for HPC Applications (Correctness), pp. 54–62. IEEE (2022)
24. Yu, L., Protze, J., et al.: ARBALEST: dynamic detection of data mapping issues in heterogeneous OpenMP applications. In: 2021 IEEE International Parallel and Distributed Processing Symposium (IPDPS), pp. 464–474. IEEE (2021)

Developing an Interactive OpenMP Programming Book with Large Language Models

Xinyao Yi[1], Anjia Wang[2], Yonghong Yan[1(✉)], and Chunhua Liao[3]

[1] University of North Carolina at Charlotte, Charlotte, NC, USA
{xyi2,yyan7}@charlotte.edu
[2] Intel Corporation, Hillsboro, OR, USA
anjia.wang@intel.com
[3] Lawrence Livermore National Laboratory, Livermore, CA, USA
liao6@llnl.gov

Abstract. This paper presents an approach to authoring a textbook titled `Interactive OpenMP Programming` with the assistance of Large Language Models (LLMs). The writing process utilized state-of-the-art LLMs, including Gemini Pro 1.5, Claude 3, and ChatGPT-4, to generate the initial structure and outline of the book, as well as the initial content for specific chapters. This content included detailed descriptions of individual OpenMP constructs and practical programming examples. The outline and content have then undergone extensive manual revisions to meet our book goals. In this paper, we report our findings about the capabilities and limitations of these LLMs. We address critical questions concerning the necessity of textbook resources and the effectiveness of LLMs in creating fundamental and practical programming content. Our findings suggest that while LLMs offer significant advantages in generating textbook content, they require careful integration with traditional educational methodologies to ensure depth, accuracy, and pedagogical effectiveness. The `Interactive OpenMP Programming` book is developed with the framework of Jupyter Book, enabling the execution of code within the book from the web browser, providing instant feedback and a dynamic learning experience that stands in contrast to traditional educational resources. The book represents a significant step towards modernizing programming education, offering insights into practical strategies for generating the textbook through advanced AI tools.

Keywords: Large Language Model · OpenMP · Interactive Book · Gemini Pro 1.5 · Claude 3 · ChatGPT-4

1 Introduction

Given the increasing complexity of supercomputer node architectures in high-performance computing (HPC), high-level programming models have become essential to enhance productivity. OpenMP is a critical programming model in parallel computing, widely used for multi-core, multi-threaded processors, many-core accelerator architectures, and a combination of them. While interest in utilizing OpenMP in HPC is growing, the OpenMP language has evolved to feature more complex syntax. The length of the OpenMP specification has expanded from 318 pages in OpenMP 3.1 to 649 pages in OpenMP 5.2, creating a steep learning curve for this high-level programming model. The OpenMP framework's complexity, stemming from its advanced execution models and the in-depth knowledge required to manage parallel tasks, poses significant educational challenges. Traditional educational resources, such as textbooks for OpenMP, often fail to incorporate the latest programming additions and lack the interactivity necessary for effective learning. Outdated content and limited accessibility frequently hinder learning efficiency.

Recently, the landscape of computing and application has been evolving with the rapid advancement of artificial intelligence technologies, particularly large language models (LLMs) such as Gemini Pro 1.5, Claude 3, and ChatGPT-4. LLMs provide a prompt-answer model of learning, offering interactive and personalized educational experiences without the need for an actual human teacher. These include grammar and syntax support, case-based learning, concept clarification, and customized exercises and quizzes. While LLMs can significantly ease the learning process for OpenMP, their utilization in this context presents unique challenges. LLMs demonstrate proficiency in handling specific tasks and adeptly addressing specific questions. However, they fall short of providing a comprehensive learning schedule covering all OpenMP aspects. In contrast to traditional textbooks, LLMs are less effective in guiding students through a structured and progressive learning process. Additionally, effective prompts are crucial to optimizing the accuracy and relevance of LLM-generated content.

To leverage the strengths of both LLMs and traditional resources while addressing their limitations, we propose the development of an interactive OpenMP book. This book aims to stay updated with the latest OpenMP advancements and implement an interactive learning experience. We utilize LLMs' powerful text generation capabilities to rapidly generate the initial version, including explanations of OpenMP constructs, programming examples, and code interpretations. Designed with a "learning by practice" approach, the book provides up-to-date code examples and allows learners to experiment with them immediately. The interactive book is open-sourced and available at https://passlab.github.io/InteractiveOpenMPProgramming/cover.html.

The main contributions of this work include:

- Generating an interactive book named `Interactive OpenMP Programming Book`;
- Proposing a method for rapidly generating OpenMP educational content using LLMs;
- Evaluating the effectiveness and limitations of LLMs in creating both conceptual and practical programming content;

– Demonstrating how well-designed prompts can significantly enhance the quality of content generated by LLMs, contributing to more accurate educational materials.

The rest of the paper is as follows: Sect. 2 discusses the background and the motivation for using LLMs to develop the `Interactive OpenMP Programming` book and identifies the deficiencies of traditional textbooks. Section 3 details the methodology employed in utilizing LLMs to create an interactive programming book, including the strategies for prompt design and content validation. Section 4 assesses and discusses the content generated by the LLMs and the content in `Interactive OpenMP Programming` book. Section 5 introduced the related work. The paper concludes in Sect. 6, where we summarize our findings, outline future research avenues, and suggest improvements for more effectively integrating LLMs into educational frameworks.

2 Background and Motivation

Learning OpenMP programming through LLMs and traditional textbooks each has its own set of advantages and disadvantages. Table 1 provides a comparison of these methods.

LLMs offer several advantages over traditional textbooks. Primarily, they provide instant feedback and interactive engagement. They could provide immediate responses to inquiries, analyze user-submitted code in real-time, and suggest enhancements. Additionally, LLMs are highly adaptable and customizable educational tools. They can tailor content and examples to match the user's skill level and learning preferences, potentially speeding up the learning process. Furthermore, LLMs can access various information sources, providing diverse perspectives and solutions. In contrast, traditional textbooks do not offer these advantages. They lack the interactivity essential for effective learning and are unable to adjust content in real-time based on students' needs.

Table 1. Advantages and Limitations of Learning from LLMs and Traditional Textbooks

Learn from LLMs	
Pros	**Cons**
- Deliver instantaneous feedback and interactive engagement. - Provide immediate responses to inquiries. - Analyze user-submitted code in real-time and suggest enhancements. - Serve as highly adaptable and customizable educational tools. - Access a wide array of information sources, offering diverse perspectives and solutions.	- Offer a relatively superficial depth of understanding of complex OpenMP constructs. - Unable to verify the accuracy of the information they generate. - Unable to execute the code in real-time. - Lack of a structured learning trajectory. - Pre-trained with fixed knowledge about a field, making it difficult to update with new information.
Learn from Traditional Textbooks	
Pros	**Cons**
- Provide a systematic and comprehensive exploration of OpenMP programming, aligning with the principle of progressive learning. - Incorporate case studies and best practices that are the culmination of years of expert experience and scholarly research. - Uphold a high standard of information accuracy.	- Lack of the essential interactivity needed for effective learning. - Struggle to keep pace with the latest programming paradigms and updates. - Require high costs for purchase, making some books less accessible.

Despite the advantages, the drawbacks of learning using LLMs cannot be ignored. The first drawback is the relatively superficial depth of understanding. From our experience with SIMD and vector architecture in OpenMP, while LLMs can introduce the basic usage of `#pragma omp simd`, they often fall short in providing detailed discussions on optimizing SIMD for specific hardware configurations. In contrast, textbooks are typically authored by experienced experts and scholars, ensuring a deeper understanding of the OpenMP content. Another issue is the absence of mechanisms within LLMs to verify the accuracy of the information they generate, potentially leading to the dissemination of incorrect or misleading content. For example, LLMs can generate explanations for `#pragma omp task depend`, but we noticed that they fail to handle data race conditions in multi-threading environments. In contrast, textbooks maintain a high standard of information accuracy. Lastly, LLMs lack structured and progressive education procedures. Traditional textbooks typically provide a more systematic and comprehensive exploration of OpenMP programming, incorporating case studies and best practices. They follow pedagogical principles, building foundational knowledge before advancing to complex topics. Although LLMs can be programmed to offer structured education, their flexibility can lead to deviations. For example, traditional learning for GPU programming starts with basic architecture and progresses to advanced topics like memory management. LLMs, however, might skip essential steps or present advanced topics prematurely based on user queries, resulting in fragmented or incomplete understanding.

A common drawback of both LLMs and textbooks is their inability to stay updated with the latest OpenMP specifications. LLMs, being pre-trained, possess fixed knowledge about a field and are challenging to update with new information. For example, in the OpenMP specification 5.2, the `depend` clause is no longer used with the `ordered` directive. Despite attempts to update ChatGPT with the latest specifications, it still occasionally generates content that incorrectly uses the `depend` clause. We find that this issue can be mitigated by directing the LLMs to learn and use specific new information. However, beginners might not be aware of whether the content generated by an LLM complies with the latest specifications, nor understand how to prompt the LLMs to produce updated content. This problem is more pronounced and difficult to resolve in textbooks. Once published, textbooks are hard to modify, and we often find that many contain outdated content that cannot be promptly updated.

Based on these pros and cons, we aim to combine the best of both worlds by using LLMs to help develop a structured, interactive textbook - `Interactive OpenMP Programming`. This involves using advanced AI tools to modernize programming education and enhance its effectiveness, thereby providing learners with a more interactive, engaging, and effective educational experience. First, the decision to employ LLMs arises from the need to address the limitations of traditional OpenMP educational resources. LLMs can quickly generate up-to-date educational content, solving the problem of outdated material in traditional textbooks. Secondly, we will analyze the depth of LLMs' understanding of different OpenMP constructs and manually complete sections where the LLM's understanding is insufficient. At the same time, we will rigorously review the accuracy of the content generated. This task is initially aimed at addressing issues with LLMs' depth of understanding of complex topics and the inability to audit the correctness of generated content. Furthermore, our exploration will provide a reference for others studying LLMs' comprehension of OpenMP. Next, we will use Jupyter Notebooks to develop an interactive, progressive textbook, where learners can execute their code directly to verify its correctness. This approach maintains the structured learning benefits provided by traditional textbooks while addressing their limitations in supporting interactive learning, the inability of LLMs to offer systematic, progressive learning, and the lack of real-time code execution. Finally, the motivation also includes exploring how to optimize LLM output through the strategic design of prompts, which is essential for enhancing the quality of the generated content. This approach ensures that the material is not only technically accurate and pedagogically sound but also tailored to the specific learning context of OpenMP programming.

3 Method

The development of the book, with the help of LLM includes the creation of outlines of the book and each chapter, and then the creation of the content and code examples of each chapter, section and subsection. We have used three LLMs in this process, including Gemini Pro 1.5, ChatGPT-4 and Claude 3. Thus our development also assessed the capabilities of each LLM in generating and developing content, examining their strengths and weaknesses. This section also includes a description of the setup and deployment of the interactive book learning environment, emphasizing how it supports incremental and interactive updates to enhance learning outcomes.

3.1 Outlining the Book and Each Chapter with the Aid of LLMs

A combined approach of human expertise and machine-generated content is recommended to effectively utilize LLMs in composing a comprehensive OpenMP programming book. The methodology involves the following steps:

Generating Outlines of the Textbook. Using various LLMs to create multiple book structures based on their interpretations of the OpenMP API 5.2 Specification and analyses of the official OpenMP API 5.2.2 Examples [4] will leverage the LLMs' capability to quickly process and synthesize extensive datasets. We used the prompt: "Please get information about OpenMP directives and clauses from the uploaded OpenMP specification and official examples. I am writing a book on teaching OpenMP programming. Please help me to generate an outline for this book." We also tried to use more prompts like "generate a more advanced outline" or "using some intended organizational approach".

However, we discovered that the frameworks produced by the LLMs did not align with our intended organizational approach. For instance, ChatGPT allocated substantial sections to discussing the foundational concepts of OpenMP and the setup processes. However, the detailed explanations and examples of the directives and the clauses were confined to merely two chapters-"Fundamentals of OpenMP" and "Advanced OpenMP". Similarly, the other two LLMs we evaluated did not perform satisfactorily. Consequently, after reviewing the frameworks generated by three different LLMs and integrating professional insights, we manually developed the book's structure. Our book emphasizes analyzing and applying various directives and clauses, illustrated through a combination of fundamental and advanced examples.

Generating Outlines for Chapters. Although the LLMs offered limited assistance in establishing the overall framework, they proved highly beneficial in crafting detailed outlines and contents for individual chapters. To ask the LLMs to generate the outline of the chapter "2.4. Synchronization of Threads Using Barrier and Ordered Directive," we first had the LLMs learn about synchronization in parallel computing scenarios from OpenMP Specification and official examples. Then, we uploaded a manually completed chapter on the `teams` construct to serve as a reference for the LLMs.

To use the proper prompts, we incorporate the CO-STAR framework, which outlines a structured approach to crafting prompts that can significantly enhance the effectiveness and professionalism of the content generated by LLMs [2]. Developed by GovTech Singapore's Data Science and Artificial Intelligence Division, CO-STAR stands for Context, Objective, Style, Tone, Audience, and Response. The prompt set is shown below:

- I am writing a book on teaching others OpenMP parallel programming. Can you help me?
- Here is a chapter I have written on teams; please analyze and learn how I created the outline.
- Now, I need to write a chapter on synchronization, mainly focusing on barrier and order constructs. Please find the descriptions of usage and related examples in the file I have uploaded.
- Please help me complete this section by first generating an outline.

The prompts are progressive and interactive, involving multiple steps, including learning from uploaded material, analyzing a previous chapter, and developing a new chapter outline. This approach generates a more detailed and contextually enriched outline. We've found that the structure generated by this set of prompts closely resembles that of the previous `teams` chapter and incorporates many terms like `explore`, `understanding`, `analysis`, and `apply` that are more apt for educational contexts. The generated and revised outlines are demonstrated in Table 2.

Assessment and Selection of the Outlines. We followed a three-step assessment process to ensure the quality and accuracy of the generated outlines. First, we conducted a cross-model review, where one LLM critiqued another's outlines, enhancing them through mutual learning. Next, according to OpenMP Specification, we manually inspected each outline's comprehensiveness and accuracy. Finally, we integrated the structures. We merged the best aspects of each outline, balancing their strengths and weaknesses to create an optimized and effective structure.

The outlines generated by different LLMs have distinct characteristics. The outline generated by Gemini Pro 1.5 is concise, focusing on practical applications and key concepts. It briefly introduces the basic usage and examples of `barrier` and `ordered` directives, explaining how to set synchronization points and maintain execution order. However, Gemini lacks comprehensive detail in practical application examples and discussions of advanced topics. The outline generated by ChatGPT 4 features clearly structured steps and examples, such as the basic usage of Barrier directives and compatibility with the `doacross` clause. This outline may offer some technical depth while maintaining good generality and overview. The outline generated by Claude 3 is a highly detailed structure covering basic concepts and uses while exploring various complex scenarios and performance considerations, such as teaching advanced uses of `barrier` and `ordered` directives like nested directives and interoperability with task scheduling. However, it might be overly complex, including some unnecessary details, especially for beginners, requiring a longer learning curve.

3.2 Content Generation, Including Code Examples Using Three LLMs

Understanding and Explaining Fundamental Constructs. This subsection outlines our analysis of how LLMs generate specific text. We show descriptions of the `barrier` directive generated by different LLMs in Table 3.

All three LLMs accurately describe the basic functionality of the `barrier` directive for technical accuracy. Claude provides a straightforward introduction to the `barrier` directive's role in thread synchronization, focusing on its basic functionality. Gemini and ChatGPT provide a detailed and context-rich explanation, emphasizing the `barrier` directive's critical role in preventing race conditions, which could be very beneficial in understanding more complex scenarios.

Considering the educational purpose, Claude offers a more generalized and accessible introduction, making it suitable for beginners just starting to learn about thread synchronization in parallel programming. ChatGPT balances a general introduction and a specific application, making it ideal for intermediate learners. With its detailed explanations of particular scenarios like race conditions, Gemini targets readers with some background in parallel programming and looking to deepen their understanding of synchronization challenges.

Generation and Explanation of Examples. Different LLMs showcase unique difficulty, depth, and correctness attributes when analyzing the generated examples. The prompt we used to generate the examples is: "Please create an example of using the *[directive name]* directive. Some of the prompts may be more specific, including demonstrating the usage of the *[clause name]* clause and demonstrating the data race."

We still focus on examples related to synchronization. Claude presents examples of high difficulty that incorporate multiple synchronization points. These examples demonstrate a deep understanding by illustrating practical synchronization uses in nested parallel contexts, offering insights into complex programming scenarios. However, it's important to note that some of these examples were not created by Claude but are directly adopted from official OpenMP examples, which were used as training material for the LLMs. Gemini primarily offers easy and basic examples, focusing on introductory scenarios. While the examples are correct, they lack depth and do not explore the complexities that more advanced users might encounter. Consequently, these examples are often insufficient for educational purposes and are typically not used in our `Interactive OpenMP`

Table 2. Outlines Generated by Gemini Pro 1.5, ChatGPT-4 and Claude 3, and the Revised Outline Used in the Textbook for Sect. 2.4. Synchronization of Threads Using Barrier and Ordered Directives

Outline generated by Gemini Pro 1.5	Outline generated by ChatGPT-4
– **Introduction** – **Barrier Directive** • Establishing Synchronization Points • Example – **The Ordered Directive: Maintaining Sequential Steps** • Enforcing Order in the Parallel Ballet • doacross Clause: Specifying Dependencies – **Implicit Barriers: Automatic Synchronization** • Removing Implicit Barriers with nowait – **Best Practices for Using Barrier and Ordered Directives**	– **Introduction** – **Barrier Directive** • Purpose of the Barrier Directive • Usage • Example: Using the Barrier Directive • Considerations – **Ordered Directive** • Purpose of the Ordered Directive • Usage • Compatibility with the doacross Clause • Example: Serial Output in Parallel Loop • Considerations – **Summary** • Takeaways
Outline generated by Claude 3	**Revised Outline**
– **Introduction** • Importance of Thread Synchronization • Overview of the Barrier and Ordered Directives – **Barrier Directive** • Purpose and Usage • Syntax and Examples • Barrier Regions • Synchronization Points – **Ordered Directive** • Purpose and Usage • Syntax and Examples • Enforcing Execution Order • Ordered Regions • Stand-alone Ordered Construct • Block-associated Ordered Construct • Interaction with Loop Constructs and Clauses • Best Practices – **Combining Barrier and Ordered Directives** • Use Cases for Combining Directives • Examples and Code Snippets • Considerations and Potential Issues – **Implicit Barriers** • Implicit Barrier Regions • Execution Model Events and Tool Callbacks – **Advanced Topics** • Nested Barrier and Ordered Directives • Interoperability with Other Synchronization Mechanisms • Synchronization in the Context of Tasking • Debugging and Profiling Synchronization Issues – **Performance Considerations** • Overhead and Scalability • Load Balancing and Synchronization Granularity • Performance Tuning and Optimization – **Summary and Conclusion**	– **Introduction** • Importance of Thread Synchronization • Overview of the Barrier and Ordered Directives – **Barrier Directive** • Purpose and Usage • Syntax and Practical Examples • Barrier Regions and Synchronization Points – **Ordered Directive** • Purpose and Usage • Syntax and Practical Examples • Interaction with Loop Constructs and doacross Clause • Best Practices and Considerations – **Combining Barrier and Ordered Directives** • Use Cases for Combining Directives • Examples and Code Snippets • Considerations and Potential Issues – **Implicit Barriers** • Overview and Automatic Synchronization • Controlling Implicit Barriers – **Advanced Topics** • Nested Directives and Interoperability • Synchronization in the Context of Tasking • Debugging and Profiling Synchronization Issues – **Performance Considerations** • Overhead and Scalability • Load Balancing and Synchronization Granularity – **Summary and Conclusion** • Recap of Key Points • Further Learning and Applications

Table 3. Generated Description of the `Barrier` Directive. Prompt: Please explain the meaning of the `barrier` directive.

Claude 3	Barrier Directive: The `barrier` directive introduces a synchronization point where all threads in a parallel region must wait until all threads have reached the barrier. This ensures all threads have completed their work before proceeding to the following computation phase
Gemini Pro 1.5	Barrier Directive: Acting as a synchronization point, the barrier directive ensures all threads within a team reach a designated point before any are allowed to proceed. This is crucial in preventing race conditions, where multiple threads accessing and modifying shared data simultaneously can lead to unpredictable and erroneous results
ChatGPT-4	Barrier Directive: This directive is used to align threads at a synchronization point before they can proceed further. It ensures that all threads in a team reach a certain point in the execution before moving on. This is particularly useful when subsequent operations depend on all threads completing certain tasks

`Programming` book. ChatGPT performs best in generating examples. It can produce both simple and more complex examples and delves into advanced performance optimization techniques. The examples are supported by comprehensive explanations that ensure a clear understanding of their application. However, ChatGPT does not generate many examples; when examples are needed to aid teaching, the descriptions remain overly simplistic, and the examples provided are insufficient. Despite mentioning optimization techniques, the capability is limited and often accompanied by inaccuracies.

The Workflow of Generating Interactive Format with the Help from LLMs. In this subsection, we will elaborate on generating and updating content for an interactive book with the help of LLMs, which we ultimately create and edit as JSON files in a Jupyter Notebook. Theoretically, it is feasible to have LLMs produce text in a specific format since generating formatted text is a strength of LLMs. However, in practice, it is not as straightforward. One of the interactive features of our designed book allows users to enter their code directly into a code input box and execute it to receive feedback. This necessitates the setting up of separate code cells, specifying the programming language (C/C++ or Fortran) and the compiler. Initially, LLMs do not always generate the format we want, often requiring repetitive debugging and constant modification of our instructions to make the LLM understand the desired format, which is quite inefficient. Moreover, different LLMs have varying levels of understanding and capability. For instance, ChatGPT can usually generate text in different formats, Gemini may not fulfill formatting requirements, and Claude can produce Markdown format but cannot separate code from textual descriptions. Therefore, we only have LLMs generate content, ideally in Markdown format, without insisting that they produce directly usable JSON files, which must be manually adjusted for format and cell type later.

Updating the `Interactive OpenMP Programming` book is straightforward. When changes are needed, we can update the content in the local repository and then upload these changes to the online repository using the standard GitHub pull request process. The online GitHub repository automatically manages the book deployment. Typically, the book is compiled locally before uploading to ensure there are no compilation errors that could hinder proper deployment. Similarly, we allow users to add content to the book or upload their code. The difference is that users need to apply before uploading. Our administrators review the content and decide whether to merge it into our book.

3.3 Interactive and Incremental Development of a Programming Book

The design of the interactive OpenMP programming book is shown in Fig. 1. On the client side, users can access the book from a browser on any web-enabled device. Besides conventional reading instructions, they can modify the corresponding Jupyter notebooks and conduct experiments. For the server side, all the book sources are stored on GitHub. This generates both the book and Jupyter notebooks. The reading materials are provided as HTML files [3]. The Jupyter notebooks, which act as a coding sandbox, are served via JupyterLab with a native kernel. There are three ways to deploy the book, each with strengths and limitations.

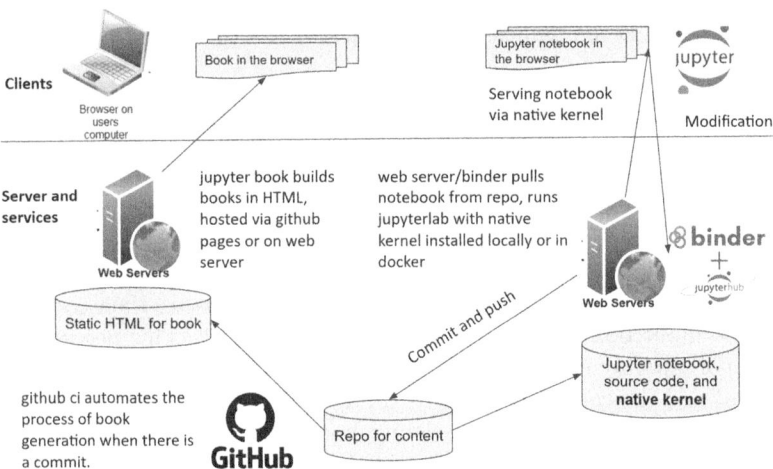

Fig. 1. Client and Server Architecture of Interactive OpenMP Programming Book

Local Deployment. We can deploy the interactive OpenMP programming book on a local Linux machine by installing JupyterBook and JupyterLab. JupyterBook generates the book website in HTML. JupyterLab runs the code examples in the book on demand. Local deployment is suitable for trial runs and development. The user can quickly modify the book content or backend server configuration and review the changes.

Self-hosting Deployment. Self-hosting is similar to local deployment in most aspects, except a server for the public or a specific private network is required. The benefit of self-hosting deployment is that we can create a more capable programming sandbox for users. For example, a local laptop may not support OpenMP GPU offloading, while a self-hosting server does. However, a self-hosting server requires more professional maintenance work. It typically must provide uninterrupted service.

Third-Party-Hosting Deployment. Another way to deploy the programming book is to utilize third-party services like Binder [1]. Instead of setting up the service from scratch on a local or remote machine under control, we can create a Dockerfile to specify what OS and software should be installed. Binder will create an online virtual machine based on the Dockerfile and set up the sandbox accordingly. However, users can't control Binder server's hardware configuration, which is typically not very powerful.

4 Assessment and Discussion

4.1 Comparing the Learning Capabilities of Different Models

We have analyzed and evaluated the capability of various LLMs to learn from uploaded materials. The results are summarized in Table 4.

Table 4. Comparison of Document Handling by Different Models

Model	Strengths	Weaknesses
ChatGPT	Can understand short documents well and comprehend desired outputs effectively	Struggles to extract useful information from lengthy documents; fails to identify detailed information or clauses of a directive
Gemini	Better performance with long documents; can extract relevant information directly from specifications	Struggles to understand the required output, resulting in overly simplistic outputs despite various methods and detailed information provided
Claude	Understands input documents and instructions well; can handle excerpted relevant content from long documents	Tends to imitate; requires substantial manual modification of generated outlines; may include unnecessary analysis in sections

We demonstrate the learning capabilities of different models through an example that illustrates their ability to acquire new knowledge and explain it effectively. The `doacross` clause, introduced in the OpenMP 5.2 specification, is used with the `ordered` directive. Although `doacross` concept was mentioned in version 5.1, it was not formally specified as a clause until version 5.2. We tasked three LLMs with analyzing content from the OpenMP specifications about the `ordered` directive and then generating descriptions of the `ordered` directive and its clauses. Ideally, they would ascertain that the doacross clause is now the only clause used with the ordered directive and understand how to use it. The primary objective of this study was to evaluate the LLMs' ability to extract and understand detailed information, with a specific focus on their comprehension of the doacross clause. Additionally, significant changes in the ordered directive have led to the removal of the use of simd, threads, and depend clauses, making doacross the sole clause used with ordered directive. Our analysis evaluated whether the LLMs could effectively learn from input files and not merely rely on pre-existing knowledge.

By analyzing the generated content, we noted that Claude's responses primarily offered general explanations and reiterations of the specification of the doacross concept. However, Claude did not provide specific insights into the doacross clause, such as its usage, functionalities, or applications. We believe that it failed to identify information specifically about the doacross clause, instead finding descriptions of the doacross concept in a different chapter. In other words, Claude does not seem to understand that doacross has been defined as a clause. Conversely, Gemini explained that the doacross is defined as a clause and this clause is used to specify explicit dependencies between iterations in parallel-executed loops. It highlighted that this enables the compiler to ensure the correctness of data dependencies as defined by developers, which is particularly crucial in scenarios with complex dependencies.

ChatGPT initially did not retrieve any content about the doacross clause when directed to study the ordered directive and its clauses. Instead, it used the depend clause incorrectly. However, when explicitly directed to focus on the doacross clause, ChatGPT demonstrated a deeper understanding and provided a more comprehensive response. It accurately recognized that doacross was defined as a clause, explained its use, and even described its compatibility with the ordered directive: the ordered directive can be effectively combined with the doacross loop scheduling to provide finer control over dependencies in loop iterations. The doacross clause allows specifying dependencies between loop iterations, which is crucial for ensuring that iteration i completes specific tasks before iteration $i+1$ can commence. It also showcased, through example code, how to use the ordered and doacross clauses to manage dependencies, applicable in scenarios requiring tightly coupled iterative operations.

The varying levels of understanding among the three LLMs concerning the newly added doacross clause present an interesting topic. Initially, we verified that all three LLMs could learn from new input materials and were not solely dependent on existing knowledge. ChatGPT does not process documents in detail, tends to overlook some content, and largely relies on existing knowledge bases. Yet, it can effectively understand and explain these details when specifically directed to extract particular content. Gemini shows strong abilities in processing the input materials; it was the only model to recognize doacross as a clause without being explicitly prompted to focus on doacross clause. However, its explanations remain limited, resembling more a rephrasing of the specification content without offering an in-depth explanation or practical demonstrations of usage. Claude reads the input but fails to understand it correctly. It identifies content related to `doacross` but does not recognize it as a clause nor grasp its application. It is unclear whether this is due to a misunderstanding or incorrect information retrieval.

Determining how much LLMs rely on user-uploaded content versus preexisting knowledge is challenging. This issue is a key area of interest in LLM algorithm design. In our work, we focus on evaluating the understanding capabilities of these models and the quality of the content they generate, without emphasizing the source of the information.

4.2 Assessment of the `Interactive OpenMP Programming` Book

Quantitative Analysis of Generated Textbook. In our published version of the `Interactive OpenMP Programming` book, there are over 200 OpenMP examples and more than 17,000 lines of text or code. We check the generated content for the text segments for accuracy and depth of understanding. This involves guiding the LLMs through several revisions or having different LLMs revise the content. We resort to manual edits if the ideal output is not achieved after multiple attempts. Typically, it takes a few minutes to generate the initial version of a chapter, followed by several hours of revisions. Completing the same volume of work totally manually usually requires over a week to finish a chapter's initial draft and revisions.

The code examples generated by ChatGPT and Gemini have been validated. They differ entirely from the official OpenMP examples, demonstrating that the LLMs do not simply copy content from input files. However, about 60% of the complicated examples generated by Claude are directly from official examples from our experience. Most simple cases are completely accurate and do not require modifications, but more complex examples often need manual corrections or optimizations, with over 70%.

Official OpenMP Examples Versus Interactive Book Demonstrations. We compared the examples using the `SIMD` directive in the `Interactive OpenMP Programming` book and the official OpenMP examples in Fig. 2. The official example is a function that processes two double-precision arrays using `SIMD` directives for parallel reduction, emphasizing modularity in a potentially larger application. It uses a private temporary variable to ensure thread safety during the sum computation. In contrast, the example in our book is a complete standalone program within a main function, utilizing a single float array and demonstrating OpenMP's SIMD capabilities in a straightforward educational format. It includes array initialization, directly adds each element to the sum, and outputs the result, making it highly accessible for learning. Unlike the official example, which returns the computed sum for use elsewhere, the example in our book prints the sum directly, emphasizing immediate visual feedback for learners.

```
#include <stdio.h>
#define N 1024

int main() {
  float a[N]; float sum = 0.0f;
  for (int i=0; i<N; i++) a[i] = i*1.0f;
  // Vectorize the loop
  #pragma omp simd reduction(+:sum)
  for (int i=0; i<N; i++) sum += a[i];
  printf("Sum:%f\n", sum);
  return 0;
}
```

(a) Code Example of SIMD in Interactive OpenMP Programming Book

```
double work(double *a, double *b, int n) {
  int i;
  double tmp, sum;
  sum = 0.0;
  #pragma omp simd private(tmp) \
              reduction(+:sum)
  for (i = 0; i < n; i++) {
    tmp = a[i] + b[i];
    sum += tmp;
  }
  return sum;
}
```

(b) Code Example of SIMD from Official OpenMP Examples

Fig. 2. Comparative Analysis of Code Examples

5 Related Work

5.1 Existing Books for OpenMP Programming

In this section, we discuss notable contributions to OpenMP programming education, highlighting their relevance to our current study while identifying unique features, commonalities, and limitations.

"Parallel Programming in OpenMP" is one of the pioneering texts [7]. Although it offers a historical and technical foundation, enriching our study's depth, the content has become significantly outdated, limiting its contemporary relevance. "Using OpenMP - Portable Shared Memory Parallel Programming" offers a comprehensive introduction to OpenMP, addressing hardware developments and comparing OpenMP with other programming interfaces [8]. "OpenMP Common Core: Making OpenMP Simple Again" simplifies OpenMP by focusing on its twenty-one essential components [11]. These books provide foundational knowledge and are rich in details and examples. However, they predominantly focus on basics and lack extensive real-world applications, with most missing in-depth optimization discussions.

"Using OpenMP - The Next Step" explores OpenMP's advanced features, such as tasking, thread affinity, and accelerators, delving into complex programming scenarios [13]. "High-Performance Parallel Runtimes" provides an in-depth analysis of parallel programming models suitable for modern high-performance multi-core processors, with detailed discussions on optimizing key algorithms [10]. "Programming Your GPU with OpenMP" focuses on GPU programming with OpenMP, emphasizing heterogeneous programming and performance optimization [9]. These books cover advanced features in OpenMP's new standards and discuss deep optimization techniques, particularly hardware-specific optimizations, including CPUs and GPUs. While they offer valuable insights for optimizing performance, their complexity may pose challenges for beginners.

A collective examination of these OpenMP programming books reveals that they adhere to educational principles, structuring content from simple to complex, gradually deepening understanding. They emphasize practical learning through extensive examples, which are crucial for learners to grasp complex concepts practically. However, common limitations include rapid obsolescence due to the fast-paced evolution of parallel programming technologies, the inability to provide real-time feedback to users, and the long development cycle of traditional publishing, which cannot quickly address limitations once published.

Our `Interactive OpenMP Programming` book leverages LLMs like Gemini Pro 1.5, Claude 3, and ChatGPT-4 to quickly generate up-to-date content, enabling real-time code execution and a dynamic learning experience via Jupyter books. This "learning by practice" approach provides immediate feedback and practical application, making the material more engaging and customizable to individual learning needs. Additionally, the `Interactive OpenMP Programming` book is open-sourced and accessible online, reducing costs and increasing accessibility compared to traditional textbooks, which often require purchase and can be less accessible.

5.2 The Use of LLM in Education and Textbook Writing

LLMs like ChatGPT have demonstrated potential in aiding various stages of writing, including organizing material, drafting, and proofreading. One of the major challenges highlighted in educational settings is the accuracy and relevance of the information provided by the LLM, particularly how it integrates into the developers' workflow without disrupting it. The study by Changrong Xiao and colleagues examines the utilization of ChatGPT for generating personalized reading comprehension exercises for middle school English learners in China [15]. Their research addresses the challenge of outdated and non-engaging educational materials by deploying ChatGPT to produce tailored reading passages and questions, thereby enhancing student engagement and material relevance. Through automated and manual evaluations, the system demonstrated its ability to generate educational content that often surpassed the quality of traditional methods. In a similar vein, Nam et al. (2024) explore the potential of using LLMs to enhance code understanding and development within an Integrated Development Environment (IDE) through their prototype tool, GILT [12]. This tool integrates directly into the IDE to provide context-aware, real-time information support, aiming to help developers understand and expand unfamiliar code more effectively. Their study involved a user study with 32 participants, showing that using GILT significantly improves task completion rates compared to traditional web searches. However, no significant gains were found regarding time savings or deeper understanding, suggesting areas for further improvement.

Another example concerning the relevance and accuracy of responses from LLMs comes from the work of Arora et al. (2024), who analyzed the usage patterns of LLMs among undergraduate and graduate students in advanced computing courses at an Indian university [6]. Their research focused on how students employ LLMs for programming assignments, particularly in code generation, debugging, and conceptual understanding. Employing a mixed-method approach, combining surveys and interviews, the study highlighted that while LLMs significantly enhance student productivity by generating boilerplate code and aiding in debugging, they also present challenges regarding response accuracy and integration with student-generated code. This necessitates substantial student interaction with LLMs to integrate and troubleshoot system components effectively. The findings emphasize the role of LLMs as supplementary tools in educational settings, suggesting the importance of proper prompts to enhance the utility and accuracy of LLM outputs in complex academic tasks. People should be very careful when verifying the accuracy of the generated code when using LLMs.

Altmäe et al. explore the use of ChatGPT in scientific writing, particularly focusing on its application in drafting a manuscript for reproductive medicine [5]. The study illustrates the potential and challenges of using AI in academic writing, highlighting ChatGPT's role in streamlining content creation, manuscripts' initial composition, and refinement. Key challenges noted include the accuracy and relevance of AI-generated content, requiring significant human oversight to ensure scientific integrity, and raising ethical concerns about authorship and the potential for AI to discourage deep learning. This exploration aligns with broader discussions on integrating AI in educational tools, as seen in other research focused on programming education. It suggests AI's utility as a supplementary aid in complex intellectual tasks, provided its limitations are carefully managed.

Literature surveys are fundamental in academia and education, providing essential overviews of existing research and identifying future research directions. The study by Wang et al. introduces `AutoSurvey`, an innovative system designed to automate the creation of comprehensive literature surveys. Employing a systematic approach that encompasses initial retrieval and outline generation, subsection drafting by specialized LLMs, integration, refinement, and rigorous evaluation, `AutoSurvey` adeptly addresses the challenges posed by the vast volume and complexity of information. By leveraging the capabilities of LLMs, the system not only enhances the efficiency and quality of literature surveys but also demonstrates significant improvements in both citation and content quality compared to traditional methods. This exploration not only highlights the potential of LLMs to drastically reduce the time required to produce high-quality academic surveys but also underscores ongoing challenges such as context window limitations and the reliability of parametric knowledge within these models [14].

The commonality among the studies above lies in their utilization of the powerful reading, understanding, and text-generation capabilities of LLMs. This aligns closely with our work. However, our research specifically focuses on generating OpenMP textbooks, emphasizing the teaching of OpenMP programming. We deeply explore the abilities of various LLMs to understand and interpret different OpenMP structures, parallel computing logics, and the generation of OpenMP examples. Additionally, we discuss how to continuously leverage LLMs to rapidly update textbook content, thereby addressing the critical issue of textbooks lagging behind during updates in OpenMP.

6 Conclusion

In conclusion, this paper has explored the innovative use of Large Language Models (LLMs) such as Gemini Pro 1.5, Claude 3, and ChatGPT-4 for creating `Interactive OpenMP Programming` book. Our research indicates that while LLMs significantly enhance the interactivity and dynamism of educational content, they must be strategically integrated with traditional educational methodologies to maintain the depth and accuracy essential for effective learning. The developed interactive book, facilitated by Jupyter Notebooks, stands out by enabling real-time code execution and feedback, which is a considerable advancement over static learning materials. The success of our approach demonstrates that LLMs can play a crucial role in modernizing educational practices, especially in complex technical domains like OpenMP programming.

Future research should focus on refining the integration of LLMs into educational frameworks, enhancing the accuracy of content through improved prompt design, and exploring the scalability of this approach across other programming languages and frameworks. We also recommend ongoing assessments of the pedagogical impact of these tools to ensure they meet educational standards and effectively support learners. By continuing to leverage cutting-edge AI technologies, educators can better prepare students for the evolving demands of the tech-driven world, making learning not only more interactive but also more attuned to the needs of contemporary students.

Acknowledgement. This material is based upon work supported by the National Science Foundation under Grant No. 2001580 and 2015254. This work was also prepared by LLNL under Contract DE-AC52-07NA27344 (LLNL-CONF-867264) and supported by the U.S. Department of Energy, Office of Science, Office of Advanced Scientific Computing Research, Scientific Discovery through Advanced Computing (SciDAC) program.

References

1. Binder. https://mybinder.org
2. Co-star framework for prompt structuring. https://medium.com/@thomasczerny/co-star-framework-for-prompt-structuring-7f9a8c221224
3. Interactive OpenMP programming book. https://passlab.github.io/InteractiveOpenMPProgramming
4. Openmp application programming interface examples. https://www.openmp.org/wp-content/uploads/openmp-examples-5.2.2-final.pdf
5. Altmäe, S., Sola-Leyva, A., Salumets, A.: Artificial intelligence in scientific writing: a friend or a foe? Reprod. Biomed. Online **47**(1), 3–9 (2023)
6. Arora, C., et al.: Analyzing LLM usage in an advanced computing class in India. arXiv preprint arXiv:2404.04603 (2024)
7. Chandra, R.: Parallel Programming in OpenMP. Morgan Kaufmann, Burlington (2001)
8. Chapman, B., Jost, G., Van Der Pas, R.: Using OpenMP: Portable Shared Memory Parallel Programming. MIT Press, Cambridge (2007)

9. Deakin, T., Mattson, T.G.: Programming your GPU with OpenMP. Context **249**, 251
10. Klemm, M., Cownie, J.: High Performance Parallel Runtimes: Design and Implementation. Walter de Gruyter GmbH & Co KG (2021)
11. Mattson, T.G., He, Y.H., Koniges, A.E.: The OpenMP Common Core: Making OpenMP Simple Again. MIT Press, Cambridge (2019)
12. Nam, D., Macvean, A., Hellendoorn, V., Vasilescu, B., Myers, B.: Using an LLM to help with code understanding. In: Proceedings of the IEEE/ACM 46th International Conference on Software Engineering, pp. 1–13 (2024)
13. Van der Pas, R., Stotzer, E., Terboven, C.: Using OpenMP# the Next Step: Affinity, Accelerators, Tasking, and SIMD. MIT Press, Cambridge (2017)
14. Wang, Y., et al.: Autosurvey: large language models can automatically write surveys. arXiv preprint arXiv:2406.10252 (2024)
15. Xiao, C., Xu, S.X., Zhang, K., Wang, Y., Xia, L.: Evaluating reading comprehension exercises generated by LLMs: a showcase of ChatGPT in education applications. In: Proceedings of the 18th Workshop on Innovative Use of NLP for Building Educational Applications (BEA 2023), pp. 610–625 (2023)

Simplifying Parallelization

Automatic Parallelization and OpenMP Offloading of Fortran Array Notation

Ivan R. Ivanov[1,2]($\boxtimes$), Jens Domke[2], Toshio Endo[1],
and Johannes Doerfert[3]

[1] Tokyo Institute of Technology, Tokyo, Japan
ivanov.i.aa@m.titech.ac.jp, endo@is.titech.ac.jp
[2] RIKEN Center for Computational Science, Kobe, Japan
jens.domke@riken.jp
[3] Lawrence Livermore National Laboratory, Livermore, CA, USA
doerfert1@llnl.gov

Abstract. The Fortran programming language is prevalent in the scientific computing community with a wealth of existing software written in it. It is still being developed with the latest standard released in 2023. However, due to its long history, many old code bases are in need of modernization for new HPC systems. One advantage Fortran has over C and C++, which are other languages broadly used in scientific computing, is the easy syntax for manipulating entire arrays or subarrays. However, this feature is underused as there was no way of offloading them to accelerators and support for parallelization has been unsatisfactory. The new OpenMP 6.0 standard introduces the `workdistribute` directive which enables parallelization and/or offloading automatically by just annotating the region the programmer wishes to speed up. We implement `workdistribute` in the LLVM project's Fortran compiler, called Flang. Flang uses MLIR – Multi-Level Intermediate Representation – which allows for a structured representation that captures the high level semantics of array manipulation and OpenMP. This allows us to build an implementation that performs on par with more verbose manually parallelized OpenMP code. By offloading linear algebra operations to vendor libraries, we also enable software developers to easily unlock the full potential of their hardware without needing to write verbose, vendor-specific source code.

Keywords: OpenMP · Fortran · offloading · parallelization

1 Introduction

The most substantial compute power found in most modern HPC systems is in their accelerators, namely GPUs [1]. Thus, it is important to achieve a high GPU utilization in order to maximize performance of scientific computing applications.

Fortran is still prevalent in the scientific community and there are vast amounts of important applications written in it. Previous Fortran codes were not written with accelerators in mind, so enabling scientists to easily make use of modern hardware with minimal effort is an important goal.

OpenMP has been widely used as a way to accelerate these programs, and the OpenMP 6.0 Specification [2] – scheduled to be released in late 2024 – will introduce a new directive with this goal in mind, called workdistribute.[1]

In this work, we present a proof-of-concept implementation of workdistribute in LLVM's Flang compiler, and show how code, which utilises array notation, can be automatically parallelized and offloaded to accelerators, with just simple annotations by the programmer. We will introduce the Flang compiler and the MLIR infrastructure it is built upon in Sect. 2. Then, we will present our approach in Sect. 4 and evaluate it in Sect. 5.

2 Background

In this section, we will outline some Fortran features which pertain to this work before introducing the new workdistribute OpenMP 6.0 directive. We will also briefly describe the LLVM project's MLIR compiler infrastructure and Fortran compiler Flang.

2.1 Array Notation in Fortran

Array notation provides easy syntax for the programmer to interact with multi-dimensional arrays in a concise and intuitive fashion, as shown in Fig. 1 **(a)**. With the new workdistribute construct, parallelization and offloading of such array notation requires only minimal source changes, as illustrated in Fig. 1 **(b)**. Programmers can also use the *slicing* notation (e.g., y(1:n/2,1:n)) to specify specific portions of the arrays to be operated on.

An intricacy of this feature is that the expression on the right-hand side (RHS) of assignments must be evaluated before being assigned to the left-hand

```
integer :: n
logical :: any_less
real, dimension(n, n) :: x, y, tmp

y(1:n/2,1:n) = 1.0
y = y + x
tmp = n * matmul(x, y + 1.0)
any_less = any(tmp(1:n/2,1:n/3) < 1.0)
```

```
integer :: n
logical :: any_less
real, dimension(n, n) :: x, y, tmp
!$omp target teams workdistribute
    y(1:n/2,1:n) = 1.0
    y = y + x
    tmp = n * matmul(x, y + 1.0)
    any_less = any(tmp(1:n/2,1:n/3) < 1.0)
!$omp end target teams workdistribute
```

(a) Fortran array notation   (b) OpenMP workdistribute

Fig. 1. **(a)** Fortan array notation allows operating on entire arrays or slices of arrays (discussion in Sect. 2.1) and **(b)** OpenMP workdistribute directive instructs the compiler to automatically parallelize the computation and optionally offload it to a target device (further discussed in Sect. 2.2)

---

[1] Note that the directive's name is coexecute in the latest technical report [2], however, it has since been renamed to workdistribute.

```
                        integer :: n
                        real, dimension(n) :: x

                        x = x(n:1)
```

(a) Array reversal (original code)

```
integer :: i, n                  integer :: n
real, dimension(n) :: x          real, dimension(n) :: x, tmp

do i = 1, n                      do i = 1, n
  x(i) = x(n + 1 - i)              tmp(i) = x(n + 1 - i)
enddo                            enddo
                                 do i = 1, n
                                   x(i) = tmp(i)
                                 enddo
```

(b) Incorrect compiler-generated code

(c) Correct compiler-generated code

Fig. 2. Using array notation in Fortran may require additional implicit allocations as storing the result of the RHS directly in the LHS when they alias would overwrite other elements that may be used later in the same array operation.

side (LHS). An example of why this is required is shown in Fig. 2 where an array notation implementation of array reversal is shown in Fig. 2c. If the result of the RHS is computed element-wise and stored directly in the LHS as shown in Fig. 2b, some of the element-wise computation will not use the original values in x, but values overwritten earlier by the same array operation. Thus, correctly generated code for Fig. 2a is shown in Fig. 2c, where we allocate a temporary array for the RHS expression before assigning it to the LHS.

In general, in order to preserve correctness, the compiler must allocate intermediate temporary arrays for all expressions that appear in the RHS. For best performance, optimizations then try to eliminate temporaries when they are not required for correctness.

2.2 The OpenMP `workdistribute` Directive

An example of the `workdistribute` directive is shown in Fig. 1 **(b)**. This directive must be nested directly in a `teams` directive which can in turn be nested in a `target` directive. The `target` directive specifies that the code can be run on a target device, while the `teams` directive indicates that a *league* of teams will be launched and they will work in parallel. The `teams` directive corresponds to the outermost level of parallelism in OpenMP. The `workdistribute` directive specifies that all teams share the work contained in it, while preserving the semantics of the Fortran code. This means that, for example, the ordering of statements is enforced and the RHS of assignments must be completed prior to the assignment to the LHS, as we discussed in Sect. 2.1.

Statements allowed inside the `workdistribute` region are array assignments, calls to array elemental operations (e.g. element-wise multiplication, math functions), calls to intrinsic functions operating on arrays (e.g. `matmul`, `transpose`, `any`, etc.), scalar operations and assignments. This means that this construct is a single block without control flow [2].

Each array element in an elemental-wise computation and assignment is a unit of work, as is each individual scalar operation. Parallelization is performed across units of work and compilers are at liberty to choose how intrinsics are implemented.

2.3 Multi-Level Intermediate Representation (MLIR)

A sub-project of the LLVM project, MLIR [3] is a compiler development framework that enables a structured intermediate representation that is easily composable and extensible. For example, unlike LLVM IR, which defines a concrete set of instructions and types, MLIR is built from the ground up to be extensible, so users of MLIR can add their own types and operations which can freely interact with preexisting ones. It allows abstractions on different levels to be freely mixed and contained in a single representation.

The basic building blocks of MLIR are *operations* and structure in MLIR is represented through region-carrying operations. For example, an `if` statement can be represented as an operation that takes a condition as an operand and contains two regions, `then` and `else`, one of which is executed according to the condition value at runtime. A group of operations and types that pertain to a specific purpose is called a *dialect*.

2.4 The Flang Compiler

Flang [4] is LLVM's Fortran compiler and it uses MLIR for its intermediate representation. This allows it to use a progressive lowering pipeline which starts at an abstract high level representation that captures the Fortran semantics and then progressively lowers that to a more concrete compute-oriented representation in LLVM IR.

Flang's optimization pipeline is generally comprised of three stages which are illustrated in Fig. 3. They roughly correspond to the dialects used at the respective stages. At the beginning, the `hlfir` (High-Level Fortran IR) dialect is used in conjunction with `fir` (Fortran IR) and `omp` (OpenMP) dialects to express a high-level abstract representation of the program.[2]

`hlfir` represents the array notation computation and array intrinsics in a way that allows high-level simplifications, for example merging multiple elemental computations, or simplifying sequences of intrinsics. `fir` is a lower level dialect that directly represents the computation while still preserving higher-level notions than traditional IRs such as loops and `if` statements and Fortran semantics for pointers and operations. This is Finally lowered to LLVM IR, where a standard optimization pipeline is run.

Fortran array intrinsics such as `matmul` and `transpose` are implemented as calls to a runtime library provided by Flang.

---

[2] Note that these are not the only dialects in use, however, they are the ones that characterize the compilation stage and its associated optimizations.

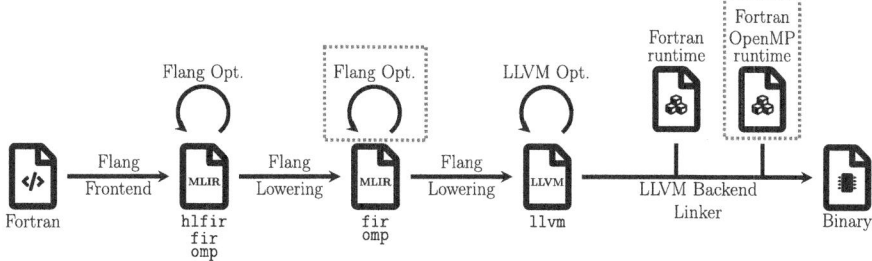

Fig. 3. Flang employs a gradual lowering strategy to preserve high-level Fortran semantics (in the `hlfir` dialect) before lowering to the `fir` dialect and finally LLVM IR. Optimizations suitable for the representation are performed at each step. The Fortran runtime provides the implementation of the array intrinsics. Most of the transformations described in this work are performed at the `fir` level and execution is supported by our OpenMP-enabled Fortran runtime, both of which are highlighted in the figure using dashed boxes.

Flang's MLIR representation allows OpenMP constructs to be represented hierarchically. This hierarchical and gradual-lowering pipeline allows us to implement the necessary transformations for performant offloading.

3 Related Work

Automatic GPU offloading has been explored in many applications and programming languages. For example, it is a standard feature in many machine learning frameworks in high-level languages. However, these still require the programmer to adopt the framework's programming style and APIs. [5,6] All arrays to be operated on also need to be converted to the types provided by the frameworks. This is also the case with NVIDIA's thrust [7], which provides high level C++ types to operate on arrays.

In C/C++ and Fortran, which are the most common languages for high performance scientific computing, accelerated libraries for similar patterns of computations that `workdistribute` allows exist [8–10], however, they still require the programmer to make extensive changes to their code.

High Performance Fortran, or HPF [11], is a Fortran extension that emerged in the 90's which supports automatic parallization and distributing of computation with annotations to native syntax similarly to OpenMP loop directives. However, while it was met with enthusiasm, it failed to achieve success and wide adoption. One of the reasons for this was immature compiler technology and slow development speed at the time [12]. Another reason cited is the difficulty of performance tuning due to the dramatic transformations carried out by the compiler [12]. Conversely, more recently, auto-parallelization and offloading of Fortran code was implemented for stencil style computation in Flang [13], showing the potential of the flexible intermediate representation.

OpenMP's `workdistribute` is similar to HPF in that it requires extensive compiler transformations which may hamper the ability of the user to tune the code. Emitting remarks about what transformations were applied may be one way to tackle this. However, `workdistribute` may be in a better place to succeed as it is being introduced into an already mature OpenMP standard and it allows easy integration into existing OpenMP code with the ability to tune some aspects of if such as memory movement.

4 Automatic Parallelization and Offloading

In this section, we will present our approach and outline how owing to the structured high level representation employed by Flang, we are able to produce a high performance implementation advantageous in comparison to traditional compilation approaches found elsewhere, for example, in clang.

4.1 Shortcomings of a Trivial Implementation

In order to preserve the Fortran semantics (Sect. 2.1), a trivial implementation would perform the following for each statement:

- Allocate temporary arrays for each expression in the RHS
- Execute a separate kernel for each expression in the RHS
- Copy the result of the RHS to the LHS.
- Deallocate the temporary arrays

Room for improvement exists w.r.t. unnecessary memory movement and allocations, cross-kernel simplifications (e.g. fusion), and using high-performance, vendor-provided libraries (e.g. cublas or rocblas for GPUs).

4.2 Overview of Our Approach

The statements that can be included in a `workdistribute` region (ref. Sect. 2.2) are be modelled by `hlfir` and optimizations on the `hlfir` level have an opportunity to greatly impact the performance of the resulting code. Thus, we would like to perform the division into units of work described above only after we have performed high-level optimizations in `hlfir`.

We achieve this by preserving the high-level structure of the `workdistribute` block and deferring materializing the separate kernels until a later stage. More specifically, we perform handling of the `workdistribute` directive at the `fir` stage of the Flang pipeline, see Sect. 2.4 and Fig. 3 for details.

4.3 MLIR `workdistribute` Operation

In order to make use of the `hlfir` optimizations, we need to preserve the information about what part of the program comes from the `workdistribute` directive through the `hlfir` pipeline. We know that `workdistribute` is comprised of a single Fortran block which contains no control flow (ref. Sect. 2.2). We introduce a new `workdistribute` MLIR operation which is a container for a single MLIR block. This block does not allow code to move outside it and allows us to precisely encapsulate the extent of our `workdistribute`. The code in this block is treated as sequential code executed on a single thread. This allows us to reuse high-level optimizations for sequential array notation code.

We adapt the existing frontend code generation to emit the contents of the `workdistribute` Fortran construct in this operation. The MLIR we get at the beginning of the Flang MLIR pipeline is sketched in Fig. 4a.

Then, we reuse the existing high-level optimizations to optimize the contents of the `workdistribute` and then bufferize `hlfir`. This will already give us many of the optimizations that we want (e.g., buffer elimination, kernel merging). This leaves us in the state shown in Fig. 4b.

4.4 Lowering `workdistribute` to Existing OpenMP Constructs

To lower the single-block `workdistribute` operation to concrete parallel OpenMP constructs we chunk the computation into appropriate kernels. Because we want to be able to replace intrinsic calls such as `matmul` and temporary memory allocations with appropriate runtime calls from the host, we need to split the target region and execute host code in-between. Splitting the target kernels is also required to synchronize across teams.

Then, we fission `workdistribute` into what will eventually become different `target` regions (i.e. kernels) or will turn into host-side runtime calls (Fig. 4c).

Now, we need to transform the `teams{workdistribute{...}}` nests. A `workdistribute loop` nest can be converted to a `distribute parallel do` nest, whereas a `workdistribute{<intrinsic>}` nest becomes just `<intrinsic>` (as the sharing of work happens *inside* the intrinsic) (Fig. 4d).

This is semantically sound, as it describes the computation that needs to happen on the target, however, it is invalid OpenMP as `teams` must be strictly nested in `target`. It also cannot be directly lowered as we do not have implementations of the intrinsics we can use on the device.

Thus, we need to fission the target region around our `teams` and transfer the rest of the computation to the host, where we can call our intrinsic functions, which will in turn perform the computation on the target device. The result of this transformation is shown in Fig. 4e. With this, we have successfully converted a `workdistribute` statement to existing OpenMP constructs which can be lowered to LLVMIR.

4.5 Enabling `hlfir` Optimizations: Alias Analysis

As we discussed in Sect. 2.2 and Sect. 4.1, implementing `workdistribute` naively results in excessive allocation of intermediate expressions and memory copying. This is especially problematic in the context of `workdistribute` as we are operating on entire arrays. In order to minimize the required intermediates, alias

```
omp.target {
  omp.teams {
    omp.workdistribute {
      %a = hlfir.elemental {...}
      %b = hlfir.matmul %a ...
      hlfir.assign %b %c
      %d = hlfir.elemental {...}
      hlfir.assign %e %d
    }
  }
}
```
(a) The `omp` and `hlfir` dialects emitted by the frontend capture the high-level semantics and structure.

```
target {
  teams {
    workdistribute {
      fir.do_loop ... unordered {
        ...
      }
      fir.allocmem ...
      call RT_Matmul(...)
      fir.do_loop ... unordered {
        ...
      }
      call RT_Assign(...)
      fir.freemem ...
    }
  }
}
```
(b) Lowering to `fir` materializes loops and allocations, and adds runtime calls.

```
target {
  teams { workdistribute {
    fir.do_loop ... unordered {
      ...
    }
  }}
  teams { workdistribute {
    fir.allocmem ...
    call RT_Matmul(...)
  }}
  teams { workdistribute {
    fir.do_loop ... unordered {
      ...
    }
  }}
  teams { workdistribute {
    call RT_Assign(...)
    fir.freemem ...
  }}
}
```
(c) We fission the `teams(wd)` nests to outline separate parallel regions.

```
target {
  teams { distribute {
    parallel { wsloop {...} }
  }}
  fir.allocmem ...
  call RT_Matmul(...)
  teams { distribute {
    parallel { wsloop {...} }
  }}
  call RT_Assign(...)
  fir.freemem ...
}
```
(d) We convert each `teams(wd)` nest to its corresponding OpenMP construct.

```
target_data {
  target { teams { distribute {
    parallel { wsloop {...} }
  }}}
  fir.allocmem ...
  call RT_OMP_Matmul(...)
  target { teams { distribute {
    parallel { wsloop {...} }
  }}}
  call RT_OMP_Assign(...)
  fir.freemem ...
}
```
(e) The `target` operation is fissioned to allow for host code execution and gets wrapped in a `target_data` to preserve the overall memory movement. Note that code in the `target_data` is executed on the host. The Fortran runtime calls get replaced with OpenMP enabled versions called from the host.

Fig. 4. Our transformation pipeline implemented in Flang takes as an input a `omp.workdistribute` nested in `omp.teams` and optionally `omp.target`, and represents it in terms of concrete parallel OpenMP operations. We omit dialect names (e.g. `omp`) and shorten `workdistribute` to `wd` for brevity.

analysis is required to proof the correctness of omitting them. In our case, however, temporaries may be allocated on the target, while other arrays may be passed into the target kernel from the host. Thus, we need to be able to reason about arrays that cross the host-target boundary.

We extend Flang's alias analysis to follow memory references across host-target boundaries. This allows the existing Flang `hlfir` lowering pipeline to avoid unnecessary temporary allocations (see Sect. 2.1).

4.6 OpenMP-Enabled Fortran Runtime

Fortran array intrinsics such as `matmul` and `transpose` are implemented as runtime calls to a library provided by Flang (*Fortran OpenMP runtime* in Fig. 3). We provide OpenMP enabled versions of the runtime functions that take as arguments arrays that are *already* on the target.

For intrinsics that have high performance implementations by the vendor, such as `matmul` which is provided by cublas and rocblas on NVIDIA and AMD GPUs, we internally defer to them. This way, we abstract the low-level detail and boilerplate associated with using them directly and enable programmers to use the native language.

4.7 Memory Movement

Memory movement for OpenMP target offloading in Fortran can be automatically generated as array types contain information about their bounds. This is in contrast with C/C++ where the sizes of the arrays must be specified by the programmer.[3] When the automatically generated memory movement is not performant enough, it can be further optimized using the standard OpenMP memory movement utilities by the programmer due to `workdistribute` being part of the OpenMP infrastructure.

5 Evaluation and Discussion

We conduct the evaluation of our approach using two experiments. Firstly, in Sect. 5.2, we compare array notation `workdistribute` against OpenMP offloading code that uses loops to express array operations to make sure our approach is up to par with idiomatic OpenMP and can benefit from vendor accelerated libraries. Secondly, in Sect. 5.3, we evaluate how our approach compares against the straight-forward, trivial implementation discussed in Sect. 4.1.

5.1 Experiment Setup and Benchmarks

Setup. We use a dual-socket system with 8-core 16-thread Xeon Silver 4215 CPUs and an AMD MI210 GPU. We run all benchmarks a total of 3 times, each with an additional single warm up iteration and take the mean runtime. For GPU evaluations we measure the memory movement time between host and device, and computation time and report both separately.

---

[3] This is already implemented in Flang and is outside the scope of this work.

```
                                      integer :: n
                                      real, dimension(n, n) :: x, y, z
      integer :: n
      real :: a                       z = matmul(x, y)
      real, dimension(n, n) :: x, y, z              cpu

      z = a * x + y                   !$omp target teams distribute &
                  cpu                 !$omp     parallel do collapse(2)
                                      do i = 1, n
      !$omp target teams distribute \    do j = 1, n
      !     parallel do collapse(2)         z(j, i) = 0
      do i = 1, n                           do k = 1, n
         do j = 1, n                           z(j, i) = z(j, i) +
            z = a * x(j, i) + y(i, j)                 x(j, k) * y(k, i)
         enddo                              enddo
      enddo                             enddo
            omp-traditional          enddo
                                             omp-traditional
      !$omp target teams workdistribute
      z = a * x + y                   !$omp target teams workdistribute
      !$omp end target teams workdistribute   z = matmul(x, y)
            omp-workdistribute        !$omp end target teams workdistribute
                                             omp-workdistribute
      (a) AXPY (n = 4 × 10⁸)
                                      (b) Matrix multiplication (n = 4096)
```

Fig. 5. We use three implementations of two common BLAS routines, *AXPY* and *Matrix multiplication*, to evaluate our approach. An array notation implementation which runs on a single core of the cpu for reference (**cpu**), a trivial implementation using traditional OpenMP offloading constructs (**omp-traditional**), and the simple array notation version, wrapped in `workdistribute` (**omp-workdistribute**). Note how `workdistribute` allows the programmer to avoid the verbosity of loop-based OpenMP code.

Benchmarks. For our proof-of-concept, we focus on two benchmarks shown in Fig. 5a and Fig. 5b. The first one is the `axpy` linear algebra operation which is a scaled vector addition, and the second one is a matrix multiplication. These are memory and compute bound, respectively.

5.2 Comparison to Loop-Based OpenMP Code

For each benchmark, we compare the array notation implementation on a single CPU core (labeled: `cpu`) and a simple straight-forward loop-based OpenMP offloading implementation (`omp-traditional`) against an implementation utilizing `workdistribute` (`omp-workdistribute`). Note how the required programmer effort for the `workdistribute` implementation is very low, involving just wrapping the array notation block in OpenMP directives. Our results are shown in Fig. 6.

We can see how the computation portion of the benchmark is on-par with the traditional OpenMP code in the `axpy` case, because the generated code is essentially the same since we are able to omit all of the redundant allocations and fuse the separate kernels. On the other hand, in the matrix multiplication case, we are able to use vendor libraries (here *rocblas* to target our AMD GPU) which boosts the performance by close to 8× while making it easier to write.[4]

---

[4] The hand-written loop-based `omp-traditional` is a trivial implementation which exhibits inefficient cache characteristics and does not make use of advanced GPU features that are essential for high-performance matrix multiplication. This is the reason for the early 100× performance difference compared to rocblas.

	runtimes	total (s)	computation (s)	memory (s)
matmul	cpu	61.6	61.6	0.00
	omp-traditional	0.440	0.312	0.128
	omp-workdistribute	0.131	0.00352	0.128
axpy	cpu	0.811	0.811	0.00
	omp-traditional	3.25	0.0110	3.24
	omp-workdistribute	3.25	0.0108	3.24

Fig. 6. We (**omp-workdistribute**) achieve superior or comparable performance compared to traditional OpenMP loop-based implementation (**omp-traditional**) on two common linear algebra operations (Fig. 5). The computation of automatically parallelized and offloaded array-notation code (**omp-workdistribute**) is overwhelmingly more performant than the original array notation code executed on a CPU (**cpu**).

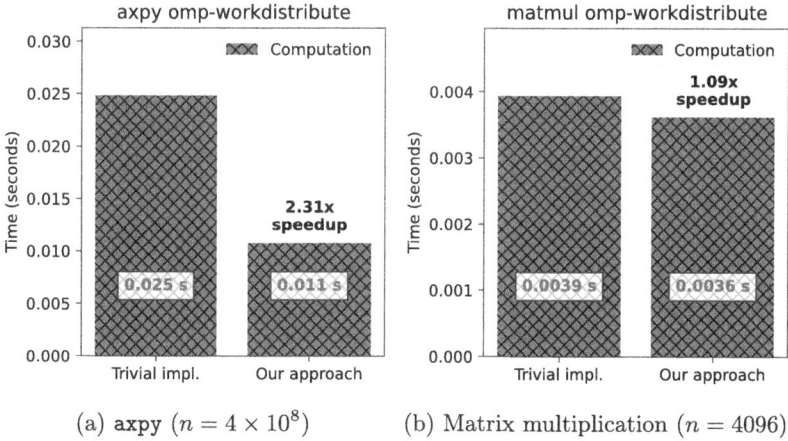

(a) axpy ($n = 4 \times 10^8$) (b) Matrix multiplication ($n = 4096$)

Fig. 7. A trivial implementation that needs to allocate temporary arrays for each expression and assignment (see Sect. 4.1) performs significantly worse than our approach which enables high-level optimizations. See Fig. 5 for the benchmarks.

Using vendor-provided linear algebra routines is cumbersome, verbose, and non-portable. On the other hand, using `workdistribute` hides the implementation details and uses abstractions available in the base language.

We can observe that on memory bound applications (e.g. `axpy`), straightforward usage of `workdistribute` will not improve performance due to the overwhelming overhead of the memory movement between the host and the device. However, as we discussed in Sect. 4.7, this can be further optimized using the existing OpenMP infrastructure and the arrays can be kept on the device across multiple target regions if the applications allows it. On the other hand, as we can see from the matrix multiplication results, for compute-heavy tasks that accelerators excel at, even the straight-forward unoptimized host-device memory movement can improve performance at close to no programmer effort.

5.3 Comparison to a Trivial Implementation

In order to evaluate the benefits of our approach, we disable the optimizations related to removal of temporary allocations (see Sect. 2.1 and Sect. 4.5), which results in generated code resembling that of a trivial implementation discussed in Sect. 4.1.

We plot the results in Fig. 7. We can see how eliminating unnecessary temporary memory allocations is especially important in memory-bound computation, cf. Fig. 7a, where we achieve a 2.3× speedup over the trivial implementation. This stems from the code in Fig. 5, i.e., we need to allocate one temporary array `tmp1` for the result of `a * x` which we compute in one kernel, then we need another temporary allocation for `tmp1 + y` which we compute in another kernel, and finally a assignment to `z` which is a redundant memory copy. Using our approach, this gets reduced to a single kernel which computes `a * x(i,j) + y(i,j)` and stores the result directly in `z(i,j)`.

For the matrix multiplication benchmark (cf. Fig. 7b), the trivial implementation still uses the vendor libraries. The relatively small speedup we get is because we eliminate the redundant allocation for the RHS and assignment to LHS and instead store directly into it.

6 Conclusion

We presented a proof-of-concept implementation of the `workdistribute` OpenMP construct which provides an easy way to automatically parallelize and offload Fortran array notation. Our approach is implemented on top of LLVM's new Fortran compiler – Flang.[5] By employing a progressive abstraction lowering strategy enabled by the MLIR intermediate representation Flang uses, we are able to perform high-level optimizations to ensure high-performance code generation. This allows us to achieve over 2× speedup on a benchmark compared to code generated by a trivial implementation.

Hiding the parallelization details also allows us to use high-performance vendor libraries to accelerate array operations without programmers needing to manually call into cumbersome APIs.

This work can enable easy GPU offloading for existing Fortran codebases and improve utilization of modern HPC systems.

Acknowledgements. This work was supported by JST SPRING, Grant Number JPMJSP2106 and the RIKEN Junior Research Associate Program.
The views and opinions of the authors do not necessarily reflect those of the U.S. government or Lawrence Livermore National Security, LLC neither of whom nor any of their employees make any endorsements, express or implied warranties or representations or assume any legal liability or responsibility for the accuracy, completeness, or usefulness of the information contained herein. This work was in parts prepared by Lawrence Livermore National Laboratory under Contract DE-AC52-07NA27344 (LLNL-CONF-867135).

---

[5] The source is made available at https://github.com/ivanradanov/llvm-project/tree/flang_workdistribute_iwomp_2024 (commit `61ae88a`).

References

1. TOP500 (2024). https://www.top500.org/lists/top500/2024/06/. Accessed 21 June 2024
2. OpenMP Architecture Review Board. OpenMP ARB Releases Technical Report 12. https://www.openmp.org/press-release/openmp-arbreleases-technical-report-12/. Accessed 25 Jan 2024
3. Lattner, C., et al.: MLIR: scaling compiler infrastructure for domain specific computation. In: 2021 IEEE/ACM International Symposium on Code Generation and Optimization (CGO), pp. 2–14 (2021). https://doi.org/10.1109/CGO51591.2021.9370308
4. LLVM. The Flang Compiler. https://flang.llvm.org/docs/. Accessed 20 June 2026
5. Paszke, A., et al.: Pytorch: an imperative style, high-performance deep learning library. In: Advances in Neural Information Processing Systems, vol. 32 (2019)
6. Frostig, R., Johnson, M.J., Leary, C.: Compiling machine learning programs via high-level tracing. Syst. Mach. Learn. **4**(9) (2018)
7. Bell, N., Hoberock, J.: Thrust: a productivity-oriented library for CUDA. In: GPU Computing Gems Jade Edition, pp. 359–371. Elsevier (2012)
8. Blackford, L.S., et al.: An updated set of basic linear algebra subprograms (BLAS). ACM Trans. Math. Softw. **28**(2), 135–151 (2002)
9. V'yukova, N.I., Galatenko, V.A., Samborskii, S.V.: Support for parallel and concurrent programming in C++. Program. Comput. Softw. **44**, 35–42 (2018)
10. Ragan-Kelley, J., Barnes, C., Adams, A., Paris, S., Durand, F., Amarasinghe, S.: Halide: a language and compiler for optimizing parallelism, locality, and recomputation in image processing pipelines. In: Proceedings of the 34th ACM SIGPLAN Conference on Programming Language Design and Implementation, PLDI 2013, pp. 519–530. Association for Computing Machinery, Seattle, Washington, USA (2013). ISBN 9781450320146. https://doi.org/10.1145/2491956.2462176
11. Richardson, H.: High performance fortran: history, overview and current developments. Think. Mach. Corp. **14**, 17 (1996)
12. Kennedy, K., Koelbel, C., Zima, H.: The rise and fall of high performance fortran: an historical object lesson. In: Proceedings of the Third ACM SIGPLAN Conference on History of Programming Languages. HOPL III. Association for Computing Machinery, San Diego, California (2007). ISBN: 9781595937667. https://doi.org/10.1145/1238844.1238851
13. Brown, N., Jamieson, M., Lydike, A., Bauer, E., Grosser, T.: Fortran performance optimisation and auto-parallelisation by leveraging MLIR-based domain specific abstractions in Flang. In: Proceedings of the SC 2023 Workshops of The International Conference on High Performance Computing, Network, Storage, and Analysis. SC-W 2023, Denver, CO, USA, pp. 904–913. Association for Computing Machinery (2023). ISBN: 9798400707858. https://doi.org/10.1145/3624062.3624167

Detrimental Task Execution Patterns in Mainstream OpenMP® Runtimes

Adam S. Tuft[1(✉)], Tobias Weinzierl[1], and Michael Klemm[2,3]

[1] Department of Computer Science, Durham University, Durham, UK
{adam.s.tuft,tobias.weinzierl}@durham.ac.uk
[2] Advanced Micro Devices GmbH, Dornach/Munich, Germany
michael.klemm@amd.com
[3] OpenMP Architecture Review Board, Beaverton, OR, USA
michael.klemm@openmp.org

Abstract. The OpenMP® API offers both task-based and data-parallel concepts to scientific computing. While it provides descriptive and prescriptive annotations, it is in many places deliberately unspecific how to implement its annotations. As the predominant OpenMP implementations share design rationales, they introduce "quasi-standards" how certain annotations behave. By means of a task-based astrophysical simulation code, we highlight situations where this "quasi-standard" reference behaviour introduces performance flaws. Therefore, we propose prescriptive clauses to constrain the OpenMP implementations. Simulated task traces uncover the clauses' potential, while a discussion of their realization highlights that they would manifest in rather incremental changes to any OpenMP runtime supporting task priorities.

Keywords: OpenMP · Scheduling · Task-based programming

1 Introduction

With the advent of hundreds of cores on a contemporary computer chip in data centres, classic data parallelism reaches scalability limits. Even if we decompose algorithms into sequences of highly parallel steps, we will eventually fail to exploit the available parallelism of a machine. Task-based programming promises to ride to our rescue. From a programmer's point of view, it imitates object-orientation's success stories. Rather than reading an algorithm as a sequence of steps where each step exploits parallel capabilities over a large data set, we decompose an algorithm into many small "mini-algorithms" over well-defined data sets, i.e., all the data they actually read and write. The tasks can then spawn further child tasks or have inter-task dependencies.

A task logically encapsulates data plus operations on these data. While programming with tasks might reflect programming's best practices, the HPC selling point behind tasks results from the fact that they help us to expose unprecedented scheduling freedom: task dependencies can often replace synchronization in-between algorithmic steps. Tasks allow us to write code with a high theoretical concurrency level.

The OpenMP® API [7] has offered task directives since version 3.0, which was released in 2008. Since then, the task features have been refined and extended to provide a state-of-the-art task-parallel programming interface. The OpenMP specification does not require a specific execution mechanism or implementation strategy for OpenMP tasks. It is deliberately unspecific in several places, and therefore offers a certain degree of freedom to its implementations. A mainstream OpenMP implementation is provided with the Clang/LLVM compiler and all of our experimental data stem from this ecosystem. Though there are alternative popular implementations such as GNU's OpenMP runtime, all share similar design rationale [6]. Whenever they yield similar execution patterns for a given task graph, our observations and concepts apply. They are generalizable.

In this paper, we study a numerical astrophysics code based upon adaptive Cartesian meshes [17] which heavily relies upon tasking [2,10]. We use it to highlight where the execution patterns from predominant OpenMP implementations are detrimental to the code's performance. Through an artificial scheduling model, i.e., a task schedule simulator, we are able to quantify what better performance alternative schedules might be able to deliver.

Once we have introduced our demonstrator and the simulator (Sect. 2), we discuss, per runtime flaw, the degree to which it is a result of the OpenMP specification or arises from implementation decisions (Sect. 3). In Sect. 4, we propose extensions to the OpenMP tasking API which would allow an application to manipulate the task execution pattern and hence to run faster. Challenging the well-intended rationale of some OpenMP implementations, our work stands in the tradition of a transition from a descriptive to a prescriptive parallelization model. We conclude in Sect. 5 that programmers should, if they want, have a stronger say in how a task graph is actually mapped onto a task schedule.

2 A Stationary Black Hole Simulation Analysed With Otter

We illustrate all OpenMP behaviour by means of a demonstrator from our astrophysical simulation suite ExaGRyPE [17]. It simulates a single, stationary black hole that is modelled via a first-order CCZ4 formulation [3]. Various numerical building blocks feed into this simulation, ranging from higher-order methods, adaptive mesh refinement, Sommerfeld boundary conditions, to tracer particles that allow us to evaluate global integrals over submanifolds.

This is an artificial yet numerically challenging setup [17]. To tackle the scenario, we need to simulate a large computational domain over a long time span exploiting all compute capabilities of the machine efficiently.

2.1 ExaHyPE's Code Architecture

ExaGRyPE is a suite of solvers built on top of ExaHyPE [11] and its meshing framework Peano. Peano's adaptive mesh refinement (AMR) is mandatory to zoom into the area around the black hole. The arising adaptive mesh is static, i.e., it does not change over time. We use plain domain decomposition along the Peano space-filling curve to decompose the mesh for multiple processes using MPI. The same non-overlapping domain decomposition is then used once more to split up the rank-local domain and to distribute the arising chunks of the domain among the available threads. Per rank, this yields a classic fork-join parallelism. Within Peano, we map it onto an OpenMP `taskloop`. Each task traverses one subdomain on the rank, triggers all the simulation computations, and eventually synchronizes the subdomain-local data (for example, halos) with other tasks and ranks. The number of these traversal tasks is typically relatively small, as the data synchronization towards the end quickly eats up all efficiency gains if we make the subdomains too small.

Algorithm 1. Pseudo code of the main traversal routine in ExaHyPE. Algorithmic steps marked with an asterix host a `parallel for` loop.

```
 1: function TRAVERSAL(...)
 2:     #pragma omp taskloop nogroup untied
 3:     for (int subdomain = 0; subdomain < K; subdomain++) do
 4:         for (int cell_in_subdomain = 0; ...) do         ▷ Traverse local subdomain
 5:             if ... then              ▷ Only some cells define (produce) enclave tasks
 6:                 while database does not contain outcome yet do
 7:                     #pragma omp taskyield    ▷ Enclave outcomes from previous traversal
 8:                 end while
 9:                 ...
10:                 #pragma omp task                              ▷ Spawn enclave task
11:                 {
12:                     ...                                       ▷ Actual work (*)
13:                     ...                                       ▷ Dump outcome into database
14:                 }
15:             else
16:                 ...                           ▷ Process actual work immediately (*)
17:             end if
18:             ...
19:         end for
20:     end for
21:     #pragma omp taskwait          ▷ Only wait for traversal tasks, not enclaves
22: end function
```

On top of the geometric data decomposition, we identify mesh cells or patches which are free of side effects [10], i.e., do not contribute towards global quantities, and are not urgent in the sense that they feed into MPI data exchange or AMR inter-resolution transfer operators. The remaining cells or patches can be spawned as separate tasks with no further in-dependencies or additional internal synchronization points. They form enclave tasks [2], which can, without a knock-on effect on MPI and the global simulation state, be executed at a later point, i.e., even after the actual traversal. The mesh traversal tasks therefore act as producers and consumers of tasks, as enclave tasks are spawned in one mesh traversal and contribute towards the solution in the subsequent mesh sweep (Algorithm 1).

Several compute steps both within the traversal and within the enclave tasks exhibit further internal concurrency. This manifests as loop parallelism resulting

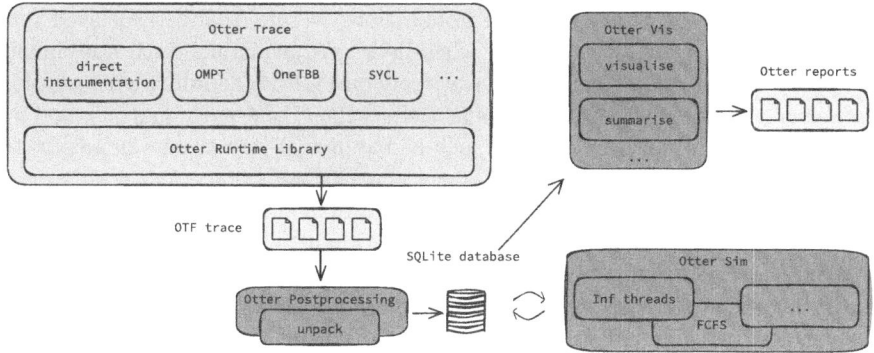

Fig. 1. The Otter tool suite and Otter's trace-simulate-postprocess workflow.

from nested loops over different Finite Volumes or sample points of the solution that evaluate the differential equations, interpolate from one mesh resolution to another, or couple different numerical schemes.

Despite the static nature of the setup and the adaptive mesh, the compute cost per cell might change in each and every time step, as we employ non-linear equation solvers with a dynamic termination criterion per cell [3,11]. With the adaptive mesh refinement, the projections along AMR boundaries are expensive and make cells adjacent to AMR more costly than others. The cost per AMR transition depends on its orientation, i.e., whether the data layout favours a direction or not. Finally, some of our ExaGRyPE solvers switch to a subgrid model around the black hole. This yields a very high load for some mesh cells compared to others. W.l.g. we use the compute cell count as the cost metric and therefore renounce the construction of a bespoke geometric load balancing. We accept that the outermost fork-join parallelism due to traversal tasks is ill-balanced.

2.2 Otter Tracing

To study task execution patterns, we rely on a tool suite called Otter (Fig. 1). Otter offers a macro API for annotating serial or partially parallelized code to highlight where tasks and loop parallelism could be introduced theoretically. It also can record existing OpenMP tasking through OMPT bindings. With both types of information, we run our simulation and let *Otter Trace* record the logical (hypothetical) task graph. This trace includes timing data, too. All trace data ends up in a modified OTF2 database [9].

Once postprocessed, scheduling simulators within the *Otter Sim* package allow us to re-play the recorded logical task graph within various idealized schedulers assuming infinite thread counts, infinite task queues serving all threads FCFS, different NUMA topologies, and so forth. *Otter Sim* can always (retrospectively) identify the critical path of a code as it has access to the whole execution trace. Therefore, we can make predictions of whether the execution time would improve if manual task annotations were actually translated into OpenMP pragmas, or if alternative schedulers were available. Such statements are optimistic: For the present studies, we rely on FCFS scheduling with a global task queue. We ignore NUMA effects as well as the critial path analysis, and we also neglect further external factors such as bandwidth constraints or task activation latencies.

Otter Vis finally translates both the traced and hypothetical data into HTML reports containing runtime metrics, graphs and figures. It allows us to compare the recorded execution pattern of a code to different simulated, hypothetical traces. Such postprocessed data can guide the parallelization of a code, but also uncovers in hindsight unfortunate scheduling decisions from a real run.

3 Execution Patterns

For our demonstrator runs, a standard 16-core AMD EPYC^{TM} Processor model 7302 serves as testbed, although we intentionally limit the number of available OpenMP threads to four. This helps us to highlight execution patterns of interest. With a larger number of threads, the resulting data can become too multifaceted, obscuring details. In all of our experiments, we have validated that the tracing induces negligible runtime overhead of less than 2%. We can trust the tracing data.

3.1 Task Spawn Guarantees

Task creation in the OpenMP API via a `task` directive introduces a task and also constitutes a Task Scheduling Point (TSP). At this point, it is at the OpenMP implementation's discretion either to execute the task immediately "in situ" (undeferred in the same thread) or to actually spawn it as a deferred task. The latter sends the task to the task pool, from which it is picked up later; potentially by another thread. While programmers can push the behaviour towards undeferred execution via `if` and `final` clauses, they can not enforce a deferred task.

This freedom is intended by the OpenMP specification. It allows an implementation to easily deal with large numbers of tasks by switching between undeferred and deferred execution as needed, depending on runtime conditions such as number of available threads, current load of the system, etc. It allows for a throttling of the task creation [1,4].

As an implementation example, LLVM's OpenMP runtime maintains a double-ended task queue per thread. Each thread enqueues created tasks in its own task queue, and always tries to pick a task for execution from the end. This leads to an effective last-in first-out execution behaviour of tasks. If there are no more ready tasks left in the thread-local queue, the thread attempts to steal tasks from queues of other threads. Stolen tasks are taken from the beginning of a queue to retrieve the longest-waiting tasks first.

In ExaHyPE, a traversal task spawns bursts of enclave tasks (Algorithm 1). Switching to undeferred mode implies that these enclave task bursts might

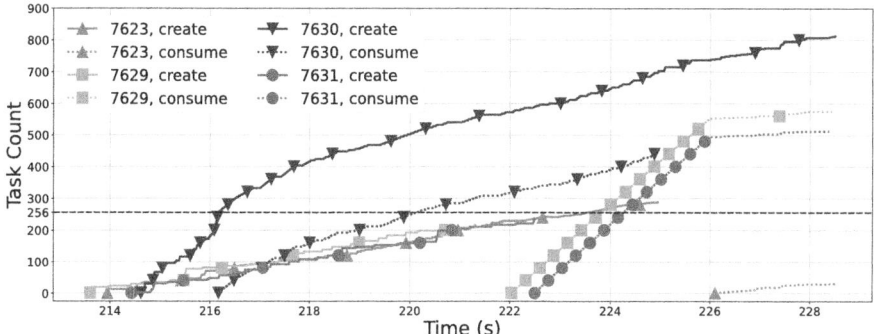

Fig. 2. Created vs. consumed enclave tasks on four threads (7623, 7629, 7630, 7631) over time for a single timestep. 7623, 7629 and 7631 produce tasks which are held in a task queue and then completed, i.e. consumed once the producing task has terminated. 7630 produces so many tasks that the producer task is suspended as further child tasks cannot be deferred. They are executed immediately. From 222 s onwards, 7629 and 7631 start to process tasks, eventually steal from 7630 and hence allow 7630 eventually to stop interrupting the producer.

be artificially constrained. Traversal tasks terminating early due to geometric load imbalances consume the tasks they have spawned before they continue to steal enclaves from other threads' queues. Traversal tasks running longer and producing many tasks see their tasks being stolen by otherwise idle threads. To enable this behaviour is the intention and motivation behind our enclave design [2]. Traversal tasks spawning a very high number of tasks might run into a situation where they exceed their task queue size, while no other threads are available to steal their tasks. They stop further task production, and instead immediately process child tasks [14]. Our testbed software stack seems to employ a queue threshold of 256 tasks. Once a thread has enqueued more than 256 tasks, the system switches into the undeferred mode (Fig. 2).

If tasks producing the lion's share of enclave tasks are also the critical tasks within their fork-join section, the switch to an immediate consumption introduces a bottleneck, as a failure to defer these tasks prolongs the critical path (Fig. 3). With *Otter Sim*, we can simulate a world where the task queues have no upper threshold, i.e., tasks are always deferred. This would reduce the runtime by up to 4.7 %. There are enough threads available towards the end of each traversal to consume all deferred tasks spawned by the critical path.

There are two workarounds to enforce this behaviour: first, we can introduce helper queues on top of the actual OpenMP runtime [10,14]. Rather than spawning OpenMP tasks directly, we hold them back in a user-defined queue, releasing them only after the production task has terminated. While there are reasons for this approach besides the manual deferring—it allows us to fuse withheld tasks into one meta task to deploy them en bloc to a GPU [16] or to vectorize aggressively [10]—it replicates OpenMP core functionality. The alternative second workaround instructs OpenMP to increase its task queues upon

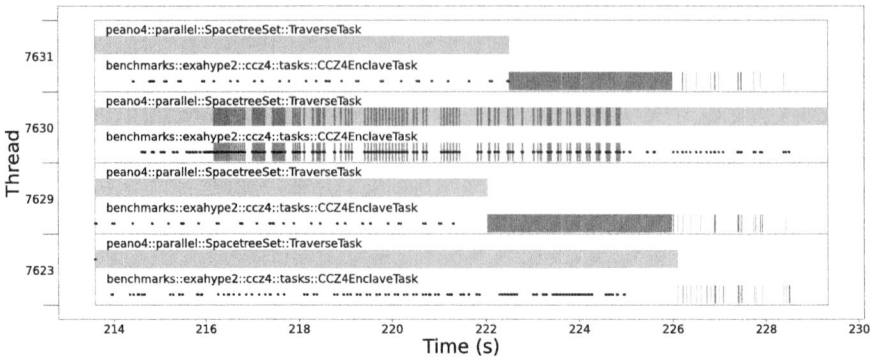

Fig. 3. Trace for task execution pattern from Fig. 2 with grey bars illustrating the traversal tasks, dots showing the creation of enclave child tasks, and narrow black bars denoting the actual enclave task execution. Bars embedded in the traversal task on thread 7630 show the task being suspended when the thread immediately executes an enclave task. All data are recorded, i.e., not simulated. The trace illustrates that the traversal task of thread 7630 is on the critical path. Not deferring child tasks prolongs this path.

demand (KMP_ENABLE_TASK_THROTTLING=0). Yet, there are good reasons for limited queue sizes. If we increase them dramatically, we have to pay a runtime and memory overhead penalty. Our demonstrator selectively identifies tasks which benefit from flexible queue sizes without asking for globally dynamic queues.

3.2 Nested Parallelism

High performance computing codes tend to combine task and data parallelism. Modern codes also tend to rely on hierarchical parallelism [12,15]. Such a code makes the concurrency fan out as the code descends along the call tree.

In the OpenMP API, the maximum number of nested parallelization levels is controlled through OMP_MAX_ACTIVE_LEVELS [7]. By default, OpenMP realizes strictly nested parallelism, i.e., our data-parallel region mapped onto a `parallel for` can only use a subset of the threads available to the enclosing section. A task that contains a `for` directive will therefore only utilize one thread to execute that region, as each task is tied to one thread.

In ExaHyPE, the subdomain traversals are realized as tasks. The domain decomposition geometrically makes some tasks responsible for the interpolation and restriction along AMR boundaries and/or the coupling of one physical model to the other. Both types of operations are very expensive. Logically, the arising projections between different solvers or mesh resolutions are embarrassingly parallel, i.e., could be mapped onto an embedded `parallel for`. Yet, we serialize any `parallel for` embedded into a task.

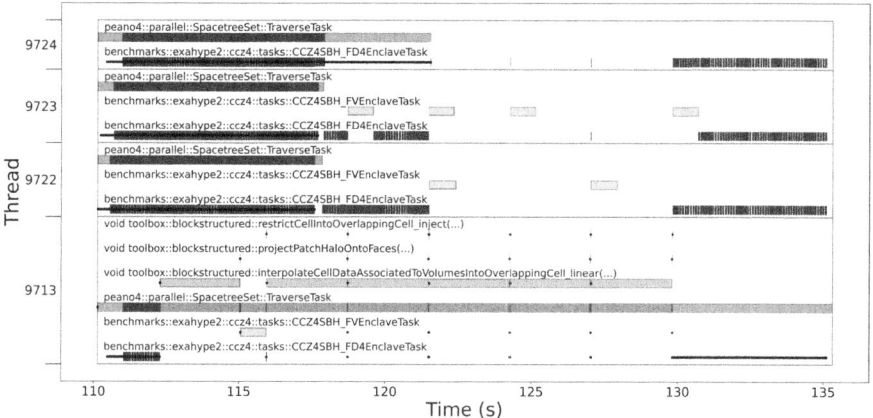

Fig. 4. Timeline of a single time step. The red bars highlight where the critical task runs into some embedded `parallel for` constructs. Recorded timings augmented by postprocessing data (critical path).

As the loops are expensive and as they often align along the critical path—in many ExaHyPE settings they are indeed responsible for making the owning task a member of the critical path—the lack of support for nested parallelism within tasks increases the makespan of the application (Fig. 4). For characteristic demonstrator setups, we could, in theory, gain up to a 43 % reduction in runtime if the loops were executed in parallel. This optimistic estimate assumes that sufficient idling threads are available whenever a critical task encounters a loop.

The OpenMP API provides no mechanism that allows a task to book multiple threads in a data-parallel fashion. This leaves us with two alternatives. On the one hand, we could use a `parallel for`, i.e., fire up a new team of threads. On the other hand, we could switch from a `for` loop to a `taskloop`. In an HPC context, a new team of threads is problematic. Typically, HPC codes spawn one thread per core right from the start to avoid oversubscription, i.e. hyperthreading resulting in overheads due to thread swapping. Mechanisms to reuse existing threads within nested regions are available (cmp. `KMP_HOT_TEAMS_MAX_LEVEL`), but do not address the present issue, if the threads are already booked out. Using a `taskloop` construct is hence more natural and, in combination with a `default(shared)` clause, a minimally invasive change to the code. Yet, creating many subtasks through a `taskloop` introduces overhead in itself, while the tasks might end up in the thread-local queue, i.e., continue to be serialized.

3.3 Fair Yields

In ExaHyPE, there are typically few traversal tasks compared to the available core count. In our experiments, the traversal tasks therefore almost never wait for the enclave tasks. All enclave tasks are completed by threads not involved in the traversal ahead of time. There are exceptions to the rule: NUMA-intensive systems such as the AMD EPYC™ processors make some developers deploy one MPI process per NUMA domain—effectively yielding a low core count per process—and dynamic load balancing might deploy more subpartitions to an MPI process than there are threads available. Our implementation therefore protects the access to enclave task outcomes with an atomic flag signalling whether the task is complete. If unset, the consumer thread yields and then polls again.

The result code starves in rare situations. Let T be the number of threads available and let $C > T + 1$ be the number of consumer tasks that traverse the domain and consume one of the E enclave task outcomes which are pending in the system. $E + C \gg T$ then is the total number of tasks. ExaHyPE can run into a situation where a consumer task yields, another untied consumer is swapped in, and the consumers all take turns checking the enclave task flags. The enclave tasks then starve.

In the OpenMP API specification, the `taskyield` construct is a hint to the implementation to introduce an additional TSP and, hence, to give other tasks a chance to be scheduled for execution. As a hint, an implementation can ignore the TSP or implement it in various ways with different performance implications [13]. For ExaHyPE, it is problematic that OpenMP's `taskyield` does not provide a fairness guarantee and notably cannot be used to drain a pending task queue incrementally. One might argue that a robust realization of our producer-consumer pattern should employ task dependencies to avoid the polling for task readiness. Yet, we note that `taskwait` with a `depend` clause is not always straightforward to use from a programmer's point of view, as all task dependency addresses have to reside within the user space. More severely, task dependencies are restricted to sibling tasks in OpenMP whereas we have parent–child relations here. ExaHyPE would benefit from a fair yielding mechanism to avoid occasional deadlocks on some hardware. At the moment, we have to manually work around such cases by adding user-defined task queues.

3.4 Taskwait Semantics

The `taskwait` and `taskloop` directives used by our traversal tasks introduce synchronization points. We use `taskwait` with `taskloop nogroup` to synchronize the set of all child tasks with the same parent task, i.e., all traversal siblings, but not their spawned enclave tasks, while the synchronization set for the `taskloop` without `nogroup` includes all descendant tasks created from within the `taskloop` region, i.e., all enclave tasks produced, too. The `taskloop nogroup` can be replaced by a for loop spawning the traversal tasks individually, which is necessary for the NVIDIA software stack that lacks support for task groups. If supported, we find it to be more elegant and slightly faster than manual task spawning.

It is up to the OpenMP implementation how the synchronization points are realized. There are two basic options. First, the runtime can process further tasks while waiting until all tasks in the synchronization set have completed execution. Second, it can actively poll the synchronization construct, possibly deciding not to execute further tasks while it waits.

Let ExaHyPE spawn K (traversal) tasks at one point, and immediately after the end of that task group issue another one with K tasks. These are two time steps. If $K - 1$ threads decide to process further (enclave) tasks at the first synchronization point, the final remaining thread might hit the end of the first task group while these threads still are busy. Only this one thread hence is available to immediately continue with the K tasks from the second task group.

While it makes sense for a thread to execute further tasks while waiting in a `taskwait` or at the end of a `taskgroup` region—this guarantees progress—it means that we add algorithmic latency to the second task group in the example. This latency is defined by the time it takes the $K - 1$ threads to finish the currently active enclave task, and to join traversal tasks of the next task group, i.e., time step.

In ExaHyPE, the traversal tasks define the critical path. If one of the traversal tasks is not immediately kicked off at the start of a task group, we risk delaying the critical path. Furthermore, we observe that such latency can lead to low occupancy further down the road, as tasks have been processed at a scheduling point where it would have been better from a performance standpoint if the underlying thread had paused for a moment and then continued with the traversal task [14]. Yet, OpenMP provides no mechanism to stop a thread at the end of a task group from continuing with other tasks. We have no mechanism to flag to the system that we are aware that there are many ready tasks but that we also know that there will be a point reached soon with a low concurrency level where these tasks can all be handled without delaying any other time-critical task. In such a case, we might be willing to accept low occupancy temporarily, as long as we can trade this to an immediate continuation along the critical path—knowing that there will be enough resources later on to handle all the postponed tasks.

4 OpenMP Extensions and Their Realization

Algorithm 2. Domain traversal loop with modified OpenMP annotations.

```
function TRAVERSAL(...)
  #pragma omp ... nogroup latency
  for (int subdomain = 0; ...) do
    ...
    while ... do
      #pragma omp taskyield throughput
    end while
    ...
    #pragma omp task defer
    ...
  end for
end function
```

With a clear description of runtime flaws, we can propose some modifications to the OpenMP API that would help our demonstrator code. We distinguish between proposals for the specification API and suggestions how to implement an altered specification (Algorithm 2).

4.1 API Modifications

ExaHyPE with its producer-consumer pattern would benefit from explicitly labelling tasks as "must be deferred", This would complement the existing semantics of the OpenMP clauses `if` and `final`, i.e., allow developers to disable task throttling [1,4,5]. In ExaHyPE, our first and foremost goal is the reduction of the critical path requiring such a flag to be prescriptive. Yet, realization constraints and task pool overflows might require it to become a weakly prescriptive annotation (see below). A possible extension of the OpenMP API would be a new clause `defer` that extends the existing clauses of the `task` directive: `#pragma omp task defer(`*condition*`)`. If *condition* evaluates to *true*, the task shall be deferred; if it evaluates to *false*, the task maybe undeferred or deferred.

ExaHyPE would benefit from the introduction of tasks that roll out embedded loops over multiple threads. Providing such a feature with spreading guarantees is difficult [15]. A plain `taskloop` with the clause `priority(omp_get_max_task_priority())` would not facilitate the feature. It would assign the resulting loop chunks high priority compared to any other task in the system and load stealing would implicitly scatter the iteration range among the available OpenMP threads. However, there is no guarantee that they are stolen. We would required a `scatter` clause.

For a `taskyield` variant, we would envisage that programmers should be able to decide that a `taskyield` region should not be an no-op, but actually pick tasks from the task pool for execution. Furthermore, it would help to mark a TSP of a `taskyield` region as either high throughput or low latency: `#pragma omp taskyield latency|throughput`, with the default being the current implementation-defined behaviour.

A low latency TSP suspends the encountering task yet brings it back as soon as possible to minimize the probability that we lose all of its cache content, following the depth-first philosophy of OpenMP implementations. It reduces the algorithmic latency of polling realized through yield. In our case, we would rather use a throughput-oriented TSP which would cause a yielding task to go to the back of a queue. Such a yield could then also provide fairness guarantees.

To facilitate low latency `taskwait` or `taskgroup` regions, the above `latency` and `throughput` clauses would also be added to these directives. It instructs the implementation that threads hitting the corresponding synchronization point are to be kept free of other tasks, as they will be needed immediately afterwards for some high priority work (`latency`). While a suspended task is waiting for tasks to complete, the implementation shall not schedule other tasks to reduce wakeup latency. It is up to the user to guarantee that this clause does not induce a deadlock or starvation, for example by having all tasks encounter a latency optimized `taskwait latency` directive.

4.2 Realization

The opportunity to manually defer tasks to the task pool independent of the execution context means that we have to provide a dynamic task queue which can grow without any constraints as a realization of an unbounded task pool. Otherwise, task pools might overflow. A weakened realization sticks to the existing implementation of task queues, but instead switches from task stealing to task distribution for "must be deferred" tasks: Whenever a thread spawns more tasks than its local task queue is able to accommodate, these tasks first are scattered over other threads' queues (similar to how tasks with data affinity are distributed [8]). If and only if this task distribution fails as well, we fall back to undeferred execution for the created task. We hypothesize that this last variant provides a reasonable compromise between runtime efficiency, small changes to existing infrastructure, and improved runtime characteristics on the demonstrator side. To avoid that an active task distribution confuses the scheduling of victim threads, it is important that the created subtasks are assigned a very low priority, i.e., are not brought forward on the target thread. Otherwise, we would replicate the motivating problem once again.

To allow parallel loops that are embedded into a task to "invade" other threads, an implementation should go the other way regarding task priorities. The loop segments scattered over the queues have to have a higher priority than the highest priority task in any respective queue, and task stealing has to take priorities into account, too. This way, we can ensure that idle tasks steal the "right" tasks from the thread issuing the parallel for, and that the stealing does not delay the actual execution of the parallel loop that kicked it off.

A fair yield which can guarantee progress in our particular case could easily be mapped onto priorities, too: If a thread queue is aware of the lowest priority task, a throughput yield would label the suspended task with a priority that is by one smaller than the currently lowest priority.

The new "low latency" clause finally requires us to eliminate the task scheduling point at the end of the loop. This will let the used threads (logically) run idle. Once we ensure that a subsequent parallel loop schedules "its own" tasks or parallel segments first, we however obtain a taskwait which prioritizes low algorithmic latency over throughput. To ensure that the subsequent loop start does not issue any other task first, we can either hardcode the scheduling or make the scheduling biased. Given the spawned task higher priorities than all other pending ready tasks introduces the required bias.

4.3 Contextualization

There are many valid reasons and rationale why OpenMP implementations fall back to task throttling if too many tasks are created [5]. Our suggestion to introduce a dedicated new clause to avoid this accepts this fact, as it suggests localized modifications to few tasks. Such a clause should have no detrimental effect on existing codes.

Our nested parallelism within tasks aligns with existing developments within OpenMP and does not sacrifice threads [15]. It notably fits to OpenMP's GPU kernel concept, where the `target` pragma lets the spawning code fan out into a new team with many threads. With a full support of nested parallelism on the host, massive tasks that should be offloaded to a GPU yet cannot be moved there for one reason or the other benefit from the full concurrency of the host processor. The feature facilitates platform- and performance-portable code.

A fair yield is a natural cousin to the existing `detach` clause, which becomes useful if we cannot easily construct or realize a completion check and instead prefer (partial) draining of the task queue.

A "do not schedule" policy at an implicit synchronization point stands in the tradition of OpenMP to grant NUMA considerations high priority. The probability is high that people use it for subsequent parallel loops with the same granularity which run over related data.

5 Conclusion and Outlook

OpenMP schedules are often not unique or enforced by the standard. We introduce four scenarios, where the LLVM implementation introduces runtime flaws: tasks are prematurely activated, tasks do not support embedded parallelism, tasks do not yield in a fair way, and waiting constructs always prioritize high throughput instead of low algorithmic latency.

These flaws result from common interpretations and rationale how to interpret and realise the standard efficiently for a magnitude of applications. Our work does not challenge the underlying implementation rationale of mainstream runtimes—indeed there are good reasons to implement things the way they are—but it suggests that users should be allowed to explicitly instruct OpenMP to realize things differently. While prescriptive OpenMP statements already enforce certain OpenMP behaviour, our work goes one step further and makes the prescriptive character cover certain realization decisions, too.

These modifications do not require major rewrites of the OpenMP runtime. Instead, the majority of them can be implemented combining task priorities with minor changes in the runtime's logic. For all changes a mature implementations of priorities is a sine qua non which can induce further scalability challenges on massively parallel systems. In combination with few further tweaks, they however will provide multifaceted tuning opportunities to codes like ExaHyPE.

GNU and other runtimes share implementation rationale with LLVM. We may therefore expect that many of the documented flaws arise there, too, likely with quantitatively different characteristics. It is future work to assess these differences systematically. Our work uses one bespoke simulation code as demonstrator. We again expect other task-heavy codes to encounter similar flaws and, hence, to benefit from the proposed extensions. The scientific challenge for future work is to quantify these effects, but also to identify if the extensions and required modifications of the runtime could potentially harm the performance of other codes. They have the potential to make runtime implementations not backward compatible from a performance point of view.

Acknowledgments. Tobias' research has been supported by EPSRC's Excalibur programme through its cross-cutting project EX20-9 *Exposing Parallelism: Task Parallelism* (Grant ESA 10 CDEL) and the DDWG projects *PAX–HPC* (Gant

EP/W026775/1) as well as *An ExCALIBUR Multigrid Solver Toolbox for ExaHyPE* (EP/X019497/1). His group appreciates the support by Intel's Academic Centre of Excellence at Durham University. The comparison of OpenMP vs. TBB and the assessment of early oneAPI OpenMP behaviour has led to some of the investigations reported here. This work has made use of the Hamilton HPC Service of Durham University.

AMD, the AMD Arrow logo, EPYC, and combinations thereof are trademarks of Advanced Micro Devices, Inc. Other product names used in this publication are for identification purposes only and may be trademarks of their respective companies. ExaHyPE (https://gitlab.lrz.de/hpcsoftware/Peano/-/releases/2024OpenMPPaper) and Otter (https://github.com/Otter-Taskification/otter/releases/tag/2024-openmp-paper) (https://github.com/Otter-Taskification/pyotter/releases/tag/2024-openmp-paper) are open source.

References

1. Agathos, S.N., Kallimanis, N.D., Dimakopoulos, V.V.: Speeding up OpenMP tasking. In: Kaklamanis, C., Papatheodorou, T., Spirakis, P.G. (eds.) Euro-Par 2012. LNCS, vol. 7484, pp. 650–661. Springer, Heidelberg (2012). https://doi.org/10.1007/978-3-642-32820-6_64
2. Charrier, D.E., Hazelwood, B., Weinzierl, T.: Enclave tasking for DG methods on dynamically adaptive meshes. SIAM J. Sci. Comput. **42**(3), C69–C96 (2020)
3. Dumbser, M., Guercilena, F., Köppel, S., Rezzolla, L., Zanotti, O.: Conformal and covariant Z4 formulation of the Einstein equations: strongly hyperbolic first-order reduction and solution with discontinuous Galerkin schemes. Phys. Rev. D **97**, 084053 (2018)
4. Duran, A., Corbalan, J., Ayguade, E.: An adaptive cut-off for task parallelism. In: SC 2008: Proceedings of the 2008 ACM/IEEE Conference on Supercomputing, pp. 1–11 (2008)
5. Gautier, T., Perez, C., Richard, J.: On the impact of OpenMP task granularity. In: de Supinski, B.R., Valero-Lara, P., Martorell, X., Mateo Bellido, S., Labarta, J. (eds.) IWOMP 2018. LNCS, vol. 11128, pp. 205–221. Springer, Cham (2018). https://doi.org/10.1007/978-3-319-98521-3_14
6. Klemm, M., Cownie, J.: High Performance Parallel Runtimes: Design and Implementation. De Gruyter, Berlin (2021)
7. Klemm, M., de Supinski, B.R. (eds.): OpenMP Application Programming Interface Specification Version 5.2. OpenMP Architecture Review Board (2021)
8. Klinkenberg, J., et al.: Assessing task-to-data affinity in the LLVM OpenMP runtime. In: de Supinski, B.R., Valero-Lara, P., Martorell, X., Mateo Bellido, S., Labarta, J. (eds.) IWOMP 2018. LNCS, vol. 11128, pp. 236–251. Springer, Cham (2018). https://doi.org/10.1007/978-3-319-98521-3_16
9. Knüpfer, A., et al.: Score-P: a joint performance measurement run-time infrastructure for periscope, Scalasca, TAU, and Vampir. In: Brunst, H., Müller, M., Nagel, W., Resch, M. (eds.) Tools for High Performance Computing 2011, pp. 79–91. Springer, Heidelberg (2012). https://doi.org/10.1007/978-3-642-31476-6_7
10. Li, B., Schulz, H., Weinzierl, T., Zhang, H.: Dynamic task fusion for a block-structured finite volume solver over a dynamically adaptive mesh with local time stepping. In: Varbanescu, A.L., Bhatele, A., Luszczek, P., Marc, B. (eds.) ISC High Performance 2022. LNCS, vol. 13289, pp. 153–173. Springer, Cham (2022). https://doi.org/10.1007/978-3-031-07312-0_8

11. Reinarz, A., et al.: ExaHyPE: an engine for parallel dynamically adaptive simulations of wave problems. Comput. Phys. Commun. **254**, 107251 (2020)
12. Royuela, S., Serrano, M.A., Garcia-Gasulla, M., Mateo Bellido, S., Labarta, J., Quiñones, E.: The cooperative parallel: a discussion about run-time schedulers for nested parallelism. In: Fan, X., de Supinski, B.R., Sinnen, O., Giacaman, N. (eds.) IWOMP 2019. LNCS, vol. 11718, pp. 171–185. Springer, Cham (2019). https://doi.org/10.1007/978-3-030-28596-8_12
13. Schuchart, J., Tsugane, K., Gracia, J., Sato, M.: The impact of taskyield on the design of tasks communicating through MPI. In: de Supinski, B.R., Valero-Lara, P., Martorell, X., Mateo Bellido, S., Labarta, J. (eds.) IWOMP 2018. LNCS, vol. 11128, pp. 3–17. Springer, Cham (2018). https://doi.org/10.1007/978-3-319-98521-3_1
14. Schulz, H., Gadeschi, G.B., Rudyy, O., Weinzierl, T.: Task inefficiency patterns for a wave equation solver. In: McIntosh-Smith, S., de Supinski, B.R., Klinkenberg, J. (eds.) IWOMP 2021. LNCS, vol. 12870, pp. 111–124. Springer, Cham (2021). https://doi.org/10.1007/978-3-030-85262-7_8
15. Sun, J., Guan, N., Li, F., Gao, H., Shi, C., Yi, W.: Real-time scheduling and analysis of OpenMP DAG tasks supporting nested parallelism. IEEE Trans. Comput. **69**(9), 1335–1348 (2020)
16. Wille, M., Weinzierl, T., Gadeschi, G.B., Bader, M.: Efficient GPU offloading with OpenMP for a hyperbolic finite volume solver on dynamically adaptive meshes. In: Bhatele, A., Hammond, J., Baboulin, M., Kruse, C. (eds.) ISC High Performance 2023. LNCS, vol. 13948, pp. 65–85. Springer, Cham (2023). https://doi.org/10.1007/978-3-031-32041-5_4
17. Zhang, H., et al.: ExaGRyPE: Numerical General Relativity Solvers Based upon the Hyperbolic PDEs Solver Engine ExaHyPE (2024). https://doi.org/10.48550/arXiv.2406.11626

Author Index

A
Araujo, Guido 49
Araya-Polo, Mauricio 64, 126

B
Barrere, Rémi 31
Bischof, Christian 97
Bonato, Vanderlei 49
Brandner, Julian 79

C
Cabarcas, Felipe 111
Cetre, Cyril 31
Chandrasekaran, Sunita 111
Chapman, Barbara 64, 126

D
Denny, Joel 111
Doerfert, Johannes 111, 197
Domke, Jens 197

E
Endeve, Eirik 16
Endo, Toshio 197

F
Francesquini, Emilio 49

G
Gratadour, Damien 31

H
Harris, J. Austin 16

I
Ivanov, Ivan R. 197
Iwainsky, Christian 97

J
Jammer, Tim 97
Jarmusch, Aaron 111
Jin, Feiyang 161

K
Kallai, Andrew 111
Klemm, Michael 210
Klinkenberg, Jannis 3
Kraus, Jan 3

L
Lee, Seyong 111
Liao, Chunhua 143, 176
Lin, Pei-Hung 143
Lisa, Nusrat Jahan 49

M
Mayer, Florian 79
Müller, Matthias S. 3

P
Pereira, Marcio 49
Petrica, Lucian 49
Peyralans, Luke 111
Philippsen, Michael 79
Pophale, Swaroop 111

Q
Quiñones, Eduardo 31

R
Rigo, Sandro 49
Rosso, Pedro Henrique 49
Royuela, Sara 31

S
Sarkar, Vivek 161
Sekender, Naveed 143
Shan, Baodi 64, 126

T
Tao, Alan   161
Terboven, Christian   3
Thavappiragasam, Mathialakan   16
Tuft, Adam S.   210

V
Videau, Brice   16

W
Wang, Anjia   176
Weinzierl, Tobias   210

Y
Yan, Yonghong   176
Yi, Xinyao   176
Yu, Chenle   31
Yu, Lechen   161
Yviquel, Hervé   49

SPRINGER NATURE

GPSR Compliance

The European Union's (EU) General Product Safety Regulation (GPSR) is a set of rules that requires consumer products to be safe and our obligations to ensure this.

If you have any concerns about our products, you can contact us on ProductSafety@springernature.com

In case Publisher is established outside the EU, the EU authorized representative is:

Springer Nature Customer Service Center GmbH
Europaplatz 3
69115 Heidelberg, Germany

The manufacturer's authorised representative in the EU is Springer Nature Customer Service Centre GmbH, Europaplatz 3, 69115 Heidelberg, Germany. If you have any concerns regarding our products, please contact ProductSafety@springernature.com

Printed and bound by CPI Group (UK) Ltd, Croydon, CR0 4YY

25/03/2026

02078195-0010